# LIVING WITH DRUGS

# LIVING WITH
# DRUGS
## DR MICHAEL GOSSOP

## SECOND EDITION

WILDWOOD
HOUSE

First published in Great Britain in 1982
by Maurice Temple Smith Ltd
Second edition published 1987 by
Wildwood House Limited
Gower House, Croft Road
Aldershot, Hants GU11 3HR
England
Reprinted 1988
© 1982, 1987 Michael Gossop

**British Library Cataloguing in Publication Data**

Gossop, Michael
  Living with drugs. —— 2nd ed.
  1. Drugs —— Physiological effect
  I. Title
  615'.7            RM300

ISBN 0 7045 3088 0
     0 7045 0566 5 (pbk)

Typeset by Robcroft Ltd, London WC1
Printed and bound in Great Britain
by Biddles Limited
Guildford and King's Lynn

## CONTENTS

# PREFACE TO THE SECOND EDITION

It is a pleasure to be able to write this preface to the second edition of *Living with Drugs*. It is less of a pleasure to report that although there have been a number of changes since the first edition both in the use of drugs and in the responses to drug taking, there have been few signs of improvement. The mid-1980s are in the throes of the greatest 'drugs panic' that Britain has witnessed since the late 1960s. Certainly the issue of drug taking is receiving a great deal of attention. The British Royal Family is concerned; the President of the United States is making emotional pleas to his nation; the British Government has targeted drugs as 'one of the most worrying problems facing our society today'. In direct competition with the prospect of nuclear war and the highest level of unemployment the country has ever seen, the drug problem is clearly doing well.

The number of casualties of drug taking appears to be still increasing. A number of 'new' drugs have appeared on the scene. Some of these drugs have been around for many years but their potential for producing altered states of consciousness has only recently become popular knowledge (as for instance, with 'ecstasy', MDMA). Other drugs have been deliberately manufactured for this purpose (the 'designer drugs'). Nor is it reassuring that a new and potentially devastating viral infection is being spread among those drug injectors who share needles and syringes.

It is very disappointing that the standard of media

reporting on drug-related issues remains generally abysmal. Television and newspaper coverage, in particular, continues to be unnecessarily sensational (perpetuating many of the myths that are discussed in Chapter 11); and too often media coverage makes no effort to differentiate between drugs. Sometimes these errors are explicit, as in claims that Drug X is instantly addicting to anyone who tries it even once. A few weeks before writing this preface this myth was solemnly presented on one of BBC television's serious documentary programmes. Sometimes the errors are implicit, as in a BBC news programme that reported a huge 'drugs seizure' with a background caption showing a line of white powder, a syringe and a rolled-up £5 note. The visual image was therefore either of heroin or cocaine. But the drug that had been seized was cannabis. A yawning chasm divides the real pattern of drug-related problems from the perceptions of those problems in the media and among politicians. It would be a small but important aid to us all in our task of learning to live with drugs if the portrayal of the problem was better informed.

# ACKNOWLEDGEMENTS

I am pleased to be able to thank some of the many people who helped me while I was writing this book, among them Mark Brutton, John Witton of the Institute for the Study of Drug Dependence, Roy Johnson of the National Council on Alcoholism, Griffith Edwards and Martin Jarvis at the Addiction Research Unit, Alex Irving of the Transport and Road Research Laboratory, Douglas Davies of the Department of Theology at Nottingham University, and Malcolm Lader and Hans Eysenck at the Institute of Psychiatry. I am also grateful to James Hunt, the former World Champion Grand Prix driver, and to the climbers Joe Tasker and Alan Rouse for talking to me about their experiences. I owe my thanks to Nan Allen, Janet Chesson and Barbara Longhurst for so patiently and meticulously preparing the typed manuscript.

# 1

## THE CHEMISTRY OF EVERYDAY LIFE

Every society has its own drugs. People have always used drugs to alter their states of consciousness, eagerly seeking out whatever naturally-occurring substances can be used as drugs, and wherever possible deliberately cultivating them. Every part of the Earth that is capable of producing drugs has been used for this purpose. Vast areas of Europe are covered by vines. The cannabis plant flourishes in Africa and Asia; and from the Middle East down through Asia the opium poppy grows – both in its wild state and under cultivation. In the cooler, wetter climate of the British Isles some of the best arable land in the country is turned over to the production of that most English narcotic, the hop. In the Americas there are plantations of the coca plant, tobacco, and cactuses containing mescaline, and throughout the world there are mushrooms containing other hallucinogenic drugs. The only people with no traditional drug of their own would appear to be the Eskimos who live in a land so bleak and uncompromising that it does not permit the cultivation of any intoxicant.

Drugs play an important part in the lives of every one of us. Drug taking is an almost universal phenomenon, and in the statistical sense of the term it is the person who does not take drugs who is abnormal. Many readers are likely to react against any suggestion that they are drug takers, to see it as some sort of accusation. The comfortable but quite mistaken orthodoxy insists that the 'normal' people who make up the majority of our society do not use drugs: set in sharp contrast to this sober normality are the 'abnormal' minority who do.

The term 'drug taking' conjures up an image of syringes, needles, heroin and all the paraphernalia of the junkie drop-out. It is surrounded by all manner of sinister implications which reinforce the view that the use of drugs is a strange, deviant and inexplicable form of behaviour – possibly even a symptom of mental illness. We have been encouraged to regard the junkies who are such a conspicuous part of Times Square in New York, Piccadilly Circus in London or their equivalent in Berlin and Amsterdam as some sort of alien breed. Consequently, we are tempted to feel that our own use of cigarettes, of alcohol, of sleeping tablets, or of tranquillisers, is quite different to their use of heroin. But are the two sorts of drug taking really so dissimilar?

The emotional reaction that is so common whenever drugs and drug taking are mentioned, is quite unwarranted, and it presents a serious obstacle to our efforts to understand this issue. Tea and tobacco contain drugs (i.e. caffeine and nicotine). Alcohol is a drug; heroin and cocaine are drugs. All are drugs in the same sense of the term, though dictionaries are particularly unhelpful in clarifying precisely what we mean by the word.

There are few satisfactory definitions of any of the terms that are used in this area. The traditional definitions of a drug tend to emphasise the chemical properties and the medical values of a specific substance. In *Butterworth's Medical Dictionary*, for instance, a drug is defined as 'any chemical substance, synthetic or extracted from plant or animal tissue and of known or unknown composition, which is used as a medicament to prevent or cure disease'. This definition is hardly adequate for the actual way in which doctors use drugs, much less for the purposes of the present discussion. Here, we are concerned most especially with the psychological (psychoactive) effects of drugs.

It is extraordinary that so little attention has been paid to the mind-altering properties of drugs. Throughout history, man has made strenuous efforts to discover and to invent substances and techniques which will help him change his psychological states. Another definition of drugs is needed which does cover their psychoactive effects. A psychoactive drug may therefore be seen as *any chemical substance, whether of natural or synthetic origin, which can be used to alter perception, mood or other psychological states.*

As definitions go, this is reasonably acceptable. The difficulty with trying to provide a definition of drugs is that drugs have no intrinsic property that sets them apart from other substances. Certainly there is no objective characteristic which can be used to distinguish them from non-drugs. People have become drunk on water which they were told was gin; they have swallowed salt tablets and shown clear signs of sedation; they have smoked inert material which they have been told was cannabis and become stoned. Should these otherwise inert chemicals therefore be classified as drugs? Certainly they were able to produce a definite psychological effect on the person who took them. In the final analysis, the concept of a 'drug' is a social artifact. What we regard as a drug depends as much upon its social meaning and the way in which people use it as upon its pharmacological or physiological properties.

An important part of what is generally called the drugs problem is the set of attitudes that society maintains towards drugs and drug taking. Much of the damage that is associated with drug taking is a result of mistaken laws and policies, and of hypocritical and self-deluding attitudes. We live in a society which tries to reconcile its disapproval of the use of drugs for non-medical purposes with the fact that vast amounts of psychoactive drugs are consumed in this way. The term 'drug taker' is used as a condemnation, as a way of identifying someone who is involved in a strange and deviant form of behaviour. There is a continuing reluctance to face up to the fact that drugs and drug takers are a part of our everyday life. Many people find it too threatening to acknowledge this, including a sizeable number of scientists, doctors and other 'experts'. Society is not made up of drug takers and non-users. We all take drugs in one way or another. The essence of the drugs problem seems to be that other people sometimes decide to take different drugs for different reasons.

When people are faced with inconsistencies of this sort, they frequently use psychological defence mechanisms in an attempt to reconcile the conflict. One of the most common of these defence mechanisms is called 'denial'. In order to resolve their conflict they deny that their own use of alcohol, tobacco or whatever, has anything in common with the illicit drugs that are used by the people they like to think of as 'drug takers'. The general reluctance to recognise that their tea, coffee, alcohol and tobacco really are drugs is a reflection of a widespread, completely irrational fear of drugs. Of course, this is not to deny that many people are badly damaged by the way they use drugs. But the generalised fear of drugs is misplaced. There are sensible as well as stupid ways to use drugs. It is a reasonable expectation that no drug should be considered completely safe; and even the least dangerous of drugs can be used in a way that is likely to be damaging to the person who is taking it. But since there is no chance that man will stop using drugs, it is imperative that we try to understand what sort of process drug taking really is. We can only do this if we re-examine some of the basic misunderstandings that surround the whole issue. At the very centre of the muddled thinking is this refusal to acknowledge that we are all drug takers.

As a continuation of this basic misconception, society clings to the notion that some of the substances we use are 'good' drugs whereas others are 'bad' drugs. LSD is a 'bad' drug. Heroin is, supposedly, the worst of the 'bad' drugs. Librium and Valium are 'good' drugs: drugs such as tobacco and alcohol tend to be classed as 'good' drugs even though we are becoming increasingly aware of their dangers. Other substances escape the 'drug' classification altogether and are regarded as non-drugs – like tea and coffee. Sometimes the 'good–bad' distinction becomes synonymous with that of 'safe–dangerous'. Society would like to believe that our good drugs are all safe, or at least comparatively safe, whereas the bad drugs should all have sinister and dangerous effects. In this way, scientific questions about the actual effects of a particular drug become entangled with issues of personal morality and subjective beliefs. This has led to some quite absurd pronouncements on the part of otherwise respected scientists and physicians: the need to justify their belief in the badness of certain drugs seems to have been so powerful that they have lost the ability to think straight on those

4

matters. By presenting personal opinions and moral views in the guise of incontrovertible scientific fact they have done more than anyone to perpetuate the myths and misconceptions about drug taking.

These 'good–bad', and 'safe–dangerous' classifications vary from time to time, and from culture to culture. During the 1960s, young people seemed to be turning to drugs in a quite unprecedented manner. LSD and cannabis were taken by millions of people. During the latter part of the decade and into the 1970s, other more sinister names such as methedrine, barbiturates and heroin began to be heard more often. The reaction of the press and of the mass media was one of righteous indignation. It seemed as if some completely new form of evil had suddenly descended upon the world. In fact, neither the widespread use of drugs nor the reaction of moral outrage that this provoked were new.

The term 'Bohemian' is often used to refer to someone who acts and dresses in an unconventional way. Few people know much about the original group of Bohemians except indirectly through Puccini's opera *La Bohème*. The Bohemians belonged to Paris of the 1840s. Like the hippies of a later age, the young men let their hair grow long, and they dressed in a manner which seemed shocking to their middle-class critics. They espoused unconventional, non-materialistic philosophies, lived in comparative poverty and flaunted their unconventional patterns of sexual behaviour. As with the hippies, drugs played an important part in their life-style. As well as drinking large amounts of alcohol, they horrified the public by their enthusiasm for a particular stimulant which they consumed in large quantities. A medical textbook published in 1909 by Sir T. Clifford Allbutt and Dr Humphrey Rolleston warned against the excessive use of this drug: 'The sufferer is tremulous and loses his self command; he is subject to fits of agitation and depression. He loses colour and has a haggard appearance . . . As with other such agents, a renewed dose of the poison gives temporary relief, but at the cost of future misery.' This drug which so shocked public opinion was coffee.

5

A reversal of roles of a different sort has taken place with regard to opiates such as heroin and morphine. Few people nowadays would hesitate in naming them as the most dangerous of drugs. Yet in America, it seems to have been a common medical practice during the early part of this century to treat alcoholics by prescribing morphine for them.

## Drug taking: a wider perspective

It is impossible to be certain how long people have been using drugs to change their states of consciousness; certainly the systematic use of drugs dates back many thousands of years. It is possible that the earliest drugs to be used would have been those that occur naturally. About four thousand plants are known to yield psychoactive drugs, but only about forty of these have been regularly used for their intoxicating effects. Interestingly, very few seem to have been known in the Old World. Prior to the voyages of exploration, Europe had comparatively little choice in its drugs. There was no tea, no coffee, no tobacco, little opium, little or no cannabis and virtually no hallucinogens. . . only alcohol. As a result, alcohol had to fill a very wide range of functions. It was used as a social beverage, as a tranquilliser, as a sedative, as a stimulant, and as an intoxicant to produce drunkenness and delirium. Alcohol became *the* European drug and it is still the dominant drug in European culture.

The voyages of exploration that opened up the Americas revealed a wide range of psychoactive drugs hitherto quite unknown in the Old World. The first voyage of Christopher Columbus discovered people on Hispaniola and Cuba who smoked cigars, and in Central and South America there was an abundance of psychoactive substances. The explorers brought these home with them. Strangely enough, the one drug that seems to have been largely unknown to the American Indians was alcohol. In return for showing such drugs as tobacco, peyote and cocaine to the European explorers, they were introduced to alcohol.

6

The general reluctance to use psychoactive drugs (and particularly drugs with hallucinogenic properties) that was built into European society at this time cannot be entirely explained in terms of the absence of the drugs themselves. Mescaline, peyote and cocaine may have been unknown in the Old World, but other drugs were available. Hallucinogenic mushrooms grow widely throughout northern Europe and there are various common substances which can be used to induce altered states of consciousness. Cannabis had been introduced into Europe with the Muslim occupation of Spain more than a thousand years ago, and although there was little interest in it as a psychoactive drug, it was being regularly cultivated for hemp fibre by the seventeenth century. So drugs were available, had there been a sufficient desire to use them.

This tendency to resist using drugs other than alcohol may have owed much to the dominant cultural influence of the Christian Church. Despite a distinctly secular attitude towards certain pleasures of the flesh, the use of drugs (other than alcohol) to modify states of consciousness has been consistently reviled by the Church. This may have been because of their links with other, more 'primitive', religions. Alternatively, it may have been because dramatically altered states of consciousness were thought of in terms of possession – usually possession by devils. Consequently, knowledge about the uses of drugs remained in the hands of various closed groups – apothecaries, alchemists, physicians and a few individuals who involved themselves with such esoteric practices as witchcraft.

Although many of the things that seem to have found their way into the witches' cauldron were probably there for their psychological significance, others contained powerful drugs. Bufotenine, for instance, is a highly toxic drug secreted by the toad. It is related to psilocin (a drug which is found in certain hallucinogenic mushrooms), and to LSD. It is also related to an extremely important brain chemical called serotonin from which it was first isolated. However, the toxic effects of bufotenine were known for centuries before its chemical discovery.

7

In 1670, the Professor of Medicine at Leipzig noted that 'Toads aroused to the point of fury are venomous', and the following suggestion is contained in a medieval recipe for poisoners: 'Place a toad in a sack with a little salt and shake well. Use the salt for giving to men.' This procedure could be guaranteed to provoke fury in even the most placid of toads, and was apparently useful for slow and chronic poisonings.

Nor was the life of the South American toad made any happier by the existence of an ancient Maya drink of heated mead into which a live toad was dropped at the last minute. Again, this was not done out of a desire to invent the cocktail olive but for the hallucinogenic drug in its skin.

Plants containing henbane and belladonna have also been used in the manufacture of salves and potions for witchcraft. Henbane contains scopolamine, and has been known for thousands of years to produce hallucinations and delirium. In the thirteenth century Bishop Albertus Magnus described how henbane was used to conjure up demons; under its influence people routinely described and believed in their visions of hell. Similarly, the thornapple, or devil's apple, which contains atropine, was said to be a major ingredient in the witches' Sabbath. Under the influence of these and other drugs, the witches flew through the night on their medieval trips. The ignorant and the superstitious mistook the hallucinations for reality, and it suited the Church to discourage the use of psychoactive drugs through their supposed link with the devil.

Of the naturally occurring drugs, those that have had most influence upon our thinking about drugs have been opium and its derivatives, notably heroin and morphine. The word 'opium' is derived from a Greek word meaning juice, and the substance itself is derived from the oriental poppy. This annual plant produces white or purplish coloured flowers. If a cut is made into the fruit capsule shortly before the flowers fall, opium oozes out in the form of a sticky solution.

One of the first references to opium is probably to be found in Homer's *Odyssey*,\* where Helen of Troy was presented with a

*There is some doubt about when Homer lived: estimates vary between 1050 and 850 BC.

gift of a drug called 'nepenthe' by the king of Egypt. By the second century AD, opium had established itself as a valuable aid to contemporary medicine. The Roman physician Galen recommended the drug theriaca, whose principal component is opium, as a treatment for many conditions including headaches, deafness, epilepsy and jaundice, as well as 'melancholy and all pestilences'. The use of opium spread from Asia Minor through Persia to India and China. It was not, however, until the second half of the eighteenth century that opium smoking became an established habit in the Far East, though it was probably first introduced to China by Arab traders as early as the eighth century.

England, too, has consumed its fair share of opium. Byron, Shelley, Keats, Lamb and Scott all took it, and William Wilberforce, George Crabbe, Thomas De Quincey and Samuel Taylor Coleridge became addicted to it. But its use was not confined to poets, writers and philosophers. It was often used instead of alcohol in the marshy Fenland areas of Cambridgeshire, Lincolnshire, Huntingdonshire and Norfolk. For most of the nineteenth century, the Fens were an unhealthy area in which to live: they were one of the main areas of the country in which malaria was endemic, and ague and rheumatic complaints were also particularly widespread. Opium was undoubtedly a useful folk remedy for such disorders, but its use was not restricted to such medical problems. Poppy head tea was often given to fractious children to calm them down, and opium was also used for recreational purposes. At the time, virtually no distinction seems to have been made between the social and the medical uses of the drug.

One custom was to drink beer with a piece of opium dissolved in it. Indeed, this custom became so well established that brewers and publicans produced opium beer in order to meet the popular taste – much to the surprise and inconvenience of travellers to the area. In 1850 Charles Kingsley described how on market days in Cambridge 'you will see the little boxes, doozens and doozens, a'ready on the counter; and never a venture man's wife goo by, that what calls in for her pennord o'elevation'. In such a dreary, foggy and unhealthy place, drugs could well provide some diversion. Another commentator at the time (one Dr Rayleigh Vicars) observed that for many people 'their colourless lives are temporarily heightened by the passing dreamland visions afforded them by the baneful poppy'.

The use of laudanum (a tincture of opium in alcohol) was also very common in England at the time and contemporary reports suggest that it may have been particularly common in women. Some women built up what would now be considered enormous habits; in one case, a woman was reported to be using a daily amount of 96 grains of the drug! This is about one hundred times greater than the amount used by most heroin addicts today. The regular use of opium was generally seen as quite normal and it appears to have provoked no marked concern.

Alcohol is one of our most extensively used drugs. Even the most primitive peoples have used it, and its history stretches back into prehistoric times. Neolithic Man knew how to make alcoholic drinks through the fermentation of cereals, and Stone Age beer jugs have been found. By 2000 BC there were taverns in Mesopotamia. In recent years, the Tasmanian aborigines were about as culturally retarded as any other known group. Yet even they knew how to tap a species of gum trees so that the sap ran down into a stone-lined hole, where it was left to undergo a process of natural fermentation. The end product was a crude but evidently quite effective intoxicant.

There are also cases of animals which have learned the pleasures of alcohol intoxication. Dogs and horses have been known to acquire their masters' taste for alcoholic beverages, and the chimpanzee will also drink them. In fact, chimpanzees seem to have clear preferences for certain drinks; sherry and port are preferred to Italian and German wines, and spirits are particularly unattractive. However, the most impressive example of alcohol intoxication in the animal kingdom is probably that of the East African elephants which would seek and eat fermenting mangoes; as a result they would become drunk and boisterous. Most drunks are worth avoiding. Fortunately, few of us ever encounter a drunk of the size and temperament of the African elephant.

The doubtful honour of being the first person ever to have his drink problem recorded goes to Noah. Genesis 9: 20-1 records that 'Noah began to be an husband man, and he planted a vineyard: and he drank of the wine, and was drunken; and he was uncovered within his tent'. Noah's sons were ashamed of this display of naked drunkenness, but his intemperance seems to have had little effect upon his health since he lived for 950 years.

Other records of the uses and abuses of alcohol have been found in ancient Egypt. Carvings have been discovered on the walls of the tombs of Beni-Hassen, which relate to the drinking habits of the Egyptian people 4,000 years ago. Some of the carvings illustrate the methods of cultivating and gathering grapes, and the operation of wine presses. Other pictures show parties at which people appear to have had too much to drink. Some of the revellers are attempting to stand on their heads. At the end of the proceedings, men are being carried home on the heads of their slaves. In the midst of such revelries, there were voices advocating moderation. One Egyptian papyrus carried the warning: 'Make not thyself helpless drinking in the beer shop . . . Falling down, thy limbs will be broken, and no one will give thee a hand to help thee up.'

In ancient Greece, Dionysus (or Bacchus) was the god of wine. Through the use of wine he was able to free the soul of all impediments of the flesh. The Greeks, however, appear to have used alcohol in moderation, and water was usually mixed with wine to reduce the strength of the drink. Plato took an especially strong line on drinking. For instance, he considered that it was barbaric to drink undiluted wine; and in the *Republic* he advocated that no one under the age of thirty should be permitted to drink wine at all. After that age it should be used only to relieve the infirmities of the flesh. It is odd that one of the few examples of immoderate drinking amongst the ancient Greeks should also have been one of their heroes – Alexander the Great. On his death, Seneca wrote, 'invincible by the toils of prodigious marches, by all the dangers of sieges and combats, by the most violent extremes of heat and cold, here he lies, conquered by his intemperance, and struck to earth by the fatal cup of Hercules'.

Among the Romans, excessive drinking was much more prevalent, particularly during the late years of the Roman Empire. Indeed, the practice of drinking vast amounts of wine became a common affair, with people trying to outdrink each other at all-night banquets. By the first century AD, the Emperor Domitian was so alarmed by the widespread drunkenness in Rome that he ordered half the vineyards to be destroyed, and prohibited the planting of any more without his imperial licence.

The discovery of distillation, and therefore of spirits, is a more recent event. It seems to have occurred about a thousand years ago, though the first coherent description of the process was made by Albertus Magnus in the thirteenth century. Some physicians and pharmacologists are ever optimistic about discovering new 'wonder drugs'. This is as true now as it was in the Middle Ages, when the alchemists were so impressed by this amazing new drug. The distilled alcohol was credited with remarkable properties. It was thought to be an antidote to senility, hence its title, *aqua vitae*, water of life.

Drunkenness existed long before man knew how to distil alcohol, but in their powerful distilled form spirits were a convenient and concentrated source of drunkenness. As the process of distillation became more efficient, spirits became cheaper and more widely available. In eighteenth-century England, the consumption of gin had reached epic proportions. Gin houses were everywhere. They advertised their delights by hanging out signs announcing that their customers could become drunk for a penny, and dead drunk for two pence. Among the added attractions, the floors of the cellars were covered with straw where those drinkers who had achieved total insensibility could be left until they were capable of rejoining the drinking. This amenity was provided free.

By 1736 the situation had deteriorated to such an extent that Parliament introduced drastic new measures in the form of the

Gin Act. This imposed severe restrictions on the sale of spirits and aroused considerable excitement both for and against the Act. This culminated in a series of riots and civil disturbances. In 1743 the Act was repealed.

Tea, coffee, cocoa and chocolate are such familiar domestic substances that most people find it hard to take seriously any suggestion that they are also drugs. Yet there is no doubt that tea and coffee are psychoactive drugs: both contain caffeine and tannin. Cocoa and chocolate also contain caffeine. Caffeine is one of a class of chemicals known as the xanthines, which produce a stimulant effect on the central nervous system and on the heart.

Like any other drug, caffeine can be used wisely, or it can be used foolishly. People who take excessive amounts of caffeine through their consumption of tea and coffee can experience various unpleasant side-effects as a result. More often than not, they fail to recognise these as toxic effects. A dose of 200 milligrams (mg.) of caffeine per day (about two cups of coffee) is usually considered large enough to have pharmacological effects which are clinically significant. It has been known for a long time that over-consumption of tea and coffee can lead to headaches and mental irritability. What is less well known is at what level of consumption a person is taking an excessive amount of caffeine. Some estimates suggest that anyone who is taking more than 600 mg. a day (five or six cups of coffee, or nine to ten cups of tea) may be running a health risk. At such levels caffeine can produce headaches, insomnia, dizziness, trembling, diarrhoea, breathlessness and anxiety symptoms. Caffeine also has various toxic effects on the heart: these can include palpitations, rapid pulse or irregular pulse rate, and when consumed in sufficiently large amounts it can lead to increased blood pressure. Many people who have found themselves suffering from these side-effects of excessive caffeine consumption must have reached for one of the common proprietary tablets used to relieve such problems. Surprisingly, some of these contain yet more caffeine, and may therefore aggravate the headache even further.

There has been some disagreement about the amounts of caffeine contained in tea or coffee. The most popular belief is that coffee contains more caffeine than tea. Several authorities suggest that coffee, as it is usually prepared, may be two or three times as strong as tea in this respect. Others have asserted that the two are approximately of equal strength. When translated into everyday terms, of course, these arguments are beside the point, since people make each drink to their own taste. An approximate comparison of the relative amounts of caffeine in various popular drinks is shown in Table 1.

*Table 1. The relative caffeine content of different drinks*

| | |
|---|---|
| Brewed coffee | 100–150 mg. per cup |
| Instant coffee | 85–100 mg. per cup |
| Decaffeinated coffee | 2– 4 mg. per cup |
| Tea | 60– 75 mg. per cup |
| Cola drinks | 40– 60 mg. per glass |

In the United States, as in many other Western countries, coffee is drunk in large quantities: the coffee break has become an established pattern of working life for many people. Cola drinks are popular among young people in all countries. In Britain, tea drinking is a ritual component of everyday life. Every one of us must have heard it said at some time or other that 'I couldn't get started properly in the morning without a drink of tea/coffee', or that 'I don't know how I would get through the day without it.'

One American survey of a group of housewives found that 26 per cent drank more than five cups of coffee every day. Even those who drank only one or two cups a day almost invariably drank a cup in the morning. When asked why, a surprisingly high proportion gave reasons that showed they were aware of its drug effects. Forty-six per cent said that 'it helps to wake you up', 42 per cent said that 'it gets you going in the morning', and about a quarter either said that it 'gives you a lift' or that it 'stimulates you'. What is even more impressive is that nearly a third of these housewives described themselves as being *dependent* upon their morning coffee. When asked what would happen if they weren't able to obtain their usual drink, those who drank five or more cups per day described exactly the sort of symptoms that make up the caffeine withdrawal syndrome – headache, irritability, loss of efficiency at certain tasks, nervousness and restlessness. People joke about being 'addicted' to their drink of tea or coffee. For some it is a joke; for others, the dependence is a fact.

Another more recent study of the use of tea and coffee in Canada produced the same sort of result – about one-third of the Canadian population may be regarded as being dependent on the caffeine provided in tea and coffee. The proportion is probably about the same in most other Western countries and in many other countries throughout the world.

Tea, coffee, and the other caffeine-containing drinks are drugs in the full sense of the term. People become dependent upon them so that they are psychologically uncomfortable if deprived of their drink. Heavier users also experience withdrawal symptoms in the absence of their drug. Whether or not one chooses to regard this dependence as a bad thing depends upon one's initial attitude towards dependence itself. Tea and coffee are comparatively cheap, freely and legally available, and their use carries no social stigma (with the exception of one or two religious groups). The main problems associated with the use of this drug follow from using it in excessive quantities.

As well as the side-effects that have already been mentioned, each of the caffeine-containing drinks can lead to restlessness and disturbed sleep. This runs against the popular belief in the effectiveness of chocolate as a 'nightcap' to help you to sleep. When it is taken in very large quantities, caffeine is a poison. It can produce convulsions like those of epileptic fits, and finally leads to death through respiratory failure. It is hardly likely, though, that any of us would take an unintentional fatal overdose. To do so would involve drinking between 70 and 100 cups of coffee at a single sitting. Any such achievement would indicate considerable determination.

# 2

## THE EFFECTS OF DRUGS

In Xanadu did Kubla Khan
A stately pleasure-dome decree:
Where Alph, the sacred river, ran
Through caverns measureless to man
Down to a sunless sea.

. . . . . . .

I would build that dome in air,
That sunny dome! those caves of ice!
And all who heard should see them there,
And all should cry, Beware! Beware!
His flashing eyes, his floating hair!
Weave a circle round him thrice,
And close your eyes with holy dread,
For he on honey-dew hath fed,
And drunk the milk of Paradise.

Opium is traditionally the drug of dreams, and these lines from Coleridge's *Kubla Khan* were inspired by opium: the rhythm of the poem reflects something of the hypnotic quality of the drug itself. There is also an intriguing allusion to opium within the poem. Coleridge had an extensive knowledge of the classics and as a lifelong opium addict he can hardly have failed to notice the references to the drug in classical literature. In the *Aeneid*, Virgil writes of *Humida mella soperiferumque papaver* (The narcotic poppy with honey-dew; Book IV, line 486).

Coleridge described how, after drinking laudanum, he fell into a drug-induced trance in which he seemed to compose two or three hundred lines of poetry. The images rose up before him as if he were the passive observer. When he awoke, he began to write them down, but was interrupted by a visitor. After returning to his writing, he found he was left with only the vaguest recollection of his original vision and could remember no more than a few scattered lines and images. Coleridge did not publish *Kubla Khan* for almost twenty years after it was written, and then only on the urging of Byron. This was probably because of his doubts about the worth of what he rather dismissively described as 'a psychological curiosity'.

The suggestion that *Kubla Khan* was inspired by opium produced intense feelings in literary circles. To some romantics, the notion that this entrancing vision could have been inspired by the drug of dreams was very appealing. Others were just as strongly offended by the idea. One recent biography, for instance, utterly rejects Coleridge's own account of how the poem was inspired, preferring instead to talk of writing poetry as 'a labour as hard and exhausting as road building'.* This same puritan reinterpretation of Coleridge's own account of the poem's origins asserts that, far from contributing to Coleridge's poetry, opium was directly responsible for extinguishing it.

In fact, both Coleridge and his puritan critics share the same misconception. Opium was not the source of his poetry nor did it lead to the death of his muse. The effects of a drug depend largely upon the psychology of the person who has taken it. Had Coleridge not experienced that particular drug-reverie of which he spoke, he might never have been inspired to write *Kubla Khan*. At the same time, the vision itself, and more particularly the translation of that experience into lines of poetry afterwards, owed more to the personality and talent of Coleridge than it did to any drug. It is patently absurd to claim that anyone can produce great poetry merely by taking drugs, though some drug takers have been convinced of the depth of their artistic vision when intoxicated.

The way in which a drug affects the person who has taken it depends as much upon the psychological characteristics of the individual (his personality, how he believes the drug will affect him, his emotional state, etc.) as upon the chemical properties of the drug itself. The idea that specific drugs have fixed and

---

* Molly Lefebure, *Samuel Taylor Coleridge. A Bondage of Opium*. London: Gollancz, 1974.

predictable effects which are the same from person to person is extremely widespread, but it remains a fallacy. In the particular case of the psychoactive drugs, such effects are the exception rather than the rule.

Few people have difficulty in understanding that different people react in different ways after drinking alcohol. Thinking of other drugs, they often forget how much the psychology of the individual can influence the drug effects. The biochemistry of a drug is only one of a wide range of factors that interact to produce the final effects. These depend to a certain extent upon the basic personality structure of the person who took it. Reactions to alcohol (and to other sedative drugs such as the barbiturates), for instance, seem to depend upon whether the drinker is an introvert or an extravert. The typical extravert is sociable, likes parties, has many friends and prefers the company of others to being alone. He looks for excitement and enjoys taking chances. The typical introvert is a quiet, retiring sort of person who is reserved and reticent except with his close friends. He tends to plan ahead rather than act impulsively, is reliable, and usually rather pessimistic. Introverts seem to be comparatively resistant to the effects of alcohol, whereas extraverts succumb to its intoxicating influence much more readily. The opposite is true of stimulant drugs like amphetamine or caffeine. Introverts react most strongly to these drugs and extraverts least.

One way of demonstrating this involves giving a sedative such as a barbiturate to groups of subjects who differ in their levels of introversion/extraversion. This has been done in several experiments, and it has been found that the amount of a sedative necessary to produce a given level of sedation varies considerably between introverts and extraverts. A standard dose of the drug sufficient to sedate more than 95 per cent of the most extraverted subjects will sedate fewer than 10 per cent of the introverted subjects.

Because of the way drugs are classified (in this case, either as stimulants or as sedatives), the way they relate to personality and behaviour is often misunderstood. It is assumed that any drug which is classified as stimulant will make the person who takes it more impulsive and excitable, whereas sedative drugs will make him quieter and less excitable – roughly speaking, that stimulants will make the user more extraverted, and sedatives will make him more introverted. In fact, the opposite is nearer to the truth. The physiological action of stimulants generally makes the user more *introverted* and sedatives make him more *extraverted*. (The physiological basis for this is quite complicated and the details need not concern us here. For the reader who is interested in this effect, a full account is given by Hans Eysenck in his book *The Biological Basis of Personality*.)

In practice, the extraverting effects of sedative drugs are already well-known. Alcohol is widely used for precisely this purpose at social gatherings such as parties. At most parties, the extraverted behaviour of the guests can be directly linked to the amount of drink that has been consumed. Drunkenness is a chemical equivalent of extreme extraversion. There is, of course, a limit to this effect. In very large quantities the sedative effects of alcohol have a disruptive effect on behaviour, and finally it produces unconsciousness.

Although the introverting effects of stimulants are less well-known, these drugs have been used in psychiatry for some years, mainly in the treatment of hyperactive children. Superficially it might seem strange that stimulant drugs have been used to calm impulsive, irritable and intractable children. The paradox, however, is more apparent than real provided one reminds oneself that drugs such as the amphetamines and methylphenidate (Ritalin, an amphetamine-like stimulant) can have an introverting effect upon behaviour. Usually between 60 and 90 per cent of hyperactive children show some improvement after being given stimulants. Unfortunately, the treatment seems to be effective only for as long as the child continues to take the drugs. Many of those who show a marked improvement while on the medication fail to maintain these gains when the drug is withdrawn. In the long-term, it seems that children who have been given this form of drug treatment do no better than those who have not.

## The user's beliefs about his drugs

Taking a drug is not a psychologically neutral event. Whether it is prescribed by a physician, bought over the counter of the local chemist, or obtained through illegal sources, the user will almost certainly have clear ideas about how and when it is appropriate to use the drug, and about the ways in which it is likely to affect his or her thoughts, feelings and behaviour. Even in those rare cases where users have no knowledge of the drug they have taken, they actively search for reasonable explanations about how the drug might be affecting them. These psychological and social influences are generated by the users themselves, by what they have been told by others, and by the immediate social circumstances in which the drug is taken; and these influences are powerful enough to alter a user's response to the pharmacological effects of the drug itself.

One study which demonstrates this was carried out at the University of Stockholm. The subjects who had volunteered to take part were divided into three groups. The first received a fairly large dose of one of the most common of the sleeping tablets currently being prescribed (200 mg. of pentobarbital) and were told that this would make them feel sleepy. The subjects in the second group were given the same sedative drug but the experimenter told them that he did not know what sort of effect it would have. Those in the third group were not given any drug at all, merely a capsule containing a pharmacologically inert powder, but they were given the same explanation as the first group – that this was a sleeping tablet that would make them feel tired and drowsy. As predicted, those who were given the active drug together with the information that this would make them feel sleepy, showed the greatest response. However, the direct drug effects alone were no more powerful than the experimenter's suggestions alone: both produced the same amount of drowsiness.

The physiological actions of drugs are not sufficient to produce the sort of psychological changes associated with the use of psychoactive drugs (e.g. euphoria). Before this can happen, the user must attach a psychological 'label' to the way he feels (though this labelling seldom occurs at a conscious level).

One of the best-known investigations of this labelling process was carried out by the American psychologists Stanley Schachter and Jerome Singer. In their ingenious study, the student volunteers were led to believe that they were taking part in a psychology experiment concerned with vision. The subjects were given an injection of adrenaline, a hormone produced in the central nervous system which causes a wide range of physiological changes in the body but no consistent psychological effects. One group was given an accurate description of the effects of the drug – that they might have a sensation of their heart beating faster, and experience some hand tremor and a warm and flushed feeling in the face. They were reassured that these effects would last only for a short time. Another group was given a misleading description of how the drug would affect them. They were told that it would cause numbness in the feet, itching sensations and a slight headache.

In the second part of the experiment, the subjects were asked individually to go to a waiting room to let the drug take effect before the start of the visual tests. In the waiting room was another 'subject' waiting for the visual tests. In fact, this other subject was really an actor who was part of the experiment. While the two are together in the waiting room, the actor starts to behave in a most peculiar fashion. He runs about the room playing basketball with a scrap of paper and a waste paper basket, makes paper aeroplanes which he throws around the room, and generally behaves in an exuberant and excitable manner.

The experiment was designed to investigate the ways in which emotional states (such as euphoria) are produced, and the real interest of the experimenters was to find out how the subjects behaved in the waiting room. The two groups in the experiment both received the same drug and were exposed to the same unusual behaviour in the waiting room. They differed only in one respect. The first group already knew how the drug would affect them; the second group did not. The results show that the people who had been misled about how the drug would affect them were more likely to be influenced by, and to imitate, the actor's behaviour: they too were inclined to become euphoric and excited.

The same experiment was then repeated, but with three groups. One received an injection of adrenaline plus an explanation of how it would affect them; the second group was given the drug but with no explanation of its effects; and a third was given a placebo injection. The subjects were then taken one at a time to the waiting room. This time the actor's performance was one of irritation and anger. Again, those who knew that their altered physiological state was due to the adrenaline were least affected by the actor's behaviour. Those who had been given the drug but no explanation of how it would affect them were more likely to become angry and irritable. The placebo group were less influenced by the events in the waiting room than those who had been given the drug but no description of its physiological effects, but more so than those who had received the drug plus an accurate description.

In this experiment, there are two factors at work. On the one hand, there is the physiological arousal (heart beating faster, tremor, etc,) caused by the drug itself and, on the other, there are the expectations and beliefs that the person has about his state of arousal. When people do not understand why they feel the way they do, they seem to relate their feelings to the particular situation in which they find themselves. It is as if the subjects who did not know how the drug would affect them had said to themselves, 'I feel strange. My heart is racing and I am trembling. Therefore I must feel angry/happy like the other person in the experiment.' Those who already knew how the adrenaline would affect them were uninfluenced by the actor's behaviour because they could attribute their altered physiological state to the drug.

The beliefs, attitudes and expectations of the drug taker are no less important outside the laboratory. In what has since established itself as one of the classic studies of cannabis smokers, Howard Becker looked at the ways in which a person learns how to get stoned on the drug. The first time someone tries cannabis, he does not usually get high. Sometimes the user feels a little strange, but is not sure how to interpret the changes he experiences. Sometimes the effects are perceived as being physically unpleasant and the novice may actually be sick. Sometimes users may claim, rather indignantly, that they do not feel any different at all. When this happens they may decide that the whole business of smoking cannabis is simply not worthwhile; or, they may be worried by their failure to experience any euphoric effects and ask others about it. In such conversations they will be made aware of specific details of their experience with the drug which they may not have noticed before, or which they had noticed but failed to identify as a part of being stoned. So the next time they try cannabis they will be better prepared to know when they are stoned.

Novices must learn the details of how it feels to be stoned, and acquire the necessary concepts to be able to identify and describe how they feel after smoking cannabis. Before that, the effects of the drug are sufficiently ambiguous for them not to know how they feel (as in the results of those experiments where the subjects did not know which drug they had taken). Inexperienced drug takers sometimes become confused and frightened by their early experiments with drugs. They may be so alarmed by the changes in their state of consciousness that they become convinced at the time that they are going insane. Yet the same alterations and distortions of consciousness which so frighten the novice may be regarded by the experienced drug taker as extremely pleasurable. Nor is there anything unique about cannabis in this respect. Drugs such as heroin also require an initial period during which the novice learns how to interpret their effects. Most people find their first experience of heroin unpleasant, and many are sick. In one study where a group of non-addicts were given either a small injection of heroin or a placebo, the placebo was reported to be more pleasurable than heroin. One can go through a whole list of drugs making the same point. Most children experimenting with their first cigarette find it a nauseous experience.

Similarly, most people find their first taste of alcohol far from appealing. In order to become a regular drug user it is necessary to learn how to enjoy the effects.

After people have learnt how to experience the effects of a drug, their beliefs and expectations about that drug may lead them to react as if they were intoxicated when they had not taken a drug at all. In one study of experienced cannabis smokers, the subjects were given cigarettes containing either cannabis or a placebo preparation of cannabis material from which the active drug had been artificially removed. Although the average level of intoxication reported after smoking the placebo was lower than for cannabis, some of the subjects felt just as intoxicated on the placebo as on the active drug. The more experienced cannabis users were the most likely to get stoned on the placebo, whereas those who had had least experience with cannabis were better able to differentiate between the drug and the placebo.

## The placebo effect

> Fillet of a fenny snake,
> In the cauldron boil and bake;
> Eye of newt, and toe of frog,
> Wool of bat, and tongue of dog,
> Adder's fork, and blind worm's sting,
> Lizard's leg, and howlet's wing,
> For a charm of pow'rful trouble,
> Like a hell-broth boil and bubble.
> *Macbeth*, IV.i. 12-19

Because psychological factors play such a large part in determining how people respond to drugs, it is possible for them to react as if they had taken a drug even when no such drug has been used. This is, of course, the placebo effect (i.e. those psychological and physiological changes produced by the placebo). Conventional definitions of a placebo usually emphasise that it should be a pharmacologically inert substance: starch, talc, and sugar powder are often used in making up placebos. These 'dummy' tablets may be thought of as 'pure' placebos in the sense that they have no pharmacological effects, but it is too restrictive to think of a placebo only as a completely inert preparation. 'Pure' placebos are not used very often except in controlled experiments; for most practical purposes it is the 'impure' placebo that is more important. This is any medicine or treatment which is prescribed because either the doctor, or the patient, or both, believe that it works, but which really has no specific effects upon the condition being treated. Many pharmacologically active drugs are used for their placebo effect in this way.

Placebos belong to that twilight world of medical science that has never quite been able to claim respectability. This is a pity, because the placebo effect is both interesting and important. It is important in practical terms because it is a major therapeutic influence (albeit an unacknowledged one) in many medical treatments. It is important in theoretical terms because it highlights the psychological component of the response to drugs.

All manner of extraordinary organic and inorganic substances, including almost every conceivable form of human and animal excretion, have been used as medicines at one time or another. Crocodile dung, the teeth of pigs, hooves of asses, eunuch fat, lozenges of dried vipers, powders made from precious stones, brick dust, fur, feathers, hair, human sweat, earthworms and spiders have all taken their place among the tools of the physician: by comparison, the witches' brew described in *Macbeth* seems positively benign. In these enlightened times, few physicians would place much confidence in such esoteric preparations. On the other hand, it has been suggested that as many as one-third of all prescriptions issued by British and American doctors may be for drugs which have no specific pharmacological effects upon the condition being treated (i.e. they are placebos).

To many people, the placebo carries rather derisory connotations which may, in part, be due to the idea that doctors use placebos as a harmless method of humouring demanding or difficult patients. Undoubtedly this does happen. But more often, placebos are not prescribed deliberately to deceive the patient, but with both the doctor and the patient believing them to be an effective medicine. Far from being the omniscient, detached scientists who know what 'really' has therapeutic value and who sometimes use placebos just to keep the patient quiet, many physicians unwittingly use valueless drugs because their personal experience tells them wrongly that they are 'getting results'.

In ancient Egypt, the physicians who prescribed crocodile dung did so not merely to have a cynical laugh at the patient's expense; nor is it entirely plausible to believe that they carried on using this unusual medication in the absence of any improvement by their patients. In the same way, patients have been purged, poisoned, punctured, blistered, bled, leeched, heated, frozen, sweated and shocked. Treatments which were administered so confidently have turned out to be either ineffective, or dangerous, or both. One can only assume that the physicians' faith in their remedies was strong enough to establish in the patient the hope and expectation that they would lead to improvement. As a result, both the patient and the physician would interpret the symptoms more optimistically after the medicine had been taken, and in many cases there would indeed be a marked improvement in the patient's condition. Nor should the reader suppose that the problems which respond favourably to placebos are imaginary or 'only psychological'. Severe post-operative pain, chest pain associated with coronary heart disease, multiple sclerosis, diabetes, radiation sickness, stomach ulcers, toothache, seasickness, arthritis and the common cold are just a few of the disorders in which placebos have produced a therapeutic improvement. Across a wide range of problems, the proportion of patients who improve after receiving a placebo averages out at about 35 per cent.

Placebo responses can be more powerful than those to active drugs. The psychological response to a drug may also profoundly alter or even reverse the direct drug effects, and as with active drugs, placebos can produce unwanted side-effects. Headache, nausea, dryness of the mouth, drowsiness and tiredness have all been reported by people who have taken a placebo. In some cases there have been major toxic reactions. After being given a placebo containing sugar powder, one patient complained of extreme weakness, palpitations of the heart and nausea; another developed a widespread skin rash (which disappeared after he stopped taking the placebo). There are even cases in which people have become addicted to placebos, and in the *Journal of the American Medical Association* an editorial warned that 'When withdrawing a placebo on which a patient has become dependent it will not help him to be told that it was only a placebo.' It is difficult to imagine a more convincing illustration of the essentially psychological nature of drug dependence than an addiction to placebos.

Nor should it be imagined that an addiction to placebos is necessarily trivial. Many active drugs are used inappropriately because the user wrongly attributes the placebo effect associated with taking the drug to the drug itself. Pain-relieving (analgesic) drugs such as aspirin and paracetamol are the world's most widely used drugs. They are also the most widely misused drugs. They are seldom taken under medical supervision, and generally they are unwittingly used for the placebo effect that goes with them. For example, they are regularly taken to suppress the symptoms of the common cold, yet aspirin has no effect upon viruses or bacteria; they are also taken to help the user to get to sleep, though their sedative properties are minimal. The United States consumes more than 9,000 tons of aspirin each year (the equivalent of about 44 million tablets every day). A study of blood donors in Connecticut found that 37 per cent of the people who gave blood had recently eaten aspirin. These drugs are at least as popular in Britain which swallows a yearly supply of some 2,000 tons of analgesics (about 4,300 million tablets), and where there are more than a million people who use them regularly each day. One criterion for identifying analgesic abuse is the consumption of more than one kilo (2·2 lb) of the drug in a six-month period.

On this basis, it has been estimated that there may be as many as a quarter of a million analgesic abusers in Britain. The heaviest user of such drugs that I have seen was a 42-year-old woman who was as obviously dependent upon them as any junkie is upon his heroin. She was using between two and three hundred aspirin tablets per week.

This form of drug abuse is encouraged by the misconception that these tablets are not really 'drugs' at all, and that they can be used as often as one likes without ill-effects. This is not so. Some 7,000 patients each year are admitted to British hospitals for aspirin-induced gastro-intestinal bleeding (usually associated with stomach ulcers). Heavy use of these drugs can also cause kidney damage, and they are one of the most common causes of accidental death among children. Such extensive misuse of these drugs reflects a deeper need to obtain instant chemical relief from each and every one of the aches and pains that are part of living.

The placebo effect can be observed in another eternal preoccupation – the search for a reliable aphrodisiac. Papyri from ancient Egypt have been found with instructions for preparing 'erotic potions', and the Greeks too wrote at length on this subject (as in the *Medea* of Euripides). There is even a reference to the subject in the Bible (Genesis 30: 14-16), where Leah used the mandrake to 'lie with' Jacob.

The mandrake holds a position of unrivalled importance in European witchcraft because of its magical properties. It was said, for instance, to utter such unearthly shrieks when pulled from the ground that whoever heard them might die. Early Christians thought it was created by God as an experiment before He created man in the Garden of Eden, and Machiavelli was sufficiently impressed by its erotic powers to write a comedy in its honour (*La Mandragola*). Despite all this, the mandrake has no chemical properties that would make it a useful aphrodisiac, though its major components (scopolamine, atropine and hyoscamine) could produce distortions of consciousness that might render the user more susceptible to persuasion. In this century, scopolamine has been used in interrogation procedures as a 'truth drug'.

In Western societies, the truffle and the oyster have a current reputation as aphrodisiac foods. Sadly, neither contains anything which is remotely likely to fire the passions. The constituents of the oyster are water (76–89%), carbohydrates (3·7–9·6%), mineral salts (0·9–3%), proteins (8–11%) and fat (1·2–2·5%). When subjected to this sort of chemical analysis, the truffle proved to be even less sexy: 77% water, 13·5% carbohydrates, and the remainder fat, albumen and salts. Few of the other reputed aphrodisiacs do much better. Even the humble potato was once regarded as an especially useful erotic stimulant.

The aphrodisiac effect of these foods and drugs is without any physio-chemical basis, though it is some testimony to the fact that they are not completely useless that these and other substances have been so persistently used in seductions. The reasons for this are psychological. The aphrodisiac is really a special sort of placebo. A good meal in relaxed surroundings can be a most effective means of turning the thoughts towards other sensual pleasures. This can be assisted by that least arcane of the seducer's devices – alcohol.

> Candy
> Is dandy
> But liquor
> Is quicker.
> (Ogden Nash)

However, even the effects of alcohol are indirect. It does not provoke sexual desire directly so much as remove the customary restraints on such behaviour. The would-be Lothario might do well to remember Shakespeare's warning about alcohol: 'it provokes the desire, but it takes away the performance' (*Macbeth*, IV. iii. 29-30).

Spanish fly is a quite different kind of aphrodisiac in that its physiological effects are supposed to work directly upon the genitals. The drug is prepared from a beautiful sheen-covered beetle found in southern Europe which is dried and heated until it disintegrates into a fine powder. This contains a drug called cantharidin which causes acute irritation of the gastro-intestinal system and an inflammation of the urinary tract. This provides some sort of genital stimulation which can be perceived as sexual desire. The use of Spanish fly is not to be recommended, as it carries a number of dangers.

In recent years, Vitamin E and ginseng have established themselves in some quarters as fashionable drugs. Claims about their effectiveness have been typically extravagant, and if one were to believe everything that has been said about them there would be few ills left to mankind. Vitamin E is ideally suited to the commercial exploitation of those in search of a panacea since it can be taken in enormous doses without producing any toxic effects. On the other hand, it has no beneficial effect either. It has been promoted and used for every imaginable disorder, from acne to cancer, from baldness to coronary heart disease. As a drug in search of an illness, it is the latest example of the age-old fallacy that health, happiness and sexual fulfilment are all available in tablet form. Ginseng also fulfils this need, though it is a more potent drug than Vitamin E. It has been known and used in China for thousands of years, and in traditional Chinese medicine its effects are explained in terms of harmonising the balance of yin and yang forces in the five bodily systems. It seems to act as a mild stimulant drug, much like coffee, and it may also possess anti-inflammatory properties. Predictably, both Vitamin E and ginseng have been hailed as aphrodisiacs (few substances have not). In the end, though, there is little evidence to show the existence of any such beast as the reliable aphrodisiac. Sexual desire is too capricious to respond obediently and automatically to the demands of a drug.

## Brain mechanisms

The significance of psychological factors in determining how someone will react to a psychoactive drug has been vastly underestimated. However, it would be just as seriously misleading to give too much weight to these factors. The psychology of the user, the social setting in which he or she takes drugs, and the specific pharmacological properties of the drug all influence how the user finally responds to the drug. Sometimes the psychological factors are most important (as with the placebo effect); sometimes social factors are the most powerful influence; and sometimes the pharmacology of the drug plays the most important role (especially at high dose levels). The emphasis given in this chapter to the psychology of the drug taker is intended to serve as an antidote to the more orthodox view that the effects of drugs are *intrinsic* properties of those substances. It is a grave mistake to imagine that we can understand the ways in which people respond to psychoactive drugs simply as a consequence of physiological reactions to a chemical substance. Nonetheless, psychoactive drugs do have effects upon the brain and bodily systems of the drug taker, and some of these effects are very interesting in their own right.

During the 1950s a young psychologist at McGill University in Canada was interested in the way in which particular areas of the brain affected learning. To test one of his ideas, he planned to apply an extremely small electric current to the brain of his laboratory animals. At that time, the technique of implanting electrodes in the brain was still extremely crude and unreliable, and through an accident one of the electrodes was implanted in an entirely different area of the brain to the one originally intended. As a result, the animal did not show the expected alerting response to the electrical stimulation, and many other scientists might have simply removed the animal and continued with the experiment. Dr Olds, however, was intrigued by the fact that the rat seemed to be interested in the part of the cage where it had received the electrical stimulation. After it had been given a few more tastes of the brain stimulation, the rat never left that part of the cage. It seemed as if it were waiting for more.

Later, when the experiment was systematically repeated, it was found that animals which had the opportunity of administering their own dose of electrical stimulation would press a lever repeatedly in order to obtain it. Some animals would deliver more than a hundred doses per minute; and if left to their own devices, they would maintain this pace for hour after hour. This only happened when the electrodes were located in a specific part of the brain – in what is called the limbic system. The functions of this area of the brain are not well understood, but it is known to play an important part in regulating the emotions. Olds' experiments represented a remarkable discovery. Never before had there been any suggestion that electrical stimulation of the brain could be pleasurable. And there seemed little doubt that the experimental animals enjoyed the experience. Animals that had not received any electrical stimulation for several days would jump out of the experimenter's hands into the test apparatus in their eagerness for more. On the rare occasions when this electrical stimulation has been tried with human subjects, it has produced feelings of euphoria and sexual pleasure. One female subject experienced repetitive orgasms after five to ten minutes of such stimulation. Not surprisingly, these areas of the brain rapidly became known as 'the pleasure centres'.

This research generated considerable excitement. To many people, it reawakened the ancient fear that others could take control of one's own mind. In his *Profiles of the Future*, Arthur C. Clarke spoke of the possibility that it could lead to 'the electronic possession of human robots' and commented that this research may turn out to have more far-reaching consequences than the early work of the nuclear physicists: 'the possibilities here, for good and evil, are so obvious that there is no point in exaggerating or discounting them'.

These early experiments fired the enthusiasm of some researchers who thought that stimulation of the pleasure centres could offer a neurophysiological explanation of drug taking. After a drug enters the bloodstream it is rapidly absorbed into the brain, and several proponents of this view of drug taking have suggested that many of the psychoactive drugs act directly on the pleasure centres of the brain. With repeated use these drugs were said to swamp the brain's ability to respond to other pleasurable forms of stimulation and the person's capacity to experience pleasure at all, except through the use of higher and higher doses of drugs. This account has a certain superficial plausibility, and it may contain some element of truth; but it has a number of serious weaknesses as an explanation of drug taking. It conveniently chooses to ignore those aspects of drug taking that cannot be explained in physiological terms. For instance, if psychoactive drugs stimulate the pleasure centres of the brain directly, this suggests that the drug experience should be one of unambiguous pleasure; and if the experimental studies are correct, it should be almost irresistible in its attractions. Yet many people find their first experience with drugs to be distinctly unpleasant: only later do they learn to enjoy the effects. Similarly, the vast majority of those who have used drugs on several occasions never become addicted to them; and even among drug addicts, very few people compulsively fill themselves with the maximum amount of drugs even when they have more than enough for their immediate needs, and eventually a sizeable number of addicts stop using drugs.

These features of drug taking are seldom recognised because they do not fit neatly into a physiological explanation. The reader may recall the legend of Procrustes, the robber who waylaid travellers and tied them to a bed. If they were longer than the bed he chopped off the offending limbs, and if they were too short, he stretched them until both bed and traveller were the same length.

In the middle of the 1970s, another scientific development revived flagging interest in the possible relationship between brain mechanisms and drug effects. Professor Hans Kosterlitz and his research team at Aberdeen University identified a number of chemical substances in the brain which had a remarkable biochemical similarity to morphine. The resemblance seemed so close that these substances were named endorphins, an abbreviation for endogenous (natural) morphine. Throughout the central nervous system, there are specific receptors programmed to react to these endorphins. It is too early to reach any definite conclusions about the significance of these complex neurochemicals. They are still a comparatively recent discovery, and the research programme surrounding them is now so intense that almost any statement is likely to be out of date by the time it is published.

One interesting possibility is that such chemicals are produced by the brain as a natural defence against pain. For instance, there have been several observations that endorphins are released in greater quantities during childbirth, and that this could account for the reduced sensitivity to pain at such times. It has been reported that the release of endorphins is often found after acupuncture intended to relieve pain. It has also been argued that endorphins could provide a neuro-chemical basis for that curious phenomenon, the placebo effect; but for the moment these comments are no more than speculative suggestions.

The existence of these chemicals and of receptors in the brain programmed to react both to them and to drugs such as heroin and morphine, would appear to have greater significance for our understanding of opiate addiction. Hans Kosterlitz has described how this recent research could provide a foundation for explaining the tolerance and withdrawal effects associated with opiate addiction. Under normal circumstances the endorphins probably maintain the balance of the nerve impulses in the brain which respond to pain and stress. The opiate drugs, however, are more toxic than their naturally occurring counterparts. As a result, the opiates overwhelm the body's natural chemicals and take over the control of these pain-inhibiting mechanisms. With repeated use, the drugs may reduce the body's sensitivity to the natural chemicals, or even reduce its capacity to produce such chemicals. The body then becomes dependent upon its outside supply of drugs in order to function normally, and when the opiates are withdrawn, the body's natural responses are inadequate. This may account for at least some of the phenomena of tolerance and withdrawal in opiate addiction. It would, however, be a mistake to elevate physiological descriptions of this sort into a complete explanation of drug taking, as some have already tried to do. It would be mistaken even to assume that a description of what happens to the neurochemical systems of the body could explain all that happens to the addict as he becomes tolerant to opiates or during the period of withdrawal from these drugs. At most, it delineates the mechanisms upon which the symptoms of withdrawal may be based.

# 3

## THE SOCIAL CONTEXT

The Vietnam War held many unpleasant surprises for the Americans: not least among these was the widespread use of drugs by American troops. By 1970, almost every enlisted man in Vietnam was being approached by someone offering him heroin – usually within the first four weeks of his arrival in the country. One soldier described how his first offer of heroin came, as he was leaving the plane on which he had arrived in Vietnam, from a soldier preparing to board the same plane to return home. By 1971, it had been estimated that almost half of the enlisted men serving in Vietnam had taken opiates (mainly heroin) on at least one occasion. Most of those who used opiates used them repeatedly and over a long period, and most of the troops who used drugs while in Vietnam used more than one type. Amphetamines and barbiturates were both widely used, and some estimates suggest that more than three-quarters of the troops in Vietnam smoked cannabis. As many as 20 per cent of the troops felt that they had been addicted to opiates. This was a cause of considerable alarm to both the military and civilian authorities. At a time when the defence of South-East Asia against the Communist menace was felt to be essential for the maintenance of the American way of life, it was not reassuring to hear that a substantial proportion of the fighting troops were using heroin. Nor was there much comfort in the thought that tens of thousands of heroin addicts might soon be discharged from their duties in the killing zones of Vietnam on to the streets of America.

Even more shocking were certain revelations about the behaviour of the troops in Vietnam (many of these were so unpalatable to the Americans at home that they were not believed). In 1968, there occurred what the official inquiry was later to refer to as the 'unusual events' of My Lai; these included

36

individual and group acts of murder, rape, sodomy, maiming and assault on non-combatants, almost all of whom were women, children and old people. The number of deaths was never clearly established, but may have exceeded 400. Other 'unusual events' of the war which understandably caused a great deal of concern were 'fragging' attacks in which officers who tried too zealously to force their men to engage the enemy were killed with fragmentation grenades. The number of reported fragging attacks increased sharply from 126 in 1969 to 333 in 1971. There were occasions on which helicopter pilots reported being deliberately fired upon by American troops, and the number of men who deserted also reflected the growing problems within the army at that time. The desertion rate more than quadrupled between 1966 and 1972, rising from 1·6 per cent to 6·5 per cent. The overall situation was such that a former officer described the army in Vietnam as being 'in a state of approaching collapse, with individual units avoiding or having refused combat, murdering their officers and non-commissioned officers. . . and dispirited where not near mutinous'.

There was some speculation that these various incidents and atrocities could have been the result of drug taking. There is no evidence to support this. It makes more sense to regard the extensive drug taking as a symptom of the breakdown of morale combined with an increased awareness and use of drugs in all sections of American society during that period. However, it remains one of the darkest ironies of the American involvement in Vietnam that the heroin sold to the troops was flown into the country in planes paid for by the US Government. Unlike almost everything else that the Vietnamese sold to the Americans, this heroin was of excellent quality. This was one of the real presents from Indochina to America, and from Nixon and his predecessors to the men of the US army.

Since the illicit heroin available on the streets of America was many times more expensive than in Vietnam and much less pure, there was a certain amount of trepidation about the chances that the new addicts would become seriously involved in crime. The Government set up a special screening system to try to identify and detoxify the addicted soldiers before their return to America. Those whose drug use was detected were obliged to remain behind for a brief period during which they were withdrawn from drugs before they were sent home.

It must have surprised everyone that when these men returned to America, only a small minority of them became re-addicted. After their discharge from the army, only 7 per cent used any opiate drugs, and less than 1 per cent felt that they had been addicted to drugs since their return. Even among those who said that they had been addicted to opiates in Vietnam, less than 10 per cent said that their addiction had continued beyond their return. Compared with the usual civilian statistics about opiate addiction, these figures are remarkably low: one might have predicted that many more of the men would have had serious problems relating to the use of opiates. What happened in Vietnam and afterwards conflicts with several popular beliefs about drug addiction. It is usually assumed that heroin addiction is an inevitable consequence of using the drug, that once it has taken hold, it is virtually impossible for the user to rid himself of the habit. The Vietnam experience shows that neither of these beliefs is true. Of the troops who used heroin, many did not become addicted. But even of those who were addicted in Vietnam, the vast majority were able to cast off their addiction when they returned to America.

This curious episode in the history of drug taking is a good example of the ways in which changes in social circumstances can have a powerful effect upon the way people use drugs. The young men who served in Vietnam were removed from their normal social environment and from many of its usual social and moral restraints. For many of them it was a confusing, chaotic and often extremely frightening experience, and the chances of physical escape were remote except through the hazardous possibilities of self-inflicted injury. As a form of inward desertion, drugs represented a way of altering the nature of subjective reality itself, and for the American serviceman, drugs were cheap and very freely available.

There are a number of separate influences at work here, each of which affects the likelihood of drug taking. During the Vietnam War, these combined to provide the conditions in which drug taking was most likely to occur. Psychologically, the experience of suddenly being removed from a safe, familiar environment to a strange, foreign and extremely threatening one, increases the pressure upon the individual to take drugs. Drugs are a useful means of coping with the mixture of fear, physical tiredness and boredom that is such a familiar feature of military life during a war. Socially, the tour of duty in Vietnam was characterised by a removal of many of the usual social and moral restraints that reduce the likelihood of drug taking. The soldiers themselves were inclined to regard their tour of duty as something separated from 'real life' and there were various social pressures to take drugs simply because so many others were using them. Last but not least, there was the physical availability of all kinds of drugs. It is difficult to imagine conditions more likely to promote their widespread use.

But the same unusual combination of factors which led to so much drug taking in Vietnam is also the key to understanding why such a high proportion of addicts managed to break the habit after going back to America. With their return, the effectiveness of all three of these influences was reduced, and as a result the pressures to go on using drugs were correspondingly less. In order to understand the ways in which people use drugs, we need to look beyond the immediate intoxicating effects, and take account of what it means to use drugs in any particular social setting. In Vietnam, the social and psychological influences acted together in a unique manner. Although this does not happen very often, there are other interesting (though less striking) examples of how the social significance of drugs can influence the way in which they are used.

The previous chapter showed how our beliefs, attitudes and expectations about drugs can have a powerful influence upon how they affect us. These attitudes and beliefs are not entirely personal, something insulated from the society in which we live. We learn about drugs from other people, from reading books and newspapers, or from watching the television. The way we think about drugs reflects the social world around us, and as a result the social context influences three central aspects of drug taking. It influences what is defined as a drug and what is not; it influences the way a person behaves after taking a drug; and it influences his subjective experience of the drug effects. We cannot hope to understand the complexities of drug taking by studying either the drugs or those who take them in isolation from the social context. In this respect, the relationship between drugs and religion is interesting since many religions offer formal guidelines about the use of drugs, and not all of these are prohibitions. Some religions, especially the more ancient ones, have an active involvement with drugs, and many anthropologists who have made a study of religion believe that all knowledge of the supernatural may be derived from the ecstatic experiences of religious visionaries and prophets. Many drugs produce convincing hallucinatory experiences and states of ecstasy, and the use of drugs for religious purposes is extraordinarily widespread. (The word ecstasy is derived from the Greek, *ekstasis*, and it means the flight of the soul from the body.)

There is no general agreement about the role of alcohol in religious experience. In his book, *The Varieties of Religious Experience*, William James wrote that 'the sway of alcohol over mankind is unquestionably due to its power to stimulate the mystical faculties', though he also spoke of drunkenness in its totality as a degrading form of poisoning. Aldous Huxley, on the other hand, was less favourably inclined toward alcohol. He could see nothing elevating in the alcohol-induced state. The only forms of worship based upon ritual drunkenness usually involved an uninhibited and belligerent euphoria. Bacchus or Dionysus was the god of wine, and his worship was characterised by wild dancing, exciting music and general excess. The ancient Roman festival of Saturnalia, too, was a period of licence when customary restraints could be thrown aside. It was a time for feasting, drinking, revelry and the pursuit of all sensual pleasures, and is considered a precursor of the Christmas festivities.

Huxley's view that alcohol is not compatible with more reflective forms of religious experience has been formalised by those religions for whom it is a proscribed drug, notably the Mormons, the Muslims and certain fundamentalist Protestant sects. The Mormons believe that their sacred text *Doctrine and Covenants* contains a series of revelations given by God to their founder Joseph Smith in 1833. Among these revelations is the prohibition of alcoholic drinks, tobacco, and even hot drinks such as tea or coffee; orthodox purists also believe that caffeine-based drinks such as Coca Cola should be included within this prohibition.

In *The Doors of Perception*, Huxley voiced another opinion which has received rather less sympathetic comment – that 'Christianity and mescaline seem to be much more compatible'. Mescaline and other drugs have played a central part in the religious experience of many cultures. When the Spanish invaded Mexico they found that the Aztecs ate the peyote cactus as a 'divine messenger' to help them communicate directly with the gods. (Mescaline is a derivative of peyote.) Peyote was unquestionably one of the most potent vision-inducing plants to be encountered by the conquerors; and the Conquistadors and the Holy Inquisition immediately began a programme intended to suppress the diabolical practices of the natives, but the sacramental use of peyote survived. During the last hundred years, the use of peyote in religious ceremonies has been adopted by many North American Indian tribes including the Comanches, Apaches and Kiowas, and it is currently used by the Indian members of the Native American Church as a sacrament in their religious services.

The use of peyote as a divine plant by the Huichol Indians of Mexico is thought to correspond most closely with pre-colonial customs. The Huichol Indians assemble each year in the desert three hundred miles from their home in the Sierra Madre mountains where they take part in a peyote hunt led by their shaman. This pilgrimage is preceded by acts of confession and purification through which the participants are initiated into the hunt, and the whole enterprise is surrounded by ritual. The peyote hunt is seen as a return to Paradise, the archetypal beginning and end of a mythical past.

Hallucinogenic mushrooms also have a long tradition of use as an aid to religious experience. When the Aryans swept down from the north into the Indus Valley some 3,500 years ago, they brought with them the cult of Soma. These early invaders of India worshipped Soma and drank an extract of it in their most sacred rites. Of more than 1,000 holy hymns in the Rig-Veda, 120 were devoted to this drug, which is now known to be the spectacular red mushroom *Amanita muscaria*, the fly agaric. The sacred psilocybin mushrooms of Mexico are also held in great reverence. The Aztecs called them 'flesh of the gods', and used them only in their most holy ceremonies; to the Indians who still use them they are 'little flowers'. Europeans are more likely to regard these insignificant little toadstools as a symbol of decay and corruption. The Catholic invaders were particularly offended by their use in religious ceremonies; the clerics and their agents were so energetic in suppressing the mushroom cults that they were driven into hiding, and for four centuries nothing was known of them. It was not until the 1930s that they were rediscovered.

There is a world beyond ours, a world that is far away, nearby, and invisible. And that is where God lives, and where the dead live, the spirits and the saints, a world where everything has already happened and everything is known. That world talks. It has a language of its own. I report what it says. The sacred mushroom takes me by the hand and brings me to the world where everything is known. It is they, the sacred mushrooms, that speak in a way that I can understand. I ask them and they answer me. When I return from the trip that I have taken with them, I tell what they have told me and what they have shown me. (A Mazatec shaman, cited in Schultes and Hofmann, *Plants of the Gods*)

Other cultures have used other drugs. Kava, which is generally prepared as a drink, is made from the root of a plant. It seems to have sedative properties something like those of alcohol, and has been extensively used by the South Sea Islanders of Samoa, Tonga and Fiji in many of their important social and religious ceremonies. Kava is taken as a way of getting in touch with the supernatural. One of the most recent studies of this drug described how it is used by men on Tanna and the islands of what were the New Hebrides as an aid to meditation and quiet reflection, 'like entering a light relaxed dream' or 'like looking into a mirror. One's mind goes beyond one's body and looks back.' As elsewhere, the Christian missionaries tried to prevent the use of this heathen drug ('The practice is a serious menace to the work of God'), and moves were duly taken to have it forbidden by law. These failed because such laws were impossible to set up and enforce, and kava drinking continues to be a popular custom on the islands.

Cannabis too has been used in religion. A large number of gods in the Hindu pantheon are thought to have a taste for drink and drugs, and bhang (a drink made with cannabis) is a favourite of Shiva. However, cannabis is more often associated with the Ethiopian Zion Coptic Church based in Jamaica. To members of this church, ganja (cannabis) is an indispensable part of their religious worship. It is smoked to help them look deeper into their own consciousness and to help them find a spirit of love, unity and justice within themselves. The Coptics, who have a literal belief in the truth of Leviticus, regard ganja as a symbol of the body and blood of Jesus, and deny that it is a drug: drug taking is forbidden by their religion as are homosexuality, oral sex, masturbation, adultery, fornication, violence and hair-cutting. Ganja is seen as the true sacrament. In contrast, wine-alcohol is the false sacrament of Christendom, causing drunkenness and crime. Although the church claims an ancestry dating back 6,000 years to the Ethiopian Coptic Church, the link between the two is revitalistic rather than historical. In its present form, the origins of the EZCC are due much more to the inspiration of Marcus Garvey whose teachings in the 1920s and 1930s set the scene for the Ethiopian movements in Jamaica (of which, the best known are probably the Rastafarians).

It is tempting to dismiss these observations as no more than anthropological curiosities. Yet the relationship between drugs and religion does extend to Western societies. Increasing numbers of people experimented with LSD and similar hallucinogenic drugs during the 1960s. On many of them the experience had a powerful impact. It offered a vivid demonstration of what William James had expressed several decades earlier:

Our normal waking consciousness . . . is but one special kind of consciousness, whilst all about it, parted from it, by the filmiest of screens, there lie potential forms of consciousness entirely different. We may go through life without suspecting their existence; but apply the requisite stimulus, and at a touch they are there in all their completeness.(*The Varieties of Religious Experience*)

After taking mescaline, Aldous Huxley came to the same conclusion. The brain functions as a reducing-valve. In order to cope with the overwhelming flow of information which bombards the senses, the brain filters it down to a trickle which can be dealt with more efficiently. The hallucinogenic drugs remove these filters.

It is currently fashionable to sneer at the hippies. Yet the hippie sub-culture was a most interesting development. In some respects it was a spontaneous religious (some would prefer to call it quasi-religious) movement with LSD as its sacrament. Of course the hippies were not a unified group. They included among their numbers drug addicts, the emotionally disturbed, social misfits, hangers-on and others who were interested mainly in the extravagant clothes and music of the movement. But beneath the surface carnival, there was still a core of hippies by whom LSD was used to pursue a new set of religious, spiritual and intellectual values. Their deliberate rejection of the spiritual and religious vacuum of what they contemptuously called 'the plastic society' is summed up in their creed 'Turn on, tune in, drop out'. This was provided for them by their high priest, Timothy Leary, a psychologist who had worked at Harvard University until his dismissal in 1963. His research and his own experiences with hallucinogenic drugs convinced him of their religious significance. Although Leary felt that these drugs did not provide an automatic ticket to religious illumination, he was convinced that they were powerful aids to such experiences. At least 75 per cent of the subjects in his experiments reported intense mystical-religious experiences, and more than half felt that these drugs provided them with the deepest spiritual experience of their lives. Leary believed that technological society fears and suppresses ecstasy and transcendental experience: religion is reduced to 'a bunch of people getting up on a Sunday morning, going down to a mortgaged building, and staring at the back of someone's neck'. In contrast, psychedelic-hallucinatory drugs could provide a quick and efficient route to religious ecstasy. He prophesied that in the future, sacramental biochemicals like LSD would be as routinely and tamely used as organ music and incense to assist in the attainment of religious experience. Leary set up two organisations along these lines: IFIF (Institute for the Investigation of Inner Freedom) and LSD (League for Spiritual Discovery). Neither flourished.

The hippies were not continuously preoccupied with the transcendental state, but the LSD experience was always there to redirect their attention back to it. The psychedelic experience is often spoken of as if it were a casual diversion. This is misleading, perhaps dangerously so; such drugs are not to be used casually. Gordon Wasson, who made such a thorough study of the religious uses of psilocybin mushrooms, also used them himself.

I am frequently asked why I do not reach for mushrooms every night. But ecstasy is not fun. In our everyday existence we divide experiences into good and bad, 'fun' and pain. There is a third category, ecstasy, that for most of us hovers off stage, a stranger we never meet. The hallucinogenic mushroom introduces ecstasy to us. Your very soul is seized and shaken until it tingles, until you fear you will never recover your equilibrium.

At the heart of many psychedelic experiences was a fundamental sense of the oneness of things, a belief that all contradictions were resolved, all opposites joined. In this, the LSD experience resembles the mystical experience, which is usually defined by its ineffability (it cannot be described or expressed), its noetic quality (to those who experience it, it is a state of knowledge), and its transiency (mystical states cannot usually be sustained for long):

But these are words . . . *And you couldn't put it into words*. The White Smocks liked to put it into words, like *hallucination* and *dissociative phenomena*. They could understand the visual skyrockets . . . But the visual stuff was usually just the decor with LSD . . . the whole thing was . . . *the experience* . . . this certain indescribable *feeling*. (Tom Wolfe, *The Electric Kool-Aid Acid Test*)

It would be a remarkable irony if an ordinary person could, merely by swallowing a pill, attain those exalted states of consciousness which often elude the most committed seekers of mystical enlightenment after a lifetime's spiritual exercises. Not surprisingly, the suggestion has evoked angry dismissals in many quarters. Whatever the true validity of the LSD experience, the hippies shared an immense knowingness, a conviction of their own superiority. Even if they could not reach the profound truth beneath the surface of things, they felt that they had at least travelled beyond the meagre frontiers of normal, rational consciousness.

For the hippies, subjective experience and the present moment were extremely important. Technology and science might be the accepted tools of progress, but they were rejected because they exacted too high a price in terms of the quality of experience. Because of its immediacy, music was an essential part of the hippie life. It did not involve rational understanding or need translation. Leary wrote: 'There are three groups who are bringing about the great evolution of the new age that we are going through now. They are the dope dealers, the rock musicians and the Underground artists and writers.' The hippies rejected the pre-packaged commercial products offered to them for a new form of music. This was played by groups like Frank Zappa and the Mothers of Invention, the Jimi Hendrix Experience, Pink Floyd, and the West-Coast acid-rock bands, Grateful Dead, Love, Jefferson Airplane, the Doors, Country Joe and the Fish. The shows put on by these bands were often elaborate, multi-media

46

happenings intended to simulate or enhance the psychedelic experience.

The hippies produced their own underground newspapers, and adopted a literature for themselves. Hermann Hesse's short novel *Journey to the East* (first published in 1932) was read and quoted by many hippies, as was another of his works, *Steppenwolf* (1927). The popularity of many such books was related to speculation about the authors' possible involvement with mind-altering drugs. In such a culturally taboo area, these books offered a reminder to the hippies that others had made similar explorations.

William Blake, the eighteenth-century mystic poet and painter, was also hailed as a fellow-spirit. Blake too hated the narrow scientific, rationalistic vision, and the hippies were enchanted by the dominant themes expressed in his writing, the denial of the reality of matter, revolt against authority, protest against restrictive moral codes and an exaltation of the spirit of love. His aphorisms were adopted as slogans of the hippie revolution, among them 'Prudence is a rich, ugly old maid courted by Incapacity' and 'The road of excess leads to the palace of wisdom'.

In his failure to allow that the hippies' life-style could be the reflection of an alternative set of social values, the Swedish psychiatrist Dr Nils Bejerot completely misunderstood what he saw of the hippies. 'Early in 1968,' he wrote in his book *Addiction*, 'I saw a shocking example of how hashish smoking can change young people's attitudes and way of life.' The shock was caused by seeing groups of young Europeans and Americans in New Delhi. 'These hippies were long haired and bearded. They wore unusual clothes and some had hung bells around their necks. A few of them had the *Tibetan Book of the Dead* in their pocket.'* Worse

* For many hippies the *Tibetan Book of the Dead* (translated by Timothy Leary) was a popular book of spiritual guidance. Its popularity can be gauged by the fact that a substantial part of it is used on the Beatles' record *Revolver*: 'Turn off your mind, relax and float downstream. It is not dying. It is not dying.'

still, they were all totally disillusioned with modern industrial society and many aimed at becoming Buddhist monks. Instead of interpreting their appearance and behaviour as part of an alternative life-style, Bejerot reduced their actions to mere symptoms of a drug-induced decay. Indeed, he went even further in that he diagnosed the lack of industrial progress in many Oriental countries as being due to their widespread use of drugs. It is curious that at a time when India was discovering Coca Cola and the delights of the Western consumer society, the hippies turned their backs on the affluent materialism of their parents and turned to the East. At their worst, the hippie tourists gave the impression of scrabbling for mantras as if for the latest clothes in a boutique sale.

One legacy of the hippies' preoccupation with extraordinary states of consciousness is that it gave considerable impetus to an industry in religious and quasi-religious cults that flourished through the 1970s and shows little evidence of decline in the 1980s. Transcendental meditation, the Krishnamurti Foundation, Buddhist groups and Yoga Centres are among the less exotic options. Others have looked to witchcraft and flying saucers to satisfy their spiritual longings. In the more sober and prosaic world of Judaeo-Christian orthodoxy, drugs and altered states of consciousness have not generally been received with much sympathy. Nonetheless, a drug (wine) sits at the heart of the Christian mystery of Communion. This is, however, used as a symbol rather than as an intoxicant.

It is a curious phenomenon that there are more drinkers among the Jews than in other social and religious groups (87 per cent of Jews use alcohol compared with 79 per cent of Catholics and 59 per cent of Protestants), and yet they appear to have fewest problems with their drinking. This is true not only of the more minor problems such as public drunkenness but also of the severe disorders such as alcoholic psychoses, liver disease and alcoholism. In one study of admissions to the New York State Hospital system, it was found that the rates of alcoholic psychoses (per 100,000 admissions) were: Irish 25·6; Scandinavian 7·8; Italian 4·8; English 4·3; Jewish 0·5. The same sort of study has been repeated several times and on each occasion the relative position of the Jews remains about the same; they have very few problems with drinking despite their high incidence of alcohol use. Alcoholism is said to be virtually unknown in Israel. This is quite contrary to the conventional wisdom that as the proportion of drinkers goes up, so the proportion of alcohol casualties (both acute and chronic) must also increase. However, the use of alcohol by the Jews is interesting mainly because it is so atypical. The fact that so many Jews drink, but so few become casualties of alcohol, has sometimes been called the Great Jewish Drink Mystery.

One of the most plausible reasons for this controlled drinking looks to the network of ritual that surrounds the way in which Jews drink alcohol. The use of wine is surrounded by religious rules which specify when, and where, and how much wine is to be taken. There are even special occasions on which Jews can break the normal taboo against intoxication. The orthodox Jew regards drunkenness with disgust, as a disgrace. Yet the festival of *Purim* is a time of licence when it is obligatory to eat, drink and be merry. The combination of the ritual surrounding alcohol with the idea of Orthodox Judaism as a total way of life helps to protect the individual from losing control of his drinking.

But however much it may reduce the likelihood of alcoholism, being an Orthodox Jew does not guarantee protection against developing a drinking problem. For those Jews who do become alcoholics, the idea that there are no Jewish alcoholics may deter them from acknowledging their own difficulties because of a sense of shame, and this may delay any move to seek help. Where abstinence is practised, there can be no drug problems. But where those who are part of an abstinent tradition attempt to use drugs, it may lead to special difficulties since they must reject all conventional restraints upon the use of that particular drug. If a Mormon chooses to drink, he is behaving in a deviant manner and his deviance is likely to create an expectation that drinking is primarily a means of becoming intoxicated, since it cannot be part of normal social behaviour. By definition, social drinking is excluded from the acceptable forms of behaviour, and psychologically, it is likely to become dissociated from other inhibitory, controlling parts of the personality of the drinker and from controls in the social system. This is not to imply that when anyone brought up within a tradition of abstinence begins to drink he will necessarily become alcoholic. It does suggest that rates of alcoholism may be comparatively high for such people.

The protective function of these rituals and social sanctions is shown by the way in which the introduction of drugs has affected societies which lack such controlling influences. The American Indians had a longstanding history of controlled use of such psychoactive drugs as peyote, yet they failed to maintain any such control over the white man's drug, alcohol. The Indians rejected or were denied full membership in American society and were correspondingly slow to acquire the white man's cultural controls defining the appropriate uses of alcohol. American Indians frequently drank to extreme drunkenness rather than to more sociable levels of intoxication, and their rates of alcoholism have remained persistently high. The Eskimos had similar difficulties with alcohol when they were first allowed to drink; their lack of previous cultural experience and guidelines for alcohol use led to pronounced abuse.

In Western societies, those who use illicit drugs face the same sort of problems. It is not surprising that some of them should become drug casualties. There are no socially-accepted rules and rituals governing the use of such drugs, no education in how to take them without damage, and no reinforcement of moderate rather than self-destructive patterns of use. Since mainstream society fails to provide any such restraints, the only rules to help the illicit drug taker control his drug taking are those available within the drug subculture itself. There have been very few studies of drug takers who keep their use of illicit drugs under control. One such investigation looked at a group of more than 100 American controlled users. The most striking feature about them was the way in which their drug taking was influenced by rituals and socially-shared expectations. Although some of them used drugs when they were alone, more than 80 per cent of their drug taking took place in a social setting, and most avoided the company of known addicts. Controlled heroin users, for instance, usually restricted their contact with addicts to those occasions on which it was necessary to obtain their drug and declined invitations to inject heroin with their addict-suppliers. Several of them drew an analogy with controlled drinking. People who adhere to rules about drinking (e.g. only drinking at mealtimes, at parties, at weekends, or not drinking during working hours or when alone) are less likely to develop an alcohol problem than those who have no such restraints and who drink whenever they feel like it. One of the drug takers in this study said that he didn't feel that he always had to have a good reason for getting high on drugs, but that if people found they were using drugs regularly without a reason, this should alert them to the dangers of slipping into a dependence on drugs.

On the other hand, not all rituals protect the individual from the hazards of drug taking; some encourage and reinforce the use of drugs.

Of his opium smoking Jean Cocteau wrote:

It is reassuring. It reassures by its luxury, by its rites,
by the anti-medical elegance of the lamps, stoves, pipes,
by the secular setting of this exquisite elegance.

In the more sordid world of heroin addiction, too, there are elaborate rituals that surround the act of injection.

It's not only a question of kicks. The ritual itself, the powder in the spoon, the little ball of cotton, the matches applied, the bubbling liquid drawn up through the cotton filter into the eye dropper, the tie round the arm to make a vein stand out, the fix often slow because a

51

man will stand there with the needle in the vein and allow the level of the eye-dropper to waver up and down, up and down . . . all this is not for nothing; it is born of a respect for the whole chemistry of alienation. (Alexander Trocchi, *Cain's Book*)

Society is not a simple monolithic organisation. It is made up of a multitude of groups, each with its own aims, interests and priorities. Most users of alcohol, coffee and tobacco can take their drugs without challenging the 'conventional' social values. It is frequently permissible to use such drugs as Valium, barbiturates and amphetamines provided that they can be obtained under the licence of a medical prescription. The committed hedonistic drug user and the addict, however, are often spoken of as if they existed outside society (whatever that means), and their behaviour is disparagingly described as a bizarre, uncontrolled and meaningless disorder. But most illicit drug users do not live outside society; they live in alternative (though subterranean) societies which are in many respects clearly at odds with conventional, middle-class values. (Whether such alternatives represent any improvement upon other, more conventional, options is another matter. They can be attacked or defended according to the premises that the reader chooses to apply.) The phrase 'alternative society' owes a good deal to the comparatively articulate dissent of the hippies during the 1960s; but even the supposedly amoral world of the street addict has its own set of alternative social rules and values. It is significant that many illicit drug users see drug taking not as a weakness or a failure, but as a challenge; and far from being an isolated event in their lives, the use of drugs is an integral part of a wider set of social values.

For many addicts, these values are derived from what could be called 'the street culture'. This provides an ill-defined but nonetheless extremely powerful view of the world and how to behave in it. 'The street' is a tough and competitive environment where only the true initiates can survive, and where there is a premium attached to keeping one's own real feelings and thoughts hidden behind a façade. One of the more obvious features of the street is its private language. The tools of the trade are not needles or syringes, they are spikes and guns, not heroin or amphetamine but smack and speed. It is a characteristic of many disadvantaged minority groups that they use a language or dialect to differentiate themselves from the majority. But it is not merely the language of the street that separates it from straight society. It also has its own moral code.

In Trocchi's novel *Cain's Book*, a friend of his wife gives the narrator some money to buy him some cannabis. Cain leaves with the money and doesn't return. In the rules of the junkie world, this is a classic burn. If the friend was not knowledgeable enough to avoid this error, he deserved to be ripped-off. The friend, however, sees this differently – as stealing – and threatens to call the police. Cain is surprised and appalled by this reaction and argues with his wife that he didn't steal the money, 'I beat him. He gave it to me.' 'You stole it, you admit stealing it.' 'Didn't steal anything, I beat that fool, can't you understand that?' Cain goes on to say that if the friend were to arrive with a gun or a knife, he would give back the money, but to call the police is outside the rules of the street. The overall purpose of these street games is to give meaning to the addict life-style. The street addict, like the rest of us, creates a social reality around himself and his sense of personal identity is closely related to his social world. The tragedy of addiction is that neither the drugs nor the street culture live up to their initial promise.

# 4

## CHEMICAL COMFORTS

### The demand for health and happiness

Aldous Huxley's *Brave New World* provided the complete drug. The product of six years' intensive research by two thousand pharmacologists and biochemists, this drug was a narcotic that also produced euphoria and hallucinations, it had 'all the advantages of Christianity and alcohol; none of their defects'. It fulfilled a variety of social functions. It was drunk from a Communion cup surrounded by quasi-religious ritual; it was routinely issued at the end of each day's work shift – four tablets a day, six on Saturdays. Its main purpose was to make everyone happy in their servitude, a way of eliminating all possibility of unhappiness, the ultimate chemical comfort.

Our own chemical comforts often carry a greater social stigma than in Huxley's fictional society. Most people are confused about their own drug taking. They are told that drugs are dangerous, yet most people are regular drug takers. They try to make sense of this by denying that many of their regular drugs are drugs at all (cigarettes, coffee, alcohol) and they exaggerate the dangers of illegal drugs which in themselves may be comparatively harmless. There are drugs that are used on a massive scale, and in order to legitimise their use, we look to the medical profession for approval.

One of the striking social developments of recent years is the way that health has been elevated to a supreme value. In the name of health and treatment, the medical bureaucracy is increasingly able to violate such important social values as the individual's freedom of choice and rights of privacy. The distinction between good and bad has been largely replaced by that of healthy and unhealthy (or as it is sometimes expressed – good for you, and bad for you).

Whatever is deemed by medical bureaucrats to be healthy is

therefore good, correct. It must be encouraged. This could relate to eating a diet low in polyunsaturated fats, drinking water containing fluoride, taking regular exercise, or wearing a seat belt when driving. Whatever is deemed unhealthy, such as smoking cigarettes, overeating, drinking too much or working under prolonged stress, is necessarily bad and must be discouraged – or if necessary stopped. Medicine has become more and more involved with aspects of social behaviour that are only vaguely and indirectly related to illness and disease. This is a perilous sort of medical imperialism that seeks to control our social affairs on such a narrow principle.

The superficial orthodoxy suggests that drugs should be used as medicine, to cure or alleviate medical problems. Between 1963 and 1978 the number of prescriptions fulfilled in England and Wales each year increased from just over 200 million to more than 300 million. Since this period has seen no conspicuous decline in the nation's general health, this trend is better seen as a reflection of the increased willingness on the part of doctors to prescribe drugs, and on the part of the general population to accept them. Some health surveys have suggested that as many as nine out of ten people who were not seeing a doctor may have been suffering from some problem deemed worthy of treatment. If a complete and unblemished state of health is so unusual, one of the decisive factors that determines whether a person approaches a doctor is his attitude towards his own physical and psychological welfare. As our expectations about health have been raised, so we have become more dissatisfied with any failure to achieve that state. As medical science has inexorably extended the definition of illness, the idea of health itself has become ever more elusive.

This is especially true of psychological medicine. Many of the 'mental illnesses' which the psychiatrist is expected to treat are not really illnesses at all. They are only illnesses in a metaphorical sense. Most are the product of a complex interaction between the special circumstances of each person's upbringing, his personality and his social environment.

But if few people are completely healthy, it must be a

worrying sign that most of the people who go to see a physician in general practice are not ill. The majority of the patients in the general practitioner's clinic are there largely for non-medical reasons. They may be lonely, anxious or unhappy because of the way their lives are going. Their difficulties are more properly regarded as social problems resulting from the circumstances in which they are living. Their expectations of life are not being met. But it is not a medical problem to be unhappy because a member of the family has died, nor to be apprehensive about facing some new challenge in one's life. These are precisely the sort of complaint that many people take to their doctor: and they are precisely the sort of complaint which commonly leads to a prescription for a psychoactive drug. Behind each of these cases is the specious assumption that problems of living can be solved, or at least 'treated', by medical means. Once this insidious principle has been accepted, there is no end to the number of problems that can be redefined in medical terms.

The public is constantly being told by the scientific optimists that there is no problem so great that it cannot be solved by science and technology. In the medical sciences, there are those who have suggested that one day all diseases may be avoidable. Endless television programmes encourage this view of medicine as a means of eliminating disease by the application of high-powered technological devices. Doctors, politicians and the general public have all acquired this taste for changing hearts, livers and kidneys in preference to changing minds: now we are being promised a pill for every ill.

We are coming to see every ache and pain as a sign that we need medical help. Until recently, we might have used plays, novels or other social and cultural devices to try to understand our pain and distress, to help us to cope with them by giving them meaning. Medical science has rendered them socially meaningless by redefining them as nothing more than mechanical breakdowns in the soft machine. They are to be solved by their removal. But because medicine deprives them of meaning, it alienates us from our own feelings: it makes us less

56

able to understand them and less able to tolerate them. The promise of freedom from pain and suffering, far from producing a happier society, is turning us into anaesthesia-consumers.

## The prescription

In a somewhat lyrical vein, Professor Trethowan has referred to 'the relentless march of the psychotropic drug juggernaut'. Almost half of all the drugs prescribed in England are psychoactive drugs or drugs which affect the central nervous system. A large proportion of these psychoactive drugs are barbiturate or non-barbiturate sleeping tablets, which suggests that a lot of people like to put themselves to sleep at night with knock-out drops. Of the remainder, most are taken for conditions which can only be described as extremely vague. Certainly it doesn't look as though they are being prescribed for specific medical conditions, and this is (or should be) worrying. If such huge quantities of drugs are being medically prescribed for what are really personal and social problems, this may establish a vicious circle in which a person who is faced by some upsetting life problem goes to his doctor, the doctor prescribes tranquillisers, and because the patient has received a prescription, he feels that his problem is really a medical one which the doctor understands and is competent to deal with. The pills produce an emotional numbness which makes the patient feel better, but they don't usually solve the problem; so when the pills run out and the original problem makes itself felt again, the patient returns to the doctor for further treatment.

Before prescribing any drug, a competent doctor should ask himself whether it might not be better to prescribe no treatment at all. If he does treat the patient, he should ask himself what he is trying to achieve, whether the prescribed drug is capable of achieving any such goals, what side-effects the drug might have, and whether the possibility of improvement overrides the likelihood of harming the patient.

In practice, these five questions often remain unanswered,

and in doing all he can, the doctor does too much. Thousands of people have been injured by the well-intentioned medicines that they have been given. A survey conducted in one large American hospital found that as many as one patient in every twenty had suffered a *major* toxic reaction to medicines. All drugs have potentially harmful effects, the more so when they are used unwisely. Any drug which is worth using at all is capable of causing harm.

It is tempting but mistaken to put all the blame on either the doctor or his patient for the over-prescription of psychoactive drugs. There is no doubt that the general practitioner feels under intense pressure to respond to the patient's problems by offering a prescription. Many patients actually request a particular drug when they go to see their doctor, and every GP must have had the totally recalcitrant patient who simply refuses to go away until he has been given a prescription. On the other hand, many doctors are all too eager to write out a prescription, especially for those vague psychosomatic disorders that are so difficult to understand.

One survey found that four out of every five doctors agreed that drugs can be very valuable in helping patients to cope with the social demands and stresses of everyday life. As examples of the sort of problem for which drugs might be offered, almost all the doctors who were interviewed agreed that tranquillisers were an appropriate treatment for marital difficulties, and more than half felt that the daily use of these drugs was a legitimate treatment for the anxious college student. In one advertisement, for instance, Librium was proposed as an appropriate treatment for a new student who finds that the changed circumstances of university life 'may force her to re-evaluate herself and her goals' and whose 'newly stimulated intellectual curiosity may make her more ´ sensitive and apprehensive about national and world conditions'. Tranquillisers have also been advertised as an appropriate treatment for the housewife with too little time to pursue a vocation for which she has spent many years in training; and even 'when anxiety and tension create major discord in

parent–child relationships'. Whatever the exact circumstances
of the consultation, about three-quarters of all visits to the
doctor result in the writing of a prescription.

Despite the central position that the prescription occupies in
medicine, we still do not properly understand its many different
functions. It is, however, increasingly clear that prescribing
depends just as much on social and psychological factors as
upon medical ones. When a patient takes his complaint to the
doctor he expects him to diagnose and treat it. But since so
many of the complaints that are brought to the modern doctor
are not really medical at all, it is quite likely that the doctor will
be unable to discover any specific cause for the complaint.

It would be mistaken to regard the prescription of
psychoactive drugs as the doctor's response to specific medical
disorders. Psychoactive drugs are generally given out for vague
and undefined problems that cause the patient dis-ease. This is
clearly recognised by the drug companies who sell their
products by emphasising the 'dual action' or 'broad spectrum
activity' of the drugs.

The conventional view of medicine suggests that the doctor
diagnoses the problem before prescribing the treatment. In this
area the whole procedure is often turned on its head with the
problem being diagnosed according to the drug that is used to
treat it. 'This is a case of Valium, there must be some anxiety.'
However, if the patient is not given a specific treatment, he may
keep returning to the surgery and become a cause of increasing
irritation to the doctor. When this happens the most likely
outcome is that the doctor will eventually prescribe a
psychoactive drug – generally a tranquilliser. Yet many of these
'difficult patients' go to see their doctor not so much for a
physical remedy in the shape of pills or medicine, as to have
someone listen sympathetically to their problems.

Far from being just a medical response to a specific
complaint, sociologists have identified as many as twenty-seven
different social functions that the prescription can play. These
include providing a visible sign of a doctor's power to heal, a
recognition that the patient is 'really' ill, an expression of the

doctor's concern, and an excuse for the patient's failure to perform his social duties. Last but not least (from the doctor's point of view), the writing of a prescription can provide a satisfactory way of signalling the end of the consultation.

Doctors may now be more aware of the potential hazards of prescribing psychoactive drugs, though this often shows itself in a strange way. Two out of every three doctors feel that *other* physicians prescribe too many tranquillisers. The drug companies have also moderated their claim about the psychoactive drugs. At one time their advertising implied that tranquillisers were non-addictive and could be safely prescribed for all manner of complaints: they are now more circumspect, and rightly so, because these drugs are far from harmless.

**Queen Valium**

Of all the psychoactive drugs currently being used, the most widely used are the minor tranquillisers. These drugs (they belong to a family of drugs called the benzodiazepines) include Valium, Librium, Ativan and Mogadon, and they are prescribed on a quite prodigious scale for an astonishing variety of complaints and ailments. They are amongst the most recent products of medical technology presented in this book. Librium was the first to be synthesised (in 1955) and it was approved for marketing in the United States in 1960; Valium was first marketed in 1963. The popularity of these drugs made them a source of enormous profit and the pharmaceutical companies immediately began a diligent search for more and more of them. In the years since Librium was first introduced, many more drugs of this class have been produced – most of them with virtually identical effects.

The United States is the great consumer of drugs. It is top of the international league table, and in 1977 it accounted for one-fifth of the entire world sale of pharmaceuticals, at a cost of 7·8 billion dollars. The prescription of drugs in America has more than doubled since the 1950s though this trend is not confined to the United States; the same thing is happening throughout the Western world. Of the prescribed drugs, the most dramatic increase has occurred amongst the psychoactive drugs, and of these, Valium is the most widely prescribed drug in the world. Valium and Librium are said to be first and fourth in the list of drugs prescribed in America with as many as one in every ten Americans taking Valium because of tension or 'nerves' during any three-month period. American physicians write approximately 50 million prescriptions for Valium every year, and these drugs are also distributed freely among hospital patients. As early as 1972, a survey of two Boston teaching hospitals found that up to 30 per cent of all medical in-patients were given Valium and 32 per cent were given a similar drug, Dalmane. The popularity of these drugs has not declined and tranquillisers remain among the most widely used drugs.

These drugs produce a number of changes in behaviour that can best be described as disinhibition. In animal experiments they reduce the negative effects of stress and frustration, but they also reduce the animal's susceptibility to punishment. They have the same effects on people, which implies that a person may be more susceptible to temptation when under the influence of drugs such as Valium. There are numerous instances of people who have been caught shoplifting while taking these drugs. It is not that the drug itself leads them to commit crimes, but that the fear of punishment, which normally has a deterrent effect, has been chemically suppressed.

It is even more worrying that these drugs can increase levels of aggression. Generally they lower aggression and hostility, as one would expect of a tranquillising drug. But under some conditions they can have the opposite effect, producing excitement, outbursts of anger and aggressive, destructive behaviour. In this, they are similar to alcohol which can make some people 'fighting drunk'. Disinhibition is precisely the sort of psychological state that makes driving under the influence of alcohol such a potentially dangerous combination. Alcohol, barbiturates and the minor tranquillisers all have similar psychological effects, and all are likely to interfere with driving skills. They may do this in one of two ways. All have a depressant effect on the brain. They slow people down. As a result they increase the chances that the intoxicated driver will fail to react quickly enough to any emergency that occurs. At a high enough dose, they may cause the driver to fail to respond altogether. But each of these drugs can also cause the sort of changes in judgement that lead to accidents. The disinhibited driver is more likely to drive too fast, to overtake without checking if it is safe to do so, or to use his car as a weapon.

The drinking driver has been surveyed and studied in great detail. He has had his body fluids and his breath analysed; he has walked up and down white lines and recited tongue-twisting phrases until it has entered into common knowledge that drinking alcohol increases the risk of having an accident. We are so familiar with Valium, Librium and the other tranquillisers that we often fail to treat them with the respect that is due to any drug. It has been known for years that tranquillisers, far from being completely harmless, can produce a whole range of unpleasant side-effects. Drowsiness, tiredness and impaired co-ordination are fairly common, and other adverse effects that are occasionally reported include confusion, depression, double vision, stammering, headache, incontinence, nausea and dizziness. The makers of Valium recognise these problems and have issued a warning that people using Valium 'should be cautioned against engaging in hazardous occupations requiring complete mental alertness such as operating machinery or driving a motor vehicle'. The risks are undoubtedly increased when such tranquillisers are used in amounts larger than was prescribed or in conjunction with alcohol (as frequently happens), yet at this moment millions of people are driving cars, trains and lorries while under the influence of Valium and its sister drugs.

A recent Canadian study found that drivers who had taken drugs were more likely to be involved in a fatal accident than drivers who were drug-free and tranquillisers were among the drugs most seriously implicated in such accidents. It is possible that this is partly caused by the sort of problem that led the person to take tranquillisers in the first place – high levels of anxiety, irritability and tension; but this probably accounts for only a small part of his accident-proneness. The rest may be attributed to the drug-induced intoxication. It is a measure of the irrationality that surrounds drug taking that this lethal state of affairs is accepted with such complacency whereas popular opinion is excited to hysteria by the casual use of illegal drugs.

The dangers of the prescribed drugs are no less than those of many of the illegal drugs. Although Valium and the minor tranquillisers are safer than barbiturate drugs in terms of their dangers in an overdose, they are just as likely to produce addiction if they are used continuously. At first the tranquillisers have a dampening effect on emotions, but after a while this fades as the person becomes tolerant to the effects of the drug. Many ordinary people who take these drugs adjust the dose not according to the doctor's instructions but according to the way they are feeling: when they feel upset or stressed, they increase the dose. This carries many potential dangers and can mark the start of drug dependence. Diazepam (the drug used in Valium) seems to have a special sinister attraction as a drug of dependence, and once the user is physically addicted, he may suffer from distressing withdrawal symptoms if he is deprived of it. These symptoms are very similar to those associated with barbiturate addiction, one of the most serious forms of drug dependence. Withdrawal begins with restlessness, anxiety and tension; the sufferer finds it very difficult to sleep and as the withdrawal reaches its peak, he may suffer from stomach cramps and vomiting; sometimes he trembles uncontrollably and has convulsions like an epileptic fit. The fact that a drug is prescribed by a doctor, and is socially acceptable to the millions of people who use it, has little or nothing to do with the damage it can cause. Tranquillisers are far from being safe drugs, and they are massively over-used. This form of drug taking is one of the hidden and more serious forms of drug abuse in our society.

## The La Roche Affair

In 1973, the cost of Librium and Valium to the National Health Service was debated in both the House of Commons and the House of Lords. This marked the culmination of a series of misunderstandings between the British Government and the Swiss pharmaceutical company Hoffmann-La Roche who held the patents for these drugs. The essence of the complaint was that the drug company was taking advantage of the National Health Service by selling Librium and Valium at vastly inflated prices. The basic chemical ingredient of these drugs was sold in Italy, for instance, at only £9 and £20 a kilogramme: in the UK the same amount of each drug was costing more than forty times as much – £370 and £922.

The British Government asked Roche to justify its profits on the basis of its costs, but when it was asked to present its accounts for examination by government auditors, it flatly refused. Since Roche does not regard its profits as a matter of public concern, there is no idea as to how much the company really makes on these drugs. However, the Swiss company did offer to return part of its profits to the Treasury 'without prejudice' (this is legal jargon for 'without admitting that we were wrong and without establishing any precedent'); and between 1967 and 1970 the company repaid £1,600,000 to the Health Service as a rebate against its high prices.

The Monopolies Commission was asked to carry out an investigation into the matter and argued that Roche was over-pricing these two drugs. Roche enjoyed a monopoly on the market for the supply of both Librium and Valium, and these two drugs represented more than two-thirds of all the tranquillisers used in the UK. As a result the company was able to fix arbitrary price levels for these drugs. The Commission recommended that the price of Librium should be reduced by 60 per cent and that of Valium by 70 per cent. In addition, the Monopolies Commission recommended that Roche should repay a further amount of the large profit it had made out of the National Health Service.

Roche rejected the findings of the Monopolies

Commission and clearly felt that it had been victimised and unfairly picked out for special treatment. It argued that since only a few of the drugs that a drug company produces are ever successful, it is necessary to use the successful drugs to support the entire research programme. In any case, even successful drugs usually return a high profit only for a short time. After that, newer, more advanced rivals appear on the scene to replace them.

In the end, Roche opened legal proceedings against the British Government and the Monopolies Commission. This set up a curious situation in which a national government was taken to court by a multinational company. As a monopoly supplier of these tranquillisers, Roche set its own price for the drugs; it also established its own levels of research expenditure and justified one by the other. The Monopolies Commission argued that the company was spending 'excessive' amounts on research and promotion. If a multinational company of this sort is allowed to set its own levels of research expenditure and then as a monopoly supplier to pass on these costs to a nation's health service, this raises interesting questions about who is playing the servant and who the master. Even at a less exalted level, there must be some limit to the price and profit levels that a manufacturer is justified in setting himself.

In the eventual settlement, Roche paid a rebate to the Health Service of £3·7 million and joined the system of voluntary price control that had been used in Britain since 1957. This system established the price of particular drugs by agreement between the Health Service and the drug company.

As a result of the Monopolies Commission report, proceedings were started against Hoffmann-La Roche in several European countries. In view of the allegations of overpricing that did so much harm to its reputation, it is paradoxical that in Canada, Hoffmann-La Roche was found guilty by the Ontario Supreme Court of trying to reduce or eliminate competition by selling Valium at unreasonably *low* prices. Between 1968 and 1974, Valium was given away to hospitals very cheaply (or even at no charge at all) in order to prevent the use of competing versions of the drug. In a four-year period, Hoffmann-La Roche reportedly gave away some 174 million doses of Valium and 26 million doses of Librium.

## Self-medication

Quite apart from the medically prescribed drugs, there are many forms of chemical comfort to which a person can turn in order to soften the stresses and strains of everyday life. The most common, of course, is alcohol. One out of every seven American adults drinks more than usual as a way of coping with a personal crisis, and men are particularly likely to turn to drink under such circumstances. Although heavy drinking is becoming increasingly common in women, they are still more likely to turn to medically prescribed psychoactive drugs as a way of relieving their psychological aches and pains.

The younger the person concerned the more likely he is to use alcohol rather than a prescribed drug to get chemical relief. Only a comparatively small number of young men use any prescribed drugs when under psychological stress. Eighty-five per cent of American men within the age range 18–29 use alcohol in moderate to heavy amounts: among men over the age of 60, only 27 per cent drink similar amounts.

Few of us enjoy being under stress, and it is natural to look for some way of reducing the pressure. For most of us, the sort of thing that causes us to feel anxious, unhappy or tense is linked to our social life. The most common life events that provoke these feelings are losing one's job, moving house, marital difficulties or the death of a close friend or someone in the family. Sometimes the roots of people's unhappiness are more elusive. They may feel depressed all the time without any obvious reason: they may feel persistently tired or tense or fidgety. By taking a drug, they can easily obtain some relief from their stress. Generally the drugs fail to resolve the original problem. The student who is worried about failing an examination for which he has not done enough work is no more likely to pass the examination if he is taking tranquillisers; the economic causes of redundancy are not altered by anti-depressant drugs, nor are parents and friends brought back to life. Indeed, the drugs may even make the original problems worse. By reducing the student's anxiety, the tranquillisers may reduce his motivation to do some revision. By suppressing feelings of grief and unhappiness, the anti-depressants may interfere with a person's ability to come to terms with his bereavement.

At the same time, it is important not to over-react to the use of drugs. There is an attitude of chemical Calvinism that seems to value suffering and to condemn the easy relief that drugs can bring. There is no great virtue in enduring psychological stress for its own sake, and there are often no easy solutions to the problems that cause so much suffering. It is too readily assumed that psychotherapy (whether of the Freudian variety or in one of its more unorthodox forms) can solve every sort of emotional problem. Those who need a panacea must continue their search. Neither drugs nor psychotherapy can resolve the problem of unhappiness.

In Huxley's *Brave New World*, Soma was used to keep the population compliant and under control. There have been uncomfortable hints that Valium and its sister drugs are being misused in this way. After all, it is much cheaper to tranquillise the distraught housewife who is confined to a remote tower block with nowhere for her children to play than it is to demolish such flats and rebuild a more human environment for her to live in. The government, the drug companies and the doctor all have a vested interest in offering a medical solution to what are really social and political problems.

Illegal psychoactive drugs are often used in the same way and for the same reasons as alcohol and as the drugs prescribed by doctors. In this respect, as in so many others, there are far fewer differences between heroin, Valium and alcohol than we like to pretend. One of the main reasons why people escalate their use of drugs to become dependent upon them (because they are all potentially addictive), is precisely because of the ease with which they can be used to relieve psychological distress.

For the bored teenager, drugs may offer the initial prospect of excitement or social acceptance. Because adolescence is such a difficult period in Western society, the teenager is especially vulnerable to the temptation of using drink or drugs to gain relief from his or her problems. In recent years, it has become increasingly obvious that far more young people get into trouble with drink than with drugs. Alcohol is easily available, socially approved of, and it solves so many of the dilemmas of youth. Shyness, insecurity, feelings of social awkwardness all evaporate after a few drinks. It is easy to relax, talk freely and confidently, and to feel extraverted and sociable after a few drinks. Anyone who has watched a party move from its sober beginnings to its less sober conclusion will appreciate how effectively alcohol works as a social lubricant. But neither heavy drinking nor drug abuse are the exclusive preserve of young people; they merely generate more righteous indignation when teenagers are involved. Anyone in psychological distress is potentially at risk if he persists in using drink or drugs as a prop. Drugs may offer temporary relief if used in this way, but in the long term, they create far more problems than they can ever solve.

In recent years, researchers have been looking at the ways in which different drugs can be used to relieve different sorts of psychological problems. Alcohol, the barbiturates and valium, for instance, can all be used as a way of blotting out feelings of anxiety or relieving stress. Just as the harassed executive may reach for a stiff drink to calm him down after a difficult day, so the adolescent labouring under feelings of nervousness and awkwardness may feel better after taking barbiturates.

For the person who is insecure or chronically shy, amphetamines supply the confidence and artificial energy that convinces the user that he is brilliant, witty and creative. Objectively he may be none of these things, but the drug-induced exhilaration is powerful enough to override any more realistic appraisal of his own performance. Many drug addicts find it difficult to express their feelings of anger and aggression in an appropriate way. Heroin helps by suppressing their aggressive feelings directly. Alcohol, Valium and the barbiturates help in a different way by producing the sort of disinhibited state that allows the person to act out his feelings of hostility and aggression. Drunks and barbiturate addicts are often a particularly irritating problem in hospital casualty departments where they stumble about, threaten the staff and generally make a nuisance of themselves.

What these drugs have in common is that they can all give a temporary chemical comfort. But in the end, none of them solve the problems of living.

# 5

## ALCOHOL

Alcohol is one of the more potent as well as one of the most widely used of all the psychoactive drugs: paradoxically, it is also the least likely to be recognised as such. Two-thirds of the American population drink alcohol. The average American spends more than 5 per cent of his annual budget on alcohol, consuming 2·6 gallons of spirits, 2·2 gallons of wine and 26·6 gallons of beer every year. The same sort of pattern emerges in most Western countries. Almost half of the British population over the age of sixteen drink regularly. More than one in ten drink every day. In 1970, the Brewers Society (the main trade association concerned with the production and distribution of alcohol in Great Britain) estimated that more than £1,700 million was invested in the alcohol industry. This was almost as much as the entire capital invested in foodstuffs. More than 700,000 people were employed in the industry. Yet in a 'league table' of alcohol consumption in twenty countries which was prepared by the US Government neither America nor Britain is even in the top ten. Top of the table is France, where almost a third of the electorate are either wholly or partly dependent upon the drinks industry for their livelihood.

Nature provides alcohol in liquid form and man has been drinking it for so long that the verb 'to drink' has come to mean to drink alcoholic beverages. There are six basic kinds of alcoholic drink: beers, cider, table wines, fortified wines, liqueurs, and distilled drinks. The ways in which these drinks are made, and their relative strengths, are shown in Table 2. They differ in their precise chemical composition, and to a certain extent in their physiological effects on the body, but the main component of all of them is ethyl alcohol, or ethanol. (In this book I have used the term 'ethanol' in its strict sense to distinguish the simple solution of ethyl alcohol from the complex mixtures of higher alcohols and other substances that make up the actual drinks that we take: the term 'alcohol' is used more loosely both to refer to the ethanol content of drinks and to alcoholic drinks in general; it seemed unnecessarily pedantic to keep referring to 'alcoholic drinks'.)

*Table 2. A table of drinks*

| Drink | Type | Alcohol content (% by volume) | Produced by |
|---|---|---|---|
| Beers | Lager | 3-6 | Fermentation of brewer's wort with hops added for flavour |
| | Ale | 3-8 | |
| | Stout & porter | 4-8 | |
| Cider | | 3·5-13·5 | Fermentation of apple juice |
| Table wines | Still wines: red, white & rosé | 8-14 | Fermentation of grape juice |
| | Champagne | 12 | Secondary fermentation with carbon dioxide retained under pressure |
| Fortified wines | Sherry, port, Madeira, vermouth | 15-20 | Wines with added brandy, neutral spirits or plant-extract flavourings |
| Distilled spirits | Brandy | 40-55 | Distillation of grape mash |
| | Whisky | 40-50 | Double distillation of fermented barley, rye or corn mash |
| | Rum | 40-75 | Distillation of fermented molasses |
| | Vodka | 35-50 | Distillation of grain |
| | Gin | 35-50 | Tasteless distillate flavoured with juniper berries |
| Liqueurs | Benedictine, Chartreuse, Kirsch, Kümmel, etc. | 25-55 | Neutral spirits with various added herbs for flavour |

Among the other alcohols are methyl, amyl and propyl alcohol. Of these, methyl alcohol is possibly the most important because it is sometimes taken as a substitute for drinks containing ethyl alcohol. Methylated spirit, for instance, contains a mixture of ethanol and methyl alcohol, and methyl alcohol is also used in some paint-strippers and anti-freeze mixtures. The intoxicating effect of methyl alcohol is much less than that of ethanol in that it makes the person less drunk after a given amount, but its side-effects are more serious. The most alarming of these are its effects on vision. These can vary from visual disturbances to total blindness. This may be followed by partial or even complete recovery, though there have been many cases in which people have been permanently blinded as a result of drinking methyl alcohol. After-shave solutions and 'eau-de-colognes' often contain another of the higher alcohols, iso-propyl alcohol, and there have been cases of people drinking these preparations for their alcoholic effect. However, few of us would willingly resort to such bizarre and dangerous methods of drinking alcohol. Let us return to our more familiar 'poisons'.

All beers are made by the fermentation of brewer's wort. This is made primarily from barley malt though other cereals may also be used. If an ale, stout or porter beer is wanted, a top-fermenting species of yeast is used, while a bottom-fermenting yeast is used for lager. European beers contain three times as much hops as American beers. The hop is sometimes said to produce a 'heady' sort of intoxication and has been described as 'the English narcotic'.

Historically, wine making is about as old as beer making with a technology which is probably even more complicated. Variations in the type of grape used, the soil of the vineyard, temperature and weather conditions during the growing period, methods of harvesting, crushing and fermenting the wine, and even the conditions of storage all affect the final quality of the wine. Wines contain literally hundreds of organic compounds. In their physiological effects, however, the differences between wines are less significant. Red wines are richer in pigment-producing compounds than white wines; they also have a higher tannin content. Whereas the still wines are fermented in a single process, the champagnes are produced in two stages of fermentation. During the second stage, the carbon dioxide produced by the fermentation is held in solution under pressure. When a bottle of champagne is chilled, uncorked, and served, the carbon dioxide content drops by about half.

Fortified wines such as port, sherry, Marsala and Madeira are ordinary wines to which a form of alcohol has been added to increase their strength. The vermouths are a similar type of drink. These are usually made from a 15–20 per cent wine with plant extracts added as flavouring. Their name probably comes from *Wermut*, a German word for wormwood, which has traditionally been thought to possess healing powers and has been added to wines since Greek or Roman times. Among the other flavourings that have been used in vermouth are bitter orange peel, camomile, thistle, cardamom and nutmeg.

Spirits have been distilled from almost every conceivable source of sugar which could be fermented. Fruits, cereals, potatoes and molasses are among the more common bases. Brandy was probably the first of the spirits to be produced commercially, and is made by the distillation of wine. The spirit is then kept in barrels for at least two years, and sometimes as long as twenty years, before blending and bottling. Calvados, a type of apple brandy, is made from apple cider in the same way that grape brandy is made from wine. In some areas where calvados is widely used, such as Brittany and Normandy, there are especially high levels of alcoholism and liver disease, and there have been suggestions that calvados contains some mysterious and highly toxic ingredient which is responsible for these problems. No such mystery ingredient has been detected.

Whisky is made from various combinations of cereals – malted and unmalted barley, corn and rye; Scotch, for instance, is made from malted barley and corn. Rum is distilled from a solution containing molasses or fresh sugar-cane juice, and the distillate may be flavoured with sherry, Madeira, wine or various fruit extracts. Gin is essentially a tasteless alcohol distillate. It can be made from any fermentable carbohydrate: barley, rye, potatoes, molasses and cane juice have all been used for this purpose. Gin derives its distinctive flavouring from a second distillation with juniper berries and plant extracts. Vodka is a similar drink but without the flavouring.

Liqueurs are among the more exotic alcoholic preparations. Most were originally made as medicines during the Middle Ages, and many of them are associated with religious orders. They were usually made from herbs which had been specially chosen for their medicinal properties, though the ingredients of some have not been revealed (Benedictine and Chartreuse, for instance). In some cases, the herbs are allowed to ferment with water and sugar and the liqueur is then distilled from this mixture. In other cases the alcohol is first distilled and then flavoured. The final preparation is usually a sweet and potent liquid, though there is another group of liqueurs known as 'bitters'; the best known of the bitters is probably angostura bitters which is used to make pink gin.

Most people use alcohol fairly intelligently and derive considerable pleasure and benefit from their drinking. But it is still a drug. Indeed it is one of the more powerful, addictive and destructive drugs that is used on a large scale. Alcohol is used widely throughout the world, but, as with any other drug, the way it is used differs from culture to culture. The Islamic faith, for instance, forbids the use of alcohol, and the majority of Muslims seem to abide by that prohibition. In other societies heavy drinking has been built into religious ceremonies. The Aztecs were required to get drunk at every major religious occasion, otherwise their gods would be displeased. Even within religions there are different attitudes and expectations about alcohol. Certain Protestant denominations of the Christian Church regard alcohol as being so repugnant that it is not allowed in their Communion ceremonies.

The Jews are especially interesting in this respect, since the use of wine plays such a central part in their religious ceremonies. Wine is taken as part of the Kiddush and Habdalah which separate the Sabbath from the secular part of the week; it is taken to honour the annual festivals, and on special occasions such as New Year's Day and Yom Kippur. It is a measure of the importance of wine in Jewish life that the incidence of alcohol use is higher among Jews than among any other religious group. Probably fewer than 10 per cent of adult Jews are abstainers, and in some surveys the percentage of abstainers has been found to be as low as 1 per cent. When set against this high incidence of alcohol use, the low incidence of alcoholism among Jews is quite remarkable; both features together make up what has been called the Great Jewish Drink Mystery (see Chapter 3).

There are also marked differences in national levels of alcohol consumption. Among the more abstemious Western nations is Norway. In certain wine-producing countries, on the other hand, notably in France, the consumption of large amounts of alcohol is part of everyday life. These comparisons between countries, however, are made on the basis of *average* levels of consumption and because of this they have only a rather general relevance to actual drinking habits within the different countries. It is possible that some countries might have comparatively large numbers of abstainers as well as of heavy drinkers. This could lead to the same average level of consumption as another country in which most people took alcohol in moderate amounts.

Alcohol is a food. Unfortunately it is not a very good food; it contains calories but no minerals or vitamins. Alcohol is also a drug. It acts on the nervous system like an anaesthetic, and in large enough amounts it is a poison which can kill. In sufficiently large doses alcohol is capable of killing any living organism, though the cases in which alcohol poisoning leads to respiratory depression and to death are comparatively rare. In smaller amounts alcohol acts as a depressant drug, though it is often mistakenly thought to be a stimulant because some people become talkative, boisterous and excitable after they have been drinking. This is not the result of any stimulant effect, however, but is really the result of alcohol releasing the inhibitions which normally restrain such behaviour, and it is better described as 'disinhibition'.

The depressant effects of alcohol are most clearly found in the central nervous system. The conscious experience of these effects is rewarding to most people, and they are one of the main reasons why people use alcohol as a drug. Unfortunately, there are also less desirable effects and the drinker must try to achieve a balance in his intake of alcohol between drinking enough to maximise the pleasurable effects and avoiding the unpleasant consequences of drinking too much.

75

In the normal drinker, a small amount of alcohol usually produces a general relaxation and relief of stress. These effects are experienced after drinking quite small amounts. At higher doses the depressant effects on the brain are more marked and the drinker often begins to show obvious signs of disinhibition at this point. He may become euphoric or tearful; he may become aggressive and 'fighting drunk', or over-friendly or amorous. The precise expression of alcohol intoxication will vary widely because it is largely determined by the individual's personality and by social and cultural expectations about the effects of drink. This is true of alcohol as it is of every other psychoactive drug. The effects that anyone experiences after taking it depend at least as much upon psychological and social factors as on any biochemical processes.

Alcohol removes the learned restraints. (Probably the nearest that the psychoanalysts have ever been to cracking a joke was to suggest that the superego – the part of the mind that operates as our conscience – is soluble in alcohol.) But other social, psychological and cultural factors determine how the drinker will then behave. If he continues to drink more alcohol, he will become increasingly clumsy and have difficulty in speaking clearly. His emotional states will become even more variable, until he becomes confused, and unable to walk or balance properly. Finally, he will pass out and fall into an alcoholic stupor; if he has taken an extremely high dose, he will die.

Two of the things that are most obviously related to how intoxicated we will become are the strength of the drinks that we have taken, and the body's capacity to absorb the alcohol contained in them.

There are several different systems used to grade the potency of alcoholic drinks. The most straightforward indicates the percentage of alcohol by volume (usually abbreviated to % v/v). Another system which is widely used, but not very easy to understand, is the 'proof' system. This owes its origin to a practice of some centuries ago. If gunpowder would ignite after being soaked with a particular alcoholic drink, this was 'proof' that the drink contained more than half alcohol. The American proof system can be translated easily into % v/v, with every two degrees of proof (American) being equal to 1% v/v. The British system is more tricky, with 57·15% v/v as the equivalent of 100 degrees proof. With three such different systems, the possibilities of confusion are considerable. All references to alcoholic content in this book are made in percentage by volume.

Alcoholic drinks have a fairly rapid effect, and up to a maximum strength of 40% v/v, the higher the concentration of alcohol, the more quickly it is absorbed into the body. Very strong drinks are absorbed relatively slowly because the high concentration of alcohol slows down the physical processing of the solution through the stomach and the intestines. Absorption is also affected by the other ingredients of a drink. In sweet drinks, the sugars slow down the rate, but the carbon dioxide and bicarbonate of sparkling wines or of a whisky and soda speed up the absorption rate. Food also slows down the absorption of alcohol. Milk is especially effective in this respect, as are carbohydrates such as bread and potatoes; the carbohydrates that are present in beer also interfere with the absorption of the alcohol content.

The rate at which the alcohol is absorbed has a direct influence on the intoxicating effects of the drink. The body can metabolise alcohol at a rate equivalent to about three-quarters of an ounce to an ounce of whisky every hour. Provided that it were taken gradually and in small amounts, it should be possible to drink as much as twenty ounces of whisky (almost a whole bottle) over a twenty-four-hour period without feeling any effect from the alcohol, or indeed, even showing any sign of alcohol in the body if physiological tests were used. The body would have metabolised the alcohol as fast as it was drunk. Should anyone be so unwise as to drink the same amount of whisky over a much shorter period of time – say one or two hours – he would be considerably indisposed by it.

The rate at which alcohol is absorbed in the body, therefore, depends on several factors, including the total amount of alcohol, the alcoholic strength of the drink itself, the time taken to drink the total amount, the presence or absence of food, and whether the food was eaten before, after, or at the same time as the drink. The absorption of alcohol is also affected by the sex of the drinker. Women show higher blood-alcohol levels than men after drinking equivalent amounts of alcohol; they absorb the alcohol faster and reach a peak level of intoxication sooner. In tests of their memory and speed of reactions women also performed worse than men after drinking. Because female hormones affect the metabolism of certain drugs, their response to alcohol is altered by their menstrual cycle and women who use oral contraceptives tend to remain intoxicated for longer than those not taking the pill.

About 90 per cent of the absorbed alcohol is metabolised by the body, and the rest is excreted in the breath, the urine and the sweat. The alcohol is metabolised by the liver, first into acetaldehyde (AcH) which in turn is broken down into acetate, carbon dioxide and water. Some drugs used in the treatment of alcoholism prevent the completion of this process so that the AcH cannot be converted and the accumulation of this substance in the blood makes the person feel sick. This experience is so unpleasant that the drinker generally has little wish to repeat it, and the drug is used to help them avoid further drinking.

## Drink and occupation

There is a rich folklore which associates certain occupations with heavy drinking and with various alcohol problems. Sailors, for instance, are notorious for their heavy drinking. It does not require any great effort of imagination to see why this should be the case. The sailor spends long periods of time in an isolated, exclusively male, work-centred environment with little opportunity to spend his wages. These work periods alternate with the free time that is spent in a port, and the contrast between work and leisure conditions encourages the sort of celebration traditionally associated with sailors. In the armed forces, drink is quite freely available and is usually subsidised, which makes it easier to develop the habit of drinking regularly and in large amounts.

For others, alcoholic drinks are even more immediately

available. Barmen, waiters and publicans are constantly exposed both to alcoholic drinks and to an environment which is calculated to promote drinking. As a result, the incidence both of alcohol-related diseases such as cirrhosis of the liver, and of alcoholism, is higher among both these groups.

Other groups which are known to be at risk in this way are journalists and businessmen who regularly entertain customers or colleagues to expense-account meals. An additional complication for such people as journalists is the stress inherent in their work. They often have to work through periods of comparative inertia when drink provides a pleasant means of passing the time; at other times they are required to work under conditions of intense physical and intellectual stress. In these conditions, alcohol can serve as a tranquilliser. Coupled with all of this, they usually have to cope with the more chronic strain of having to work to a deadline. One consequence of these conditions is the comparatively high rate of alcoholism in the profession.

Of course journalists have no monopoly on occupational stress. The practice of medicine puts many different sorts of stress on the doctor, and as a profession, physicians are not noted for their aversion to alcohol. The more dramatic manifestations of this are often to be found in those cradles of medicine – the medical schools. Unfortunately, doctors are not trained to understand the non-medical uses of drugs, and their understanding of the problems that can be associated with alcohol is often equally poor.

Problem drinkers are not just the alcoholic down-and-outs who stumble around our cities. The majority of people with a drink problem continue to work. Often their colleagues are aware of their drinking, but for various reasons they turn a blind eye to it. In some cases, the standard of work that the person is capable of producing suffers; occasionally a crisis develops and it becomes impossible to carry on as if the problem did not exist. Sadly, this often leads to mutual misunderstanding, rejection and recrimination which could probably have been avoided by a more open recognition of the problems at an earlier stage. However, it is easier to suggest this than actually to do it. There is an understandable tendency for any group to avoid making any unnecessary trouble for itself – such as by identifying one of its members as a problem drinker. In any case, there are no definite criteria which can be used to decide when a particular level of drinking becomes 'problem drinking'.


## Drink and driving

Most people in the United States, Britain and Europe drive a car. Most of them drink alcohol. At some time or other, most of them do both.

In 1904, the *Quarterly Journal of Inebriety* carried an editorial condemning the use of alcohol by drivers of automobile wagons. 'The general policy and diminished power of control of both the reason and senses are certain to invite disaster in every attempt to guide such wagons.' Since that time, the internal combustion engine has transformed our lives. None of us can escape the ubiquitous motor car, and because of this, the question of drink and driving has become more and more important to each one of us.

The costs of drunken driving are enormous both in personal and in economic terms. In the United States, roughly half of all road traffic deaths involve heavy use of alcohol, on the part of the drivers or pedestrians involved, and during the late 1960s more people were killed on the roads of America by alcohol than were killed in the Vietnam War. The number of highway deaths each year at that time was about 60,000. The Blennerhassett Committee which recently submitted its report on drunken driving to the British Government estimated the annual costs of road traffic accidents due to drinking at about £100 million.

The first scientific investigations of how alcohol affected driving ability were conducted in America during the 1930s. Measures of blood alcohol concentration showed that drivers who were involved in fatal crashes often had high levels of alcohol in their systems. About half of the drivers who were involved in fatal crashes had been drinking large amounts of alcohol. Of the other drivers who were stopped at the same times and places as the accident, only a few (between 1 and 4 per cent) had drunk enough alcohol to give them blood alcohol levels above 0·1 per cent.

The same sort of result has been obtained in more recent research studies. In Britain, about one-third of the drivers killed in fatal accidents in 1976 had blood alcohol levels above the legal limit; on Saturday nights, the proportion of fatal accidents involving drivers with blood alcohol levels above the legal limit rose to an appalling 71 per cent. 63,000 people were convicted of drunken driving offences during 1976.

At a blood alcohol level of 0·08 per cent (the legal limit in Britain), the risk of having an accident suddenly starts to increase rapidly. At this level, the risk of an accident is about twice as high as for the sober driver: at 0·15 per cent the risk has increased to ten times the normal level, and by 0·2 per cent it is twenty times as high as for the non-drinking driver. After larger amounts of alcohol, the driver cannot counteract the effects of drink merely by making a special effort. Worse still, once the driver begins to feel the intoxicating effects of alcohol, he is inclined to become over-confident and take unnecessary risks, and drink probably leads to as many accidents because of errors of judgement as because of its physically debilitating effects.

Any road traffic accident is the result of a whole series of events, all of which combine to produce the final crash. It is a mistake to look for a single cause in such a complicated situation. The driver's personality, his level of driving skill when sober, and the road traffic conditions at the time all play a vital part. But having taken account of these factors, there can be little doubt that alcohol in large, or even in fairly moderate, amounts, increases the chances of the driver being involved in an accident. In the sort of 'near misses' that happen so often during ordinary driving, the alcohol may make just enough difference to the driver's reaction times, to his skill, or to his judgement, to produce a serious accident.

In 1967, the British driver was introduced to the use of the breathalyser as a result of the Road Safety Act. This was preceded by an intensive publicity campaign, and the introduction of the breathalyser had an immediate and dramatic effect. Road casualties fell by 11 per cent, and deaths on the road by 15 per cent. Within a few years, however, its deterrent effect had disappeared. This was probably due, as much as anything, to the realisation by drivers that their chances of being caught were comparatively low. In order to counteract the rising figures of drunken driving, the Government looked again at the possibility of random breath tests. In 1968, a poll conducted by the Automobile Association on the acceptability of random breathalyser tests showed that only 25 per cent were in favour, whereas 68 per cent were against random tests. By 1975, another poll showed that opinion had moved in the opposite direction: 48 per cent were in favour of random tests, and 37 per cent were opposed to them. It is not clear why such a marked change in public attitudes should have occurred during this period, but it looks as if the Government may now change the law to introduce random testing.

### The hangover

One of the most common and more immediate forms of retribution that is experienced as the result of heavy drinking is the hangover. 'Who hath woe? who hath sorrow? who hath contentions? who hath babbling? who hath wounds without a cause? who hath redness of eyes? They that tarry long at the wine; they that go to seek mixed wine . . . At the last it biteth like a serpent and stingeth like an adder.' (Proverbs 23: 29-30, 32).

As well as woe, sorrow and so forth, this unpleasant state is characterised by headache, dizziness, fatigue, nausea, and digestive disturbances, and it is almost always the consequence of too much alcohol. Among the few real exceptions to this are people whose state of physical health does not permit alcoholic drinks, even in moderation. People with liver disorders, for instance, may suffer from headaches and indigestion after only a few drinks and the effects of alcohol on stomach ulcers can be extremely painful. It is doubtful, however, whether these adverse effects of alcohol should really be considered in the same category as the hangover which follows excessive drinking.

Alcoholic drinks consist mainly of ethyl alcohol and water, but they also contain small amounts of other substances called congeners. These congeners include other forms of alcohol, ethyl acetate, various sugars, salt, acids, minerals and B-group vitamins, and the concentration of these components varies in different drinks. Although most people are unaware of their existence, the congeners are important to the drinker because they give the characteristic flavour and colouring to the different drinks. They also contribute towards the hangover. When the higher alcohols have been distilled off from brandy, people who were given this congener-concentrate to drink developed headaches and drowsiness which persisted for up to eighteen hours. No such symptoms were recorded in another group who drank a solution containing a comparable amount of ethanol.

The congener content of various drinks seems to affect not only the likelihood of waking up with a hangover after a given amount of alcohol, but also the severity of the hangover symptoms themselves. This has usually been tested experimentally, having volunteer subjects drink either a high-congener or a low-congener drink. Vodka and bourbon are the two drinks that have generally been used in experiments because they are so different in their congener content. Vodka, for instance, is very nearly a neutral spirit and may contain as little as 3·3 grammes per 100 litres. Bourbon, on the other hand, contains a massive 286 grammes. At a given dose of ethanol both drinks can produce hangovers, but people who have drunk too much bourbon are likely to feel much worse than the vodka drinkers.

One of the congeners which has been associated with such hangover symptoms as headaches, sweating, and feeling of sickness, is acetaldehyde (AcH). Interestingly, AcH occurs in higher quantities in white than in red wines, which is contrary to certain folklore about red wines causing worse after-effects. On the other hand, calvados, which has the reputation of being a particularly fierce form of brandy, contains extremely high levels of certain congeners (notably the esters).

One of the reasons that people regularly give for drinking beers and lagers – and one that features in several advertisements – is to quench a raging thirst. Paradoxically, alcohol has the opposite effect. It produces dehydration, and after excessive drinking this is felt as one of the symptoms of the hangover. It has been suggested that after drinking too much, it is possible to reduce the severity of the hangover by drinking large amounts of water to counter the after-effects caused by the drying action of the alcohol.

## Alcoholism

When a persistent heavy drinker begins to treat his hangover with further alcohol, he is running a serious risk of becoming a dependent drinker. This 'hair of the dog' treatment may lessen the immediate physical and mental distress, but it helps to establish a pernicious habit. As with the person who has learnt to use drugs as a psychological prop to deal with real or imaginary difficulties, this sort of 'morning-after' drinking is often a further step to long-term dependent alcohol use. In Britain the usual estimates put the number of alcoholics somewhere between 200,000 and 400,000. In America, there are probably about 6 million alcoholics – roughly 1 per cent of the population, though some estimates have put the number as high as 20 million.

As with other forms of drug dependence, there is general confusion about what we mean by the term alcoholism. Doctors and researchers are often just as confused about this as the man in the street. During the past century there has been a shift of perspective. Alcoholism was once regarded primarily as a sin and a vice; it is now more frequently seen as a disease. In fact, this polarisation of attitudes towards alcoholism is quite unhelpful. The person who has become dependent on alcohol (or on other drugs for that matter) should not be seen as morally weak nor necessarily as being sick. By focusing attention on alcoholism merely as a bad habit, the moral viewpoint underestimates the extent to which alcohol can become a central feature of the alcoholic's life; and because of this, it also underestimates the difficulties inherent in the individual's attempt to stop drinking. The disease conception of alcoholism falls into the opposite error; it encourages a view of alcoholism as a specific illness over which the alcoholic has no control. Alcoholism is not a specific disorder; in almost every case, it is a complex mixture of social, psychological and physical problems. Although several eminent specialists in this field have expressed the belief that it is still more humane to regard the alcoholic as 'sick' than as morally weak, the disease concept of alcoholism can be equally misleading since it can encourage both the doctor and the alcoholic patient to ignore the active role that the individual plays in determining his own drinking behaviour.

The idea that alcoholism is a disease also encourages many heavy drinkers to feel that they need not worry about their own drinking habits despite the problems produced by their drinking. Because of this it is often a better idea to remove the medical mystique from the problem by thinking simply in terms of drinking problems. These can vary from drunkenness and the familiar hangover through problems with social relationships and various psychological difficulties, to full medical disorders such as liver damage. The more of these complications from alcohol use that the individual experiences, the more concerned he ought to be to change his drinking habits. Certain problems are especially significant. Regularly drinking more than was intended, being intoxicated at inappropriate times, the conviction that alcohol is a necessary aid to functioning properly or the feeling that one's drinking is not really under voluntary control – any of these things should be treated as danger signs. The drinker who recognises his own attitudes and behaviour among these problems would be well advised to consider changing his drinking patterns.

Of course, the notion of 'drinking problems' is itself rather vague. In the first place, it does not specify whose problems are involved. If a person is drinking so much that he is damaging his health, and is unable to give up his heavy drinking, there is little difficulty in deciding whose problem is involved. But in many other cases the drinker would be quite happy to go on drinking if only others would let him. Whose problem is it then? Drunkenness, for instance, is just such a public nuisance.

During the twenty years between 1957 and 1977 there was a steady rise in the incidence of drunkenness offences in England

and Wales. This was most marked for males (rising from about 370 to 540 per 100,000 of the population). The most marked increase during this period was for young men aged between 18 and 21, which more than doubled, rising from just over 600 per 100,000 to almost 1,500. For various reasons, drunkenness offences among women are far less common than they are among men, but the rise in convictions among women aged 18 to 21 was even more dramatic in this period, increasing from about 35 per 100,000 to almost 100.

Drunkenness is one of the more visible drinking problems, but it is rather different from the chronic forms of alcohol intoxication. These are not really about getting drunk at all. A man who is chronically intoxicated on alcohol may not show any of the acute effects that are usually seen in the drunk. The most common features of alcoholism are usually described as: (i) an increased physiological tolerance to alcohol; (ii) withdrawal symptoms and craving when alcohol is not available; (iii) inability to drink moderately: many alcoholics seem to lose control over their drinking after having one drink and go on to drink to excess.

The acute withdrawal syndrome that is provoked in alcoholics when they are deprived of their drug has been a known part of the human condition for thousands of years. It is also one of the most severe drug withdrawal states, far more serious, for instance, than that provoked by heroin withdrawal. Symptoms can include insomnia, tremor ('the shakes'), a general state of confusion, and auditory, tactile or visual hallucinations. These hallucinations (the DTs, *delirium tremens*), have been the topic of many jokes over the years (usually featuring pink elephants), but for the person involved they are a terrifying experience. Withdrawal from alcohol can also provoke seizures in which the unfortunate alcoholic suddenly falls into an epileptic fit with convulsions. These fits almost always occur during the first forty-eight hours after drinking has stopped.

The third feature that has been mentioned – loss of control – has been the subject of considerable controversy. It fits quite well with the 'disease' model of alcoholism, in so far as it suggests that the individual is powerless to control his own drinking; and it is also consistent with the popular belief that the only realistic goal for an alcoholic is total abstinence. Many of the people who believe that they have lost control when they drink, try to cope with this by 'going on the wagon' for days, weeks, or even longer between their binges.

The true significance of this loss of control phenomenon is that the drinker *believes* that he cannot control his drinking. Because he believes he has no control, this affects his behaviour when he uses alcohol and further reinforces his belief. This loss of control feature of alcoholic drinking is really a psychological and attitudinal effect, and as such it is dependent upon individual learning and social influences.

In recent years it has been established that alcoholics need not choose between abstinence and alcoholism. Many people who have formerly been dependent upon alcohol were able to return to normal drinking. When these findings were first published by Dr D. L. Davies of the Maudsley Hospital they provoked an outburst of hostile criticism. Since then, other researchers have obtained the same results, and there is no longer any doubt that at least some alcoholics can learn to control their intake of alcohol and develop normal drinking habits.

These three features – increased tolerance, craving and withdrawal symptoms when alcohol is not available, and loss of control – seem to be more common in North America and in Anglo-Saxon countries. In France, on the other hand, the predominant pattern of alcoholism reflects the first two features, but instead of feeling that he has lost control of his drinking after the first drink, the French alcoholic drinks steadily but cannot do without his drink. Instead of binges alternating with periods of abstinence, the pattern is one of constant heavy drinking without marked intoxication. A survey carried out in France asked what amount of wine a workman could consume *every day* 'without inconvenience'. The response was a staggering 1·8 litres (almost two and a half bottles of wine, or 6 ounces of ethanol). A quarter of the people in the survey described wine as 'indispensable' to their lives.

One of the most interesting comparisons to be made between

European countries is that between the rates of alcoholism in France and Italy. Although both countries produce and consume large amounts of wine, the incidence of alcoholism in France is five or six times as high as that in Italy. This is not simply related to the prevalence of drinking, because wine is used by a larger proportion of the population in Italy than in France. Sociologists have noted several differences that could have an influence. Among these are the French belief that drinking large amounts of wine is somehow associated with virility; the Italians do not share this belief. The French are also more tolerant of drunkenness, seeing it as amusing or at least as tolerable, whereas the Italians regard it as a personal and family disgrace. There are also differences in national attitudes towards drinking among children. The Italians are inclined to regard the matter unemotionally and as a normal and unexceptional part of the child's social development; French parental attitudes, on the other hand, tend to be more rigid and are usually either strongly in favour or strongly opposed to drink.

Until recently the communist countries of Eastern Europe played down their problems with alcohol. However, alcohol consumption in the Eastern bloc is amongst the highest in the world. Vodka is consumed in large amounts in Russia, where for reasons better known to the Russians it is known as 'The Green Snake'; and a public campaign has recently been mounted against the problem of drunkenness. In Poland the nation's three million hard-core drinkers account for something like half of the total amount of alcohol that is drunk by a population of 34 million. The Baltic port of Szczecin had such a bad reputation as a Polish version of Sodom and Gomorrah that a form of total prohibition was introduced in the area for a time. The results were much the same as in the United States between 1920 and 1933. From 1 January 1980 another system designed to restrict the availability of alcohol is being tried in Warsaw with a ban on the sale of drinks containing more than 4·5 per cent alcohol during weekends, holidays and pay-days. Yugoslavia has also introduced restrictive measures by placing a ban on all forms of advertising designed to promote the use of alcohol (and tobacco).

Heavy use of alcohol over a prolonged period of time certainly increases the risk of developing various physical illnesses, but there are no convenient signposts to show at what point someone moves from moderate and acceptable levels of drinking to a pattern of heavy drinking which may cause damage to health. It seems as though this threshold may be lower than it was once thought to be. Converted to standard units of alcohol, one unit is equivalent to half a pint of beer, one glass of wine or a single measure of spirits. The Royal College of Psychiatrists has suggested that the limits to safe drinking are about 50 units per week for a man and about 35 per week for a woman. Anyone who regularly drinks more than that amount is at risk of establishing a pattern of addictive drinking, and probably also of damaging his or her liver. Among the diseases associated with long-term heavy drinking are inflammation of the stomach and diseases of the pancreas as well as damage to the heart, liver and nervous system.

Cirrhosis of the liver is a good example. If different countries are arranged in order of their consumption of alcohol per person, this also puts them in roughly the same order of their death rate from cirrhosis. Of the non-communist countries, France, Portugal and Italy are at the top of the liver disease table. At the bottom of the table are the United Kingdom, Eire and the Netherlands. It is rather surprising to find the UK at the bottom of the table since its *per capita* consumption is comparatively high – higher, for instance, than that of the USA which has a higher incidence of cirrhosis. In New York State, cirrhosis is the third most frequent cause of death for adults in their productive years; in California it is the fourth most frequent cause. In Ontario, Canada, it is the most rapidly increasing cause of death among people over the age of twenty-five.

For the average drinker, of course, this catalogue of alcoholic disasters seems remote, and he finds it difficult to reconcile his own enjoyment of wine or beer with the havoc that alcohol can wreak. None the less, it is the same drug, alcohol, that is involved. But it is a mistake to focus only upon the drug. It is not the alcohol that causes drunkenness and alcoholism; it is the unintelligent way in which the individual uses alcohol that is responsible.

# 6

## TOBACCO

In 1604 King James I published his *Counterblaste to Tobacco*, one of the first and most strident condemnations of 'This Filthy Custom'. 'A custom loathsome to the eye, hateful to the nose, harmful to the brain, dangerous to the lungs, and in the black stinking fumes thereof nearest resembling the horrible Stygian smoke of the pit that is bottomless.' Like one of his successors, King James was very clearly not amused.

It can be taken as snuff or it can be chewed; it can be smoked in pipes, as cigars or as cigarettes. Each of these forms has been popular at one time or another, but during this century one has increasingly established its supremacy over the others – cigarette smoking. For the Western world, the discovery of tobacco can be directly traced to Christopher Columbus' voyage to the New World in 1492. Columbus himself was far too preoccupied by his lust for gold to take much notice of the curious customs of the natives, and it was not until later voyages that the smoking of tobacco was given any real consideration. At first, the Spanish sailors found it an unpleasant experience, but they soon became enthusiastic smokers themselves.

The dubious honour of being the first man to smoke tobacco in Europe belongs to Rodrigo de Jerez, a companion of Christopher Columbus. On his return to Spain, he so alarmed his countrymen by breathing smoke that they concluded the Devil had entered him, and hurried off to the priest who in turn referred the matter to the Holy Inquisition. As a result, de Jerez spent some years in prison. When he was let out, he may have been considerably piqued to find that smoking had established itself as a popular pastime.

The current preoccupation with the adverse effects of smoking is not new. In 1526, Oviedo the Spanish historian described it as 'a bad and pernicious custom' and King James'

*Counterblaste* is hardly a recommendation of the habit. James I combined his distaste for tobacco with his financial acumen and imposed a tax on it. Others adopted more drastic measures. In Russia, Turkey, Persia and parts of Germany it was punished by death. In Transylvania the smoker was dealt with more leniently: all his money and possessions were confiscated by the state. Torture and mutilation have also been used to persuade smokers not to harm themselves by smoking. Since its discovery many physicians have been convinced that smoking was harmful, though the nature of the supposed damage has changed. It was once thought to 'blacken the brain'. Indeed this was said to have been demonstrated beyond all doubt by autopsies carried out on the bodies of smokers.

The tobacco trade has always been a lucrative enterprise and during this century vast industrial and political influence has come to be linked with this drug. If you pop into your local tobacconist's shop you will be confronted by an impressive array of brightly packaged cigarettes, cigars, and tobaccos. Everything seems to point to an enormous variety of choice for the consumer. The facts of the matter are rather different.

Seven large multinational tobacco corporations control almost all aspects of cigarette production in the Western world. Their control extends from growing the leaf to selling the packets of cigarettes. Between 85 and 90 per cent of the leaf tobacco in international trade is already directly or indirectly controlled by only six multinationals. The efforts of these companies to control the consumption of cigarettes are mainly concentrated in advertising. In their attempt to conceal the full extent of their advertising costs, the multinational tobacco companies have all acted in unison to keep details of this expenditure from an investigation by the Federal Trades Commission. The best estimate is that, each year, these firms spend about 1·8 billion dollars on advertising.

It is difficult to see how the public could benefit from this massive expenditure. Rather than providing information, cigarette advertising mainly produces confusion and vagueness. The advertisements themselves are little more than emotionally-loaded image-boosters, and one could be forgiven for believing that the main effect of such advertising is to debase and corrupt society's understanding of this form of drug taking. One of the purposes of such advertisements seems to be to protect the market position of the established multinational tobacco companies by erecting massive barriers to the entry of any rival.

But apart from excluding potential rivals, advertising seems to be concerned with exploiting already-existing tastes and directing them towards specific brands. One of the classic studies of the effects of advertising suggested that 'if underlying conditions are favourable to an increase in demand for a product . . . the use of advertising tends to enhance and accelerate the rising trend of demand. In the case of declining trend in demand . . . advertising is powerless to halt or reverse the trend. It can do no more than temporarily delay it.' Recent research into advertising is inconclusive. Adverts do not appear to have any clear causal effects on behaviour, and variation in demand seems to depend much more upon such straight-forward factors as the price of the product and the income of the consumer. Where cigarette advertising has been banned, as in Italy and Norway, this has not stopped the increase in smoking. The same increase can be seen in Eastern Europe where there is no cigarette advertising.

The multinational tobacco companies are also said to have more questionable techniques of protecting their profits. A recent United Nations report described how another component of the marketing of tobacco involves 'global corporate bribery'. The same report suggests that pay-offs (some involving millions of dollars) have been issued to politicians and political parties both in the United States and elsewhere in the world by several of the largest multinational tobacco companies.

There is a common feeling nowadays that drug taking can be controlled by taxation. This idea seems appealing, but like other systems of drug control that attempt to impose themselves upon the consumer, it may raise as many problems as it solves.

## Tobacco

Since 1960, tobacco taxes have steadily increased. In 1975, the total tax revenue from tobacco in the United States was almost twice that from alcohol. As a result, the tobacco lobby can apply immense political pressure for its own ends. One of the other interesting developments that has followed the rise in tobacco taxation is the development of the black market. About 30 per cent of all cigarettes on international sale come from the black market. In Italy, bootleg cigarettes make up 35 to 40 per cent of all sales, and in Afghanistan about 65 per cent are contraband. In the United States, the tax on a packet of cigarettes varies from state to state. The combined state and city taxes in New York City make it the most expensive place in the country to buy cigarettes. North Carolina, on the other hand, is one of the cheapest places. A single truck-load of cigarettes bought in North Carolina and brought to New York could easily produce a profit of more than 60,000 dollars. As a result of this bootleg trade in cigarettes, more than half of the traditional wholesalers have been put out of business during the past decade, and criminal conspiracy charges have been brought against nine members of the Wholesale Tobacco Distributors in New York. All five of New York's Mafia families are said to have moved into cigarette marketing operations. Their annual profits may be as much as 100 million dollars. It is thought that the Mafia involvement in this lucrative trade will continue to increase.

Americans smoke 620 billion cigarettes every year, one sixth of the entire world output. In 1978, they paid some 15·8 billion dollars for this doubtful privilege. About one-third of the American and British adult population are smokers. The trend in America and in the industrialised countries, however, is towards a gradual reduction in the consumption of cigarettes. In the Third World, there is a rapid increase in consumption; this is a great potential market for the tobacco companies. Now that there is an increasing awareness of the potential hazards of smoking, the advertising and marketing practices of the tobacco companies have come under special scrutiny in the West. In the Third World, where there is less awareness of the risks and fewer regulations, the opportunities are much greater, and it seems unlikely that there will be any alteration in the present increase in smoking in these countries.

## What is tobacco smoke?

A burning cigarette is a miniature chemical factory. From the fifteen or so major constituents of tobacco, almost two thousand compounds are produced by combustion. These vary with the type of tobacco plant from which the leaf was gathered and the way in which it was cured. But the mixture that eventually reaches the smoker's body depends upon more than just the chemistry of tobacco. It depends upon the way in which the smoker smokes it. The more vigorously he puffs on the tobacco, the higher the temperature at which it burns: this affects the chemical products of combustion. The smoker who keeps a cigarette between his lips when smoking will inhale more of the 'side-stream' smoke than someone who holds the cigarette away from his mouth: side-stream smoke that curls away from the end of a burning cigarette is more concentrated than the main-stream smoke inhaled through the cigarette itself. Cigarette smoke also becomes more concentrated as the cigarette burns down. Cigarette smoke is less irritating to the lungs than cigar and pipe smoke, and because of this it is the most likely to be inhaled. However, the ingredients of tobacco smoke can act in the mouth, in the air passages or in the lungs. The components of tobacco smoke that are of most medical interest are nicotine, carbon monoxide and tobacco tar.

There has never been any doubt about the remarkable and insidious attractions that tobacco has for some people. In 1527, a Spanish bishop described how the native habit of smoking was taken up by Europeans: 'When reproached for such a disgusting habit, [they] replied that they found it impossible to give it up. I cannot understand what enjoyment or advantage they derive from it.' To the non-smoker, it seems inconceivable that countless millions of people should persistently inhale the smoke of dried leaves. It produces no obvious intoxication, and the initial experience of inhaling cigarette smoke is almost

94

always unpleasant. Many people are actually sick the first time they smoke. Despite this, it is amazing to find that for every hundred teenagers who smoke more than a single cigarette, eighty-five will continue to smoke and only fifteen will not. Cigarette smoking is one of the most addictive of all drug habits. It is more likely to produce dependence than using either barbiturates or alcohol: the nearest drug habit, in terms of the risk of becoming dependent, is injecting heroin. Its high addictive potential is further increased by the fact that, unlike many other types of drug taking, smoking improves the smoker's performance in normal social and work settings.

Nicotine is a powerful drug with a variety of effects, many of which are unpredictable. Generally speaking, it is a stimulant drug: among its other effects, it stimulates the secretion of adrenaline and noradrenaline, which produces an increase in heart rate and blood pressure. Yet when smokers are asked why they smoke they usually say something like 'It relaxes me', or 'It helps to calm me down'. In other words, they are suggesting that smoking has primarily tranquillising or sedating effects. In large doses it can produce vomiting, tremor and convulsions. It is also one of the most powerful poisons and is used in a number of agricultural pesticides. The fatal dose for a man may be as low as 60 mg., though it seems to be less dangerous when swallowed in the form of tobacco. A strong cigarette may contain 20 mg. of nicotine, though only a small amount of this reaches the brain when it is smoked (perhaps 2 mg.). Death from nicotine poisoning, as with cyanide poisoning, occurs within minutes (both cyanide and ammonia are also present in tobacco smoke, though, mercifully, only in very small quantities).

Nicotine reaches the brain within a few seconds of each puff and the average smoker may deliver something like 70,000 separate doses of the drug to his brain every year. Several experiments have shown that when smokers are given cigarettes containing very little nicotine they tend to smoke more, and when they are given cigarettes with very high nicotine levels they smoke less. All of this might be thought to point directly to nicotine as the crucial addictive agent in smoking. However, the effect that nicotine has had on smoking in these experiments has often been extremely crude and variable. In one study, the strong cigarettes contained more than four times as much nicotine as the weak ones, yet the smokers who were given the low-nicotine cigarettes smoked only about a quarter as many more than the high-nicotine group. There are other problems involved in this sort of experiment. It is difficult to vary the nicotine content of cigarettes without altering other constituents. Nicotine and tar are closely related, and since tar is largely responsible for the flavour of the cigarette this could produce a bias in the results which was not directly related to nicotine at all. Some studies have even used cigarettes made of dried lettuce leaves with nicotine added to them. These tasted so unpleasant that the subjects in the experiment probably smoked fewer of them because of their vile flavour rather than because of their drug content. Another way of investigating the role played by nicotine involves giving measured doses of nicotine to smokers and then seeing how this affects their smoking.

One of the best recent experiments of this sort was conducted by Dr Channi Kumar and his colleagues at the Institute of Psychiatry in London. A group of volunteer smokers was divided into three groups which received different doses of nicotine: one group received a high dose, the second a low dose, and the third only a nicotine-free placebo. In the first part of the study, the three groups were asked to inhale from cigarettes containing different amounts of nicotine (or no nicotine at all) at fixed intervals. In the second part of the study a few weeks later, instead of receiving their nicotine by smoking, they were given the different doses of drug directly by injection. The experimenters took various physiological measures to check that the drug had had an active effect. Throughout both parts of the study, all the subjects were allowed to smoke whenever they wanted to. The results clearly show that inhaled doses of smoke postponed and reduced further smoking and that this was related to the content of the smoke. When the results of the second part of the experiment were analysed, they showed, contrary to all expectations, that the intravenous doses of nicotine had no effect on the person's subsequent smoking. This result is strong evidence against the idea that smoking can be explained simply in terms of the smoker's need for nicotine. Nicotine clearly has some effect on smoking and it may turn out to be quite an important effect, but there are other aspects of smoking that provide powerful rewards for the smoker. The psychological and social significance that the habit has for the smoker is one of the most important but least understood aspects of smoking.

## Smoking and illness

The American smoker is informed that 'The Surgeon General has determined that cigarette smoking is dangerous to your health'. Similarly, cigarettes sold in Britain carry a health warning such as 'Smoking can damage your health'. In 1976, the Minister of Health demanded that this should be changed to: *Danger: Cigarettes cause lung cancer, bronchitis and heart disease.* The cigarette manufacturers were able to use their considerable political influence to have this rejected and have argued that the adverse effects of smoking have not been established.

The argument that smoking is a direct cause of these diseases is not new. In one form or another it has been with us for centuries. King James asserted that smoking caused damage to the lungs and to the brain, and physicians claimed to have demonstrated how it 'blackened the brain'. The American anti-cigarette lobby that demanded prohibition was convinced that smoking was a certain cause of moral degradation. Smoking is clearly as much a moral and political issue as a scientific and medical one, and as in so many other cases where the two have become entangled, rational argument is often the first victim. The great smoking debate is characterised, as it always has been, by dogmatism, impatience and self-righteousness as much as by impartial investigation of the issues. The facts themselves, however, are quite clear. Smokers are at much greater risk of contracting lung cancer. They run a much greater risk of developing chronic bronchitis and emphysema. Similarly, smokers are twice as likely to die of coronary heart disease as non-smokers. No one disputes these observations: there has, however, been some argument about how to explain them.

One of the weaknesses of the evidence linking smoking with lung cancer and with heart disease is that it is based on correlational statistics – these simply show that the two often go together. They do not show how they are caused. As an example, correlational statistics show that people who take tranquillisers are more anxious than people who don't. This does not prove that tranquillisers *cause* anxiety. The same is true of smoking and illnesses; *both* may be due to other factors. The same sort of statistics show that smoking is positively correlated with suicide: this does not prove that smoking causes suicide. Smoking is negatively correlated with Parkinson's disease and diabetes: this does not show that smoking prevents these diseases.

Nonetheless, correlational studies can help to draw attention to possible causal links even if they do not confirm them. There can be no doubt about the official medical view of the matter. The Royal College of Physicians has stated this as clearly as anyone could hope: 'Cigarette smoking is now as important a cause of death as were the great epidemic diseases such as typhoid, cholera and tuberculosis' (*Smoking and Health Now*). At least 320,000 Americans and 50,000 Britons are said to die unnecessarily each year as a result of smoking (some estimates put the numbers even higher), and the Royal College is convinced that there is a direct causal link between smoking and various fatal and disabling diseases.

For most of this century, there has been a steady increase in the number of smokers and in the incidence of lung cancer. This is usually put forward as support for the causal view (i.e. smoking causes lung cancer). However, there are problems involved in this interpretation. Medical diagnoses are far from being completely reliable; in fact, for some diseases they are extremely unreliable. During the past century there have been many changes in diagnostic practice in relation to such diseases as lung cancer. A medical article written in 1904 found that out of 178 cases of lung cancer detected by autopsy, only 6 were diagnosed while the patient was alive. Without an autopsy they would have remained undetected. With modern techniques, many more of these cases would have been recognised. So a good deal of the apparent increase in lung cancer may actually be due to improved diagnostic techniques (radiology, broncoscopy, sputum examination and surgery). This leads on to another problem: although lung cancer is less likely to be missed by modern medicine, it can still be falsely diagnosed. Pathologists are often in disagreement with doctors in clinical practice on the question of this particular diagnosis, and it has been suggested that the interest in lung cancer stimulated by the new techniques may have led doctors to diagnose lung cancer too often. There are fads and fashions in diagnosis as in other non-medical areas of life.

The most recent study of the accuracy of medical diagnoses (published by Drs Cameron and McGoogan in the *Journal of Pathology*, 1981) confirms that there are still many inaccuracies in the identification of illnesses. In about 40 per cent of all cases, the diagnosed cause of death was found to be incorrect when an autopsy was carried out, and despite the vastly improved modern techniques of screening for lung cancer, this is one of the most frequently misdiagnosed forms of cancer; generally, these are errors of under-diagnosis. In the Cameron studies the disease was confirmed at autopsy in 59 per cent of cases. Under-diagnosis was about three times as common as over-diagnosis (31 per cent and 10 per cent respectively). Coronary heart disease is also subject to many diagnostic errors, and it is probably used as a convenient label whenever the cause of an unexpected death is not known. Heart attacks (acute myocardial infarctions) were misdiagnosed in 36 per cent of cases: it was offered incorrectly (over-diagnosed) in 19 per cent of cases, and missed (under-diagnosed) in 17 per cent.

These results raise serious doubts about the validity of using death certification as a basis for estimating public health trends.

And although they suggest that the massive increase during this century of deaths from lung cancer cannot be explained as a result of over-diagnosis, there are other disturbing possibilities. For instance, if there were a systematic bias such that lung cancer or coronary heart disease were over-diagnosed among smokers but under-diagnosed among non-smokers, this would invalidate the conclusions of many studies on smoking and health.

Assuming that no such bias does operate, errors in the diagnosis of lung cancer should be no different for men than for women. The period 1890–1920 saw a massive increase in the numbers of men who smoked. It was not until 1920–1940 that women began to smoke in any numbers, during which time there was no marked increase in smoking among men. It is usually assumed that there is a delay of something like thirty years before the effects of smoking begin to show themselves as lung cancer. If smoking does indeed cause cancer, we would expect the incidence of the disease among men to show a rapid increase long before it appears for women. Between 1911–1915 men were twice as likely to die of lung cancer as women. This risk gradually increased. By the 1950s, men were ten times more likely to die of this disease. By this time, however, the sex ratio had begun to decrease. All of these changes are consistent with the patterns of smoking by men and women earlier in the century; they are also consistent with the suggestion that smoking causes lung cancer.

Cigarette smoke is known to contain chemicals which can cause cancers when they are applied in sufficient concentrations to some wretched laboratory animal; it also contains other chemicals which can encourage the development of cancer. The precise constituents of tobacco smoke that cause cancer have not been identified with any certainty, though it is suspected that they are likely to be found in the small droplets that condense out as tar. One of the research groups that is most strongly convinced that cigarettes are a direct cause of lung cancer is that at Oxford University which conducted the investigations of the smoking habits of British doctors. In a paper published by the Royal Statistical Society of London, Richard Doll argued that we are all exposed from birth to agents that are capable of causing the disease, and that these agents interact to multiply the degree of risk. Industrial studies have shown that among workers who are exposed to asbestos or irradiation, smokers are at even greater risk than usual of contracting lung cancer. Of these various agents, Doll and his colleagues are convinced that cigarette smoke is most clearly implicated as a cause of this disease.

If smoking does cause lung cancer we might expect heavy smokers to contract the disease *earlier* than light smokers. But although heavy smokers are more likely to develop lung cancer than light smokers, the amount smoked seems to make no difference to the age at which a person contracts lung cancer. Light smokers are afflicted with the disease at about the same age as heavy smokers. On the other hand, there does seem to be a clear mathematical relationship between the incidence of lung cancer and both the number of years during which a person has smoked cigarettes and the average number of cigarettes smoked per day.

The experimental work that has been done with animals strongly supports this view that duration of exposure to cigarette smoke is a crucial factor in causing cancer; and in human studies, among people of a given age, those who started to smoke earliest are most likely to develop lung cancer. A sixty-year-old who has smoked more than twenty cigarettes a day since his early teens runs a thirty-three times greater risk of contracting the disease than a non-smoker; if he started smoking in his early twenties he is at fifteen times the risk of a non-smoker, and if he started smoking after he was twenty-five years old, he runs an eight times greater risk. When information from different countries is compared, with this time-lag taken into account, there is a close relationship between the number of manufactured cigarettes sold (per adult) in 1950 and the incidence of lung cancer in 1975. The United States has the unfortunate honour of being the world's leading cigarette-smoking nation as well as having the highest incidence of lung cancer.

It is sometimes said that the way in which cigarette tobacco is cured has an influence upon the health of the smoker. The most common brands of cigarettes sold in Britain and America contain Virginia tobacco This is a tobacco that has been flue-cured by heating for five to seven days and it is chemically different from the tobacco used in some European cigarettes which has been air-dried. Flue-cured tobacco has a sugar content which may be twenty or thirty times as high as that of air-cured tobacco, and its smoke is acidic and easier to inhale than that of the alkaline air-dried tobacco. It is not inconceivable that these different tobacco-curing processes might relate to the smoker's chances of contracting lung cancer. When one compares countries such as France and Britain, which differ in terms of the type of cigarette tobacco that is generally smoked, France has a lower incidence of lung cancer. This can easily be explained in terms of the fact that the French consume fewer cigarettes than the British: the incidence of lung cancer in France is just as one would expect from a knowledge of the number of smokers in the country. Nonetheless it is odd that so little is known about this question of curing proccesses. For the moment it is not clear whether or not flue-cured Virginia tobacco is intrinsically more harmful than air-dried tobacco, or whether it could be harmful in a less direct way because its acidic smoke is easier to inhale.

One of the curious anomalies in the evidence linking smoking and lung cancer relates to inhalation. It seems a matter of common sense that inhaling tobacco smoke should be worse for you than not inhaling it, and several studies have been published which suggest that this is so. This view of inhaling has now become so well-established that it is difficult to imagine how the facts could be otherwise. Yet when the statistician Sir Ronald Fisher looked at this question he found that the incidence of lung cancer among his sample of smokers who inhaled was 10 per cent lower than among those smokers who did not inhale! A French study produced a similarly surprising result. Although light and medium smokers who inhaled were more at risk than those who did not, the incidence of lung cancer among heavy smokers who inhaled was little more than half that of the non-inhalers. Nor are these the only studies which have produced this result. It was even confirmed by one of the studies most often used as evidence that smoking does cause these diseases, the twenty-year investigation into the smoking habits of British doctors. Smokers who inhaled were at no greater risk of contracting lung cancer, cancer of the oesophagus or cancer of any other respiratory site than were smokers who did not inhale. Again, the death rate for lung cancer was actually lower for heavy smokers who inhaled. One attempt to make sense of this peculiar finding suggested that smokers who say they do not inhale are actually slow inhalers whereas those who say they do inhale are fast inhalers. Fast inhalation may be associated with a lower risk of cancer because it deposits less tar on the vulnerable upper airways.

Lung cancer is the most notorious smoking-related disease. It is, however, far less common than coronary heart disease which is now the leading cause of death in many developed countries. Although we know that smokers are more likely to die of this disease than non-smokers, there has been some argument about the nature of this relationship. It has been suggested that the observed association between the two is not due to cause and effect but to the presence in the population of people who have inherited a predisposition to both smoking and heart disease.

One of the most interesting experimental techniques in psychology and medicine involves the study of twins, particularly identical twins. Identical twins are nature's gift to experimentation since they share the same genetic endowment. If we can find a large enough number of identical twins where one twin is a smoker and the other is not, then this provides an extremely valuable test of whether genetic factors, smoking, or both, contribute towards the various diseases to which smokers are so prone. If genetic factors are partly responsible for the common basis of smoking and disease, the twin who does not smoke will still be at risk of becoming ill, even though he does not smoke. In a Swedish study of more than 23,000 twin pairs, it was quite clear that identical twins are more likely either to be both smokers or both non-smokers than is the case for two people with different genetic endowments: they are also more alike in such other aspects of their drug-taking as their use of tranquillisers, sleeping tablets, and alcohol. They even show a greater similarity in terms of the number of cups of coffee that they drink during the day, and in such other aspects of their behaviour as sleeping difficulties and feelings of stress. The Swedish study showed beyond any reasonable doubt that smokers are genetically different from non-smokers. The differences between them cover a wide range of personality characteristics and behaviours, many of which are known to be implicated in the smoking-related diseases. For instance, susceptibility to stress is partly determined by genetic factors and this is known to be related to coronary heart disease.

The Swedish study also produced an interesting suggestion that the death rate for people who are under stress is *lower* among smokers than among non-smokers. Again, the numbers involved are small and it is difficult to know what this result means, but it could indicate that for those people who are already under stress, smoking may compensate for the stress by helping to relieve tension.

It would, however, be unwise to conclude too readily that smoking does not increase the risk of heart disease. There is a considerable body of evidence from other investigations that does implicate smoking as one of the contributory factors in coronary heart disease, though the relative risk of the smoker developing this disease is less than for lung cancer or chronic bronchitis. A recent report in the *New England Journal of Medicine* (Vol. 304, 1981) compared the effects of smoking on heart disease when such differences as age, sex (coronary heart disease is more common among men), alcohol consumption, prior symptoms of heart disease, and obesity were taken into account. Persistent smokers were found to be more than twice as liable to heart disease as people who had once smoked but who had since given it up. In the age range 45–55, smokers are more than four times as liable to this disease than non-smokers.

Most studies have also shown that this liability is dose-related – the more cigarettes the person smokes, the greater the risk of heart disease.

But whatever doubt there is about the causal relationship between smoking and heart disease (and many smoking researchers would argue that there is no longer any doubt at all), for respiratory problems the evidence is indisputable. Cigarette smoking is the most important cause of chronic bronchitis; and again, the degree of risk is related to the number of cigarettes smoked. Among men who smoke more than twenty-five cigarettes a day, the death rate from bronchitis and emphysema is more than twenty times higher than for non-smokers. The highest death rate in the world for bronchitis and emphysema is in England and Wales where it is estimated that about 25,000 people die each year from these diseases because of their smoking. On this question, the results of the Swedish twin study are quite clear. When one identical twin is a smoker and the other is not, the smoker is more likely to develop such symptoms as persistent cough, shortness of breath, and severe chest pains. This difference between smokers and non-smokers is just as evident in ordinary twins as it is in identical twins, so the effect seems to be independent of genetics and can be attributed to the smoking. It is probably due to those substances in tobacco smoke which irritate the respiratory system by creating mucus and by clogging up the self-cleaning processes of the lungs and bronchial tubes.

It is sometimes difficult to make sense of the detailed evidence relating smoking to ill-health. There are certainly many areas that we do not fully understand, but in this it is no different from most other areas of research. It is possibly too soon to say definitely whether or not smoking is a cause of coronary heart disease in otherwise healthy individuals. The causal link between smoking and lung cancer seems to be more clearly established, though here, too, there are many details about the pathological mechanisms that are unknown. The strongest evidence is that linking smoking with various respiratory disorders, some of which may have serious, disabling and possibly fatal consequences (e.g. chronic bronchitis).

There are also the hazards associated with the high concentrations of carbon monoxide contained in cigarette smoke. When the smoke is inhaled, the carbon monoxide is diluted to about 3–6 per cent, thus exposing the smoker to levels of carbon monoxide about twice as high as those encountered in the most polluted city traffic conditions, and eight times those permitted in industry. One of the main dangers associated with carbon monoxide is the way that it replaces oxygen in the blood; and the heart, which has a great demand for oxygen, is among the first parts of the body to suffer. Under most normal circumstances, this may have no obvious effect on a young and healthy person. However, it can limit the athletic performance of smokers; it can interfere with the growth of the unborn child among pregnant mothers; and among patients with arterial disease or those recovering from a heart attack it may impose a fatal stress on the weakened heart.

In short, smoking is almost certainly the most physically destructive of all forms of drug-taking. There may still be some uncertainty about precisely how dangerous it is, but as a general health hazard there can no longer be any doubt.

Whether or not these potential health risks prevent people either from starting to smoke or from continuing the habit is another matter. Most smokers acknowledge the health risks associated with smoking, and some even accept the most pessimistic interpretation of the evidence, yet they go on smoking. When drugs offer sufficiently powerful psychological rewards, these can override health considerations. Alcohol, too, is known to carry considerable risks to health, and at a meeting of the American Medical Association it was once proposed that alcohol should carry a similar warning to that on cigarette packets.

Direction for use: use moderately and not on successive days. Eat well while drinking and, if necessary, supplement food by vitamin tablets while drinking. WARNING: May be habit forming; not for use by children. If this beverage is indulged in immoderately it may cause intoxication (drunkenness), later neuralgia and paralysis (neuritis) and serious mental derangement, such as delirium tremens and other curable and incurable mental diseases, as well as kidney and liver damage.

Strong stuff! But in the end, health warnings do not have any great deterrent effect upon the use of drugs. People do not use drugs *because* they are safe, nor do they necessarily stop using them because they know they are dangerous.

Already there are rumblings to the effect that smoking should be totally prohibited. The Norwegian Medical Doctors Association is applying pressure on the Norwegian Government to ban the use of tobacco by the year 2000. An alternative tactic against smoking, and arguably a more effective one, may be to focus upon reducing the social nuisance and possible health risks that smokers inflict upon others. Smoking clearly involves some risk to health, and most authorities are agreed that the risk is considerable. Whatever the degree of risk, it is important that the individual should be provided with a clear, factual account of the effects of smoking. After that, it is up to him to decide whether or not to face the possible hazards.

However, unlike most other forms of drug-taking, the smoker also inflicts his habit on others in a very direct way. Non-smokers who sit in a room polluted by tobacco smoke are forced to become smokers merely by breathing. In a small, enclosed space such as a railway compartment, a car or a small office in which there are several heavy smokers, the non-smoker may inhale as much smoke in an hour as the smoker inhales from each cigarette, and those with asthma, allergies or chest complaints may have to endure acute discomfort under such circumstances. A recent article in the *British Medical Journal* (1981) claimed to have shown that the health of non-smokers could be seriously damaged by exposure to other people's smoking. This looked at the health of more than 91,000 Japanese wives. All were non-smokers. The author claimed that a woman married to a cigarette-smoker was more likely to develop lung cancer than one married to a non-smoker, and that the risk of developing lung cancer increased with the number of cigarettes smoked by the husband. Unfortunately, this study contains a mathematical error which, when corrected, alters the results in such a way that they no longer support the author's conclusions. Had it been shown that the innocent non-smoker was at greater risk of contracting such serious diseases as lung cancer if exposed to the fumes of the cigarette smoker, this would have given extra weight to the argument for restricting the individual's freedom to smoke in public places.

The California ballot for the 1980 Presidential election contained an anti-smoking referendum. Specifically at issue was Proposition 10. If accepted this would have made it an offence to smoke in any enclosed public space, and offenders would have been issued with the equivalent of a parking ticket and fined fifteen dollars. Several other states in America have already passed similar laws. The issue had been put before Californian voters two years previously when it was rejected by 54 per cent to 46 per cent. On both occasions, the tobacco companies ploughed millions of dollars into a campaign to sway public opinion against such measures. In 1978, the companies are reputed to have spent more than six million dollars, and about two million in 1980. As in 1978, the investment was repaid and Proposition 10 failed. The reason for this investment is that the stakes are high. Despite the fact that California is way down the league of cigarette-smoking states in terms of the percentage of the population who are smokers, Californians still spend more than one and a half billion dollars on cigarettes each year.

But whether or not the argument for limiting smoking in public is linked to evidence about the proven medical hazards of exposure to cigarette smoke, it is, in any case, unpleasant for someone who chooses not to smoke to have to tolerate such air pollution. We are more familiar with other measures to limit air pollution. England has had laws against air pollution since the thirteenth century. By the nineteenth century, the Industrial Revolution had produced conditions worse than ever before. These persisted well into the present century and some are with us today. One, thankfully now extinct, was the dense yellow fog known as a 'London particular'. This was certainly unpleasant and is difficult to imagine how it could have been anything but harmful to health. The 1952 London fog produced such a disastrous crop of deaths that it provided a powerful stimulus for the passage of the Clean Air Act. Some prominent physicians have drawn parallels between the evidence relating to air pollution and to smoking. Even now we remain as unsure about the precise ways in which air pollution can damage health as we are about smoking.

## The search for a safer cigarette

The search for a safer cigarette dates back to the mid-1950s when the notion that cigarette smoking might have physically damaging effects began to gain ground. By the 1960s it had become the established view. As people became more and more nervous about the effect that smoking might have on their health, so the filter-tip revolution occurred. The filter-tip cigarette was originally devised as a means of capturing a larger share of the consumer market. Its success was due to the way in which it also came to symbolise the possibility of a less harmful cigarette. In the early 1950s, tipped cigarettes accounted for less than 1 per cent of the market. By the mid 1970s they made up 95 per cent.

For the tobacco companies, this was a challenge to their ingenuity. For instance, as the fashion in smoking moved to filter-tip cigarettes, there was a corresponding preference for cigarettes with a narrower column (i.e. the manufacturer needed to put less tobacco in each cigarette). And although cigarettes have become longer, so have the filter-tips. The other advantages of using filter-tips are that the tobacco can be more loosely packed, and it is easier to use the sort of waste material that would once have been discarded. As a result of all these changes, cigarettes now contain only about half as much tobacco as they did in the 1930s.

Cigarettes are also weaker than they were. In the 1950s, the average cigarette delivered more than twice as much tar and nicotine as in the mid-1970s. This has happened in America,

Britain and most European countries. Since this change coincided with the switch to filter-tip cigarettes, these two developments mean that the smoker today is inhaling considerably less tar and nicotine than his counterpart thirty years ago. The move towards low-tar, low-nicotine cigarettes is, however, limited by the taste of the smoker. It is possible to extract virtually all of the nicotine from a cigarette. Tar is rather different. Whatever material is burned in a cigarette will produce tar. In principle, this could be filtered out, but since the tar carries the flavour, the resulting no-tar cigarette would have no appeal to the smoker. It would deliver nothing but a flavourless and chemically inert warm gas.

There is some evidence that filter-tip cigarettes may be less harmful than the non-tipped variety, probably because of the way in which they reduce the tar content of the inhaled smoke, but there is also a paradoxical effect in that many brands of filter-tip cigarettes deliver more carbon monoxide than plain cigarettes. By reducing the amount of one of the harmful agents in cigarette smoke, filter-tip cigarettes, instead of producing a 'safer' cigarette, may have merely altered the balance of the harmful constituents. Dr Michael Russell of the Addiction Research Unit in London has argued that some filter-tip cigarettes (those with unventilated filters) may be more dangerous than non-tipped cigarettes in terms of the carbon monoxide that the smoker inhales. In Russell's view, people smoke mainly for nicotine but die to a large extent from tar and carbon monoxide, and he has proposed that the search for a less harmful cigarette might be better directed towards one that delivered low tar and low carbon monoxide but a medium dose of nicotine.

Some of the reasons why low-tar cigarettes have a low-tar yield are quite surprising. The expectation fostered by the multinational tobacco companies is that these cigarettes contain some new and specially-developed low-tar tobacco. This is partly true. The nicotine and tar content of tobacco can be reduced in several ways, one of which is through the selective breeding of the plants, and by special methods of cultivation. A less well-publicised reason why these cigarettes produce low levels of tar is that they contain smaller amounts of tobacco.

One American consumer magazine made a direct comparison between low-tar and ordinary cigarettes by buying packets from local stores and unwrapping the contents; these were left to stabilise under room conditions for two days. After this time, the contents were weighed. The low-tar cigarettes contained less than two-thirds as much tobacco as the ordinary brand. In addition, low-tar cigarettes contain a high level of reconstituted 'tobacco sheet'. This is made by salvaging the sweepings and stems, in other words the remnants that have been discarded during the manufacture of other cigarettes. The makers are also using 'puffing' techniques for inflating the volume occupied by the tobacco. This usually involves injecting Freon, a refrigerated gas which vaporises at room temperature, into the tobacco and allowing it to expand. One can only gasp in amazement at the genius that could persuade people to choose a low-tar, low-nicotine cigarette that is also a low-tobacco, low-quality cigarette. The manufacturers must still be laughing.

Among the other developments in this field is the search for an effective tobacco substitute. A new smoking material (NSM) cigarette was tried in Britain in the 1960s. This owed a great deal to the desire of ICI to find new uses for cellulose and the hopes of Imperial Tobacco that they could find some way to protect themselves from fluctuations in the supply of the natural product. Most substitutes are nicotine-free and contain less tar than tobacco smoke; they also produce smoke which is less complicated in its chemical components than tobacco smoke. In the long term, they may offer a less harmful alternative to cigarettes containing tobacco. For the moment, however, no satisfactory or commercially successful tobacco substitute has been found. Men have tried smoking cabbage leaves, tomato leaves, spinach, wild hydrangea, cocoa beans and lettuce leaves – with varying degrees of pleasure. Few of these seem likely to replace tobacco. None the less, the search for a tobacco substitute continues.

# 7

## CANNABIS

Marihuana, hashish, pot, weed, bush, tea, Mary Jane, grass, shit, dope, bhang and ganja are a few of the different names for preparations of the plant, *Cannabis sativa L*, otherwise called Indian hemp. The drug can be eaten, drunk, or, as is more common in Europe and America, smoked. Cannabis is the general term for the different preparations of this herbaceous annual plant, of which there are different varieties, with somewhat different physical, as well as chemical, characteristics. Most botanists agree that these should be regarded as belonging to a single species, though others suggest that there are really three species.

Cannabis is closely related to the hop, and grows vigorously both in its wild state and under cultivation. Indeed, it is so vigorous that it still grows wild in countries where systematic efforts to eradicate it have been going on for centuries. It was one of the first plants to be cultivated by man for its non-food properties, and is thought to have originated in Asia. The earliest Indian Vedas which were composed before 1400 BC refer to the chemical virtues of cannabis, and those who worship the Hindu deity Shiva have used bhang in their religious practices.

The cultivation of cannabis seems to have been introduced into North America in 1606 by Louis Hébert, an apothecary. Apart from yielding a drug, the plant also produced the fibre which was used at that time to provide sails and rigging for ships of the Royal Navy. King James I commanded his American colonies to cultivate the plant, and in 1630 cannabis was a staple crop of the East Coast. The government of Virginia awarded bounties to those producing cannabis and imposed penalties on those who produced other crops. On the whole, the early colonists seem either not to have known, or to have had no interest in, its intoxicating effects.

The drug probably first reached Europe more than a thousand years ago following the Muslim invasion of Spain. François Rabelais, the eminent French physician and satirist of the sixteenth century, wrote of it in his book *Gargantua and Pantagruel*, but it was not until quite recently that it inspired any serious interest. This probably dates back to the invasion of Egypt by Napoleon's expeditionary force in 1798. On their return to France, many of the troops brought cannabis with them, and by the middle of the nineteenth century the medical profession had begun to show an interest in the drug. It had also intrigued a small group of writers, artists and intellectuals, and in 1844 Paris saw the founding of the Club des Hachischins. Théophile Gautier and Charles Baudelaire both wrote of their fantastic hallucinatory experiences after eating large amounts of the drug. This they took in the form of 'a green sweetmeat, the size of a nut and singularly odious' (Baudelaire). Gautier also writes of 'a piece of greenish paste or jam, about the size of one's thumb'. However, it was not until very much more recently that the drug became used by more than a small minority of the intelligentsia in Europe. This seems to have occurred with the developments of the mid-1960s, and it was probably as much the result of American cultural influences as of any other single factor.

There are an estimated 200 million to 250 million people throughout the world who use cannabis. Most of them live in Asia and Africa, but over the past twenty years or so the West has seen a remarkable surge of interest in the drug. By the 1970s, it was suggested that as many as 24 million Americans had tried the drug and about 8 million had continued to use it on a regular or occasional basis. The numbers now may be even higher. In 1977 more than half of the US population between the ages of eighteen and twenty-five had used illegal cannabis. Even in Britain a BBC survey suggested that there might be 4 million people who have tried it. Another survey of drug use at British universities found that about one-third of the students had tried cannabis. (There are about 270,000 undergraduate students currently enrolled at British universities.)

Cannabis is a unique drug. It defies attempts at precise pharmacological classification since its effects are so various. Under different conditions it can act as a stimulant, as a sedative, as an analgesic or as a mildly hallucinogenic drug. It has superficial similarities with many other drugs, but on the whole, the differences between cannabis and other drugs are more striking than the similarities. In its chemical composition, cannabis is an exceedingly complex substance. The main active ingredients of the drug are the cannabinoids – a group of compounds which, for the sake of simplicity, are generally referred to as THC. This is an abbreviation for tetrahydro-cannabinol, which seems to be the most important psycho-active constituent. The potency of the drug varies according to the plant from which it was taken, and genetic factors play an important role here. Stronger cannabis is generally grown from the seeds of plants which were themselves high in THC. The plant can be grown from suitable seed in most temperate conditions and cannabis of reasonable potency has been grown in England and Canada.

So many people have insisted that hashish, the resinous form of cannabis, is stronger than marihuana (grass), the herbal form, that this has become a generally accepted truth. Some people have gone further and argued that hashish and mari-huana have different effects. Neither of these ideas is correct. The active drug is the same in both forms of cannabis, and there is no necessary reason for hashish to be more potent than grass, though it often is the stronger of the two. However, the active THC content of hash seems to be less stable, and over a period of months its potency declines more rapidly than that of marihuana.

It is always a somewhat hazardous procedure to describe the subjective effects of a drug, and this is especially true of a drug such as cannabis where the effects are even more variable than those of most other psychoactive drugs.

'What does one experience? What does one see?
Wonderful things, eh? Amazing sights?' . . .

This is an ill-informed notion, a complete misunderstanding . . . The brain and organism on which hashish operates will produce only the normal phenomena peculiar to that individual – increased, admittedly, in number and force, but always faithful to their origin. A man will never escape from his destined physical and moral temperament: hashish will be a mirror of his impressions and private thoughts – a magnifying mirror, it is true, but only a mirror. (Charles Baudelaire)

Bearing this in mind, there is a surprising consensus among cannabis users about the effects that they do experience. The most common of these seem to be a general sense of relaxation and peacefulness coupled with heightened sensory awareness. All the senses seem to be more acute, but most cannabis smokers report that the experience of listening to music is particularly intense and pleasurable under the influence of the drug. Many users become euphoric and find that the most mundane events and objects are sources of considerable amusement. Other common effects include a changed sense of the passage of time; time usually is described as appearing to be stretched out and to be passing more slowly. Users also describe an increased sense of sexual pleasure, and the drug has often been used as an aid to imagination and fantasy.

Erich Goode, the American sociologist, has pointed out that almost all the reported effects of cannabis are *whimsical* in nature – 'happy, silly, euphoric, relaxed, hedonistic, sensual, foolish and decidedly unserious'. The drug is often used in connection with activities which are themselves highly pleasurable – eating, listening to music, watching a film, having sexual intercourse, meeting friends, etc. Cannabis is used as a means of intensifying the level of enjoyment. To this extent it is accurately described as a recreational drug. Cannabis is seldom used (or it is used far less) during serious work-related activities, because most users recognise that it interferes with these.

Users overwhelmingly describe their experience in pleasurable terms. This is not to say that the drug does not also produce some effects which are actually or potentially unpleasant. Confusion, irrational thoughts, increased tension, impaired memory, sadness, rapid heart rate, dizziness and nausea have all been reported as occasional effects. None the less, it remains true that most users, most of the time, enjoy their cannabis experiences.

Those who wish to prevent people from being able to use cannabis generally use one or both of the following arguments: that cannabis may be pleasurable but is physically or psychologically dangerous; that cannabis itself may be comparatively harmless, but leads to other more dangerous forms of drug taking.

## Physical hazards of cannabis use

The medical and scientific journals have published a number of papers which set out to prove that the use of cannabis is not completely safe. Of course it is not completely safe. No drug is completely safe. In sufficient quantities, common salt can be lethal. It is possible to find isolated cases of people who have suffered damage as a result of ingesting almost any substance, including food and water.

The short-term physiological effects of cannabis are fairly unremarkable. One of the most common effects is a reddening of the eyes. This seems to have no real clinical significance, and contrary to popular belief cannabis does not produce dilation of the pupils. The drug also causes dryness of the mouth, an increase in pulse rate, and at high doses a slight increase in blood pressure. These effects disappear within a few hours unless the dose is repeated. Cannabis does not produce any significant changes in hormonal activity or in blood biochemistry. Nor does it seem to have any effect on the liver or kidneys. Its effects upon the electrical activity of the brain are equally unremarkable, and in some studies of brain wave activity it has proved very difficult to detect any changes at all. The changes that do occur in the brain seem to be predominantly changes in brain chemistry, but the significance of these has yet to be established.

In terms of its lethal dose, cannabis is an exceptionally safe drug. The safety of a drug, in this respect, is calculated as the difference between the effective dose and the lethal dose. In the case of the barbiturate drugs, for instance, this difference is comparatively small. With cannabis it would be virtually impossible to ingest enough of the drug for it to have a lethal effect. It has been estimated that the lethal dose could be as high as 40,000 times that of the effective dose. Cannabis is one of the least toxic drugs known to man, and there is no evidence that anyone has ever died as a direct result of taking an overdose of it.

In terms of its chronic effects, there is very little reliable information. It has been suggested that cannabis smoking might lead to bronchial and respiratory disorders in long-term heavy users. Equally there has been some concern that chronic cannabis smoking might have some of the same health risks as those that are now linked with tobacco, notably lung cancer. The tar yield from marihuana, for instance, is similar to that of tobacco. But as yet no firm evidence has appeared to link cannabis with lung cancer. There is, however, a recently published study of chronic cannabis smokers in Costa Rica which produced the startling suggestion that cannabis smokers who *also* smoke cigarettes appear to have healthier small airways in their lungs than people who *only* smoke cigarettes (this is consistent with the claim sometimes made by cannabis users who suffer from asthma that cannabis alleviates their asthma attacks). This result is surprising and needs to be approached with some caution because of the limited nature of this Costa Rica study, but the authors suggest that cannabis smoking may offer some slight protection against the harmful effects of tobacco smoke.

On the question of lung damage, it is unfortunately necessary to add that several governments, notably the Mexican government, have been spraying cannabis crops with highly toxic weed killers such as paraquat. Paraquat has no odour and no known taste, and it is invisible to the eye. As a result several people have suffered irreversible lung damage through consuming cannabis which has been poisoned as a result of these legally sanctioned anti-cannabis campaigns. Yet in an outline of its plans for the 1980s, an American Drug Enforcement Administration official complained that if it were not for the existence of certain unnecessary restrictions, it would be prepared to use even more powerful poisons.

As with every other illegal drug, there have been several sensational reports linking cannabis with brain damage, genetic damage and deformed babies. There is no convincing evidence associating cannabis with any of these effects: though on the last point, pregnant women might be well advised to avoid any unnecessary drugs during their term of pregnancy. This is certainly true of the first few months, during which time the foetus is especially vulnerable. Since cigarette smoking is known to have some adverse effects on the baby, cannabis smoking might have similar effects.

To understand why the idea that cannabis causes brain damage developed, we must look at how science *actually* works. Whereas science may be a rational procedure, scientists remain as human, fallible and irrational as anyone else. When the needs and emotions of the scientist are sufficiently strong they can influence his work to produce the conclusions that he wants to reach. In Nazi Germany there was a rush to provide 'scientific evidence' about the genetic inferiority of the Jews. In Stalinist Russia, there was the remarkable case of T. D. Lysenko whose completely spurious theory of heredity dominated Russian science for decades. Lysenko refused to acknowledge the existence of genes and proposed that heredity was a general property of living organisms. The theory held up the promise of being able to produce hereditary changes in a particular direction by environmental means: and because this was such an appealing idea it enabled Lysenko and his followers to reject the actual results of scientific experiments in favour of what they already 'knew' to be correct. This bias, though on a lesser scale, is constantly present in science, and in recent years psychologists have begun to investigate how this 'experimenter effect' operates. There are a number of scientists who have a deep-rooted need to show that cannabis is an evil and dangerous drug. To prove that, would be to justify their dislike of the drug and their need to keep it illegal.

One example of the sort of research that is supposed to have 'shown' that cannabis causes brain damage appeared in that most prestigious medical journal, *The Lancet*;* but when examined in detail, the investigation shows nothing of the sort. Among its scientific weaknesses are the following:

(1) All the patients in the study were known to use drugs other than cannabis. Every one of them had an extensive history of drug use. All had used LSD: one is even described as having taken an overdose of LSD. No detailed information is given about their use of alcohol, which is already *known* to cause the sort of changes in the brain that were found (though two out of ten were described as heavy drinkers). Therefore any abnormalities in these patients could have been due to drugs other than cannabis.

(2) The patients were drawn from an abnormal sample who were not representative of long-term cannabis users. One had had a schizophrenic illness, another had a possible psychotic illness, and three had a history of head injury. All of them were people who had sought medical or psychiatric help because of various troubling symptoms. Four already had neurological problems; two were attending a drug addiction centre; one had a history of drug abuse and had recently taken an overdose of drugs other than cannabis, and the other three were receiving psychiatric treatment. Any abnormality is probably completely independent of the cannabis use, and even the authors of this paper admit that their sample could have been abnormal before they started to use cannabis.

(3) The technique used to measure brain damage (air encephalography) has not been perfected, and neuroradiologists

---

* Campbell, Evans, Thomson & Williams. Cerebral atrophy in young cannabis smokers. *The Lancet*, (4 December 1971), 1219-1224.

acknowledge that it is impossible to define exactly the difference between normal and abnormal levels.

In fact, the article is entirely inconclusive. But because it reached the conclusions that many people wanted to hear, they disregarded all of these faults. Typical of the responses that the paper generated is a letter (also published in *The Lancet*) arguing that this 'evidence' should be used to justify 'the continuation and strengthening of *every possible measure* to suppress cannabis'.

## Psychological hazards

Most psychoactive drugs produce adverse reactions amongst some individuals. In a study of more than 5,000 patients, as many as one in every ten showed an adverse reaction to the psychoactive drugs that were being medically prescribed for them. When we are dealing with the non-medical use of drugs, the problem is further complicated by the fact that the beliefs and expectations of the individual play an even more crucial part in determining how he will experience the drug effects. What is seen as a highly pleasurable hallucinatory experience by one person, may be seen as a terrifying symptom of impending madness by another.

Although adverse reactions to cannabis are fortunately quite rare, about three-quarters of them take the form of a panic attack in which the user experiences intense anxiety. Often this is caused by the user coming to believe that he is going mad, or dying. Such panic attacks are usually limited to novice or inexperienced users who have taken a relatively large amount of the drug, or who are exposed to sudden unpleasant forms of stress.

At low doses, the subjective effects of cannabis are similar in some ways to those of alcohol. But at higher doses, the effects are quite different, and for the inexperienced user they may be quite unexpected. The experienced smoker recognises these as effects of the drug. But if the novice mistakenly interprets them as signs of madness, this can provoke a panic attack. Such reactions are generally self-limiting, and for a matter of minutes or for a few hours. The best treatment is to reassure the user that what he is experiencing is the effect of the drug and nothing more sinister. If the user is taken to a mental hospital and treated as if he were suffering from some psychiatric illness, this is likely to intensify and to prolong the reaction.

The possibility that cannabis might provoke a serious, long-term psychotic illness like schizophrenia has also been suggested, though the evidence supporting the existence of a specific 'cannabis psychosis' is essentially anecdotal. Many such reports have issued from Third World countries. The first full-scale enquiry into the effects of cannabis was the Indian Hemp Commission of 1893-4. To many people it seemed unnecessary to re-open this question of whether cannabis caused insanity: some even suggested that the Commission deliberately chose to ignore what had already been proved. Certainly the statistics sent in from mental hospitals all over India cited cannabis drugs as one of the chief causes of mental illness. In an article in the *Indian Medical Gazette*, one of the foremost experts at the time, Surgeon Lt-Col. Crombie, had described cannabis as 'the actual and immediate cause of . . . insanity'.

However, when the commission re-examined the evidence that had been used to justify this conclusion, it was found to be extremely weak. The statistics were not based on any medical diagnosis, but were simply comments entered by the admissions clerk, and were usually taken from the policemen or whoever brought the patient to the asylum. The examining magistrate required some specific cause of illness to be shown and it was standard procedure to enter 'hemp drugs' as the cause whenever the patient had been known to use them. When the commission made a detailed examination of specific cases even Lt-Col. Crombie was forced to admit that the cannabis could not have caused the illness. The commission concluded that 'it may well seem extraordinary that statistics based on such absolutely untrustworthy material should be submitted year after year in the asylum report'.

Almost a century later, the quality of the evidence from Eastern countries is not much better. In 1972, the Canadian Le Dain Commission concluded that 'thorough controlled studies in these countries, which isolate the long-term effects of cannabis from the powerful and pervasive socio-cultural, economic, nutritional and hygienic conditions described have yet to be reported'.

In the West, there is very little to support the idea that cannabis causes a psychotic illness. Since California probably contains as many cannabis users as any other part of the Western world, it is interesting to look at the incidence of cannabis psychosis there. A study of students at the Berkeley University campus in 1968 found no cases of this supposed disorder despite the fact that at least a quarter of the 40,000 students there had tried the drug. Another survey of more than 700,000 medical admissions in California found that only nine were related to cannabis, and none required treatment for more than eight days. The question here is not whether cannabis smokers *can* develop a psychosis. Undoubtedly they can. The incidence of psychotic illness in the general population is about 1 per cent, so it would be no surprise if 1 per cent of cannabis smokers developed such a disorder. The important question is whether the use of cannabis *increases the risk* of developing a psychotic disorder. Although this is theoretically possible, there is no evidence that the use of cannabis itself increases any such risk. It is more likely that if a psychotic reaction does develop after smoking cannabis, this owes much more to the pre-existing personality difficulties and psychiatric problems of the individual.

Exactly the same issues are involved in the suggestion that cannabis leads to a general withdrawal from 'straight' society (otherwise dignified by the scientific-sounding term 'amotivational syndrome'). The psychological studies that have been carried out have produced conflicting results. Some found no differences between users and non-users; others found that cannabis smokers were sometimes less successful in situations requiring high levels of drive and ambition, or in performing routine and repetitive tasks. An article in the *Journal of the American Medical Association* (1971) expressed doubt that there was any relationship at all between cannabis use and educational performance. Cannabis users did no better than non-users; nor did they do any worse. This was true, regardless of the amount of the drug involved. Interestingly, 18 per cent of the chronic users planned to work for their doctorate (against only 11 per cent of the non-users). However, where differences of this sort do emerge, they are best seen in terms of the psychological characteristics of the individuals taking part in the study rather than as the direct result of any drug effect. It is comparatively easy to remember this when the results suggest that drug takers do better than non-users. It is soon forgotten when the results point to some psychological deficit among users. In the case of the 'amotivational syndrome' there are many reasons why the individual who does not want to involve himself with routine or competitive tasks should choose to take cannabis rather than alcohol.

## The escalation theory

In the absence of any convincing evidence that cannabis is an especially dangerous drug, another justification for preventing people from using it is that although it may not be dangerous in itself, it can lead on to other more dangerous forms of drug taking. In its usual form, the escalation theory states that smoking cannabis leads to heroin addiction.

The reason why so many people have been convinced that cannabis use leads to heroin addiction is that many (though not all) heroin addicts begin their drug career by smoking cannabis. Sometimes there is a similar link between other drugs and cannabis in that cannabis is often one of the first *illegal* drugs that people take. If, for the moment, we ignore the question of legality, then most heroin addicts and other heavy drug users began by taking alcohol or tobacco (or even tea or coffee). Few people would care to argue the case that smoking cigarettes or drinking alcohol causes heroin addiction.

123

The escalation theory is riddled with errors – both of logic and of fact. In its report to the British Government, the Wootton Committee stated that there was no reason to believe that the use of cannabis led to other more harmful forms of drug taking. The Home Secretary of the day, James Callaghan, disagreed. So did some members of the medical profession. Dr Tylden, a London psychiatrist, called the report 'a junkie's charter' and stated that cannabis was the main cause of heroin addiction among young people in Britain. Many people continue to believe the escalation theory because they would like it to be true.

There is one slight vestige of truth in the escalation idea, but this has much more to do with the *reasons why* people want to take drugs and the social circumstances in which they take them than with any property of cannabis itself. Many people who use cannabis have a general interest in the use of drugs to change their states of consciousness. Because they must obtain cannabis illegally they are likely to come into contact with members of the drug subculture who have access to other drugs. It is not entirely surprising, therefore, that some cannabis users should experiment with these drugs, perhaps on the grounds that if cannabis is illegal and it has not harmed them, maybe the other drugs will be equally pleasant and forgiving in their effects. A few may go on to become dependent upon these, but under the circumstances, it is remarkable that so few cannabis users progress to other drugs. There are currently only a few thousand opiate addicts in Britain (there are about 6,000 addicts known to the Home Office at the time of writing this book), yet there are millions who have tried cannabis.

An intriguing piece of evidence against the escalation theory concerns the use of cannabis by West Indians in Britain. Although cannabis is used fairly widely by some members of the West Indian community, there is very little problem associated with heroin addiction in this group. In the twelve years since it opened, only one West Indian addict has been seen at the Drug Dependence Unit at the Maudsley Hospital in London.

## Medical uses of cannabis

Although this book is primarily concerned with the non-medical use of drugs, it is interesting to note a revival of interest in the medical potential of cannabis. During the nineteenth century cannabis preparations had been used to treat a wide variety of disorders. The *American Dispensatory* of 1851 recommended extracts of hemp as a treatment for gout, rheumatism, tetanus, convulsions, depression and delirium tremens. In England, Dr J. R. Reynolds, who was Queen Victoria's physician, described cannabis as 'one of the most valuable medicines we possess', and a nineteenth-century chemist's brochure recommending 'Indian Cigarettes' as a treatment for asthma described how 'a refreshing sleep soon removes all the alarming symptoms. . . . To facilitate the use of Indian Cigarettes and enable the patient to benefit by them under all circumstances, whether travelling or walking, they are sold in elegant little cigar cases which can be carried in a breast-pocket with the least inconvenience.' With the rapid developments that occurred in drug research during the twentieth century, interest in many natural medicines declined, and during the past sixty or seventy years it has been generally assumed that cannabis is primarily a recreational drug with no specific medical application. Recent research, however, has suggested that cannabis may have two particularly valuable uses.

Glaucoma is a disease of the eye caused by increased levels of pressure inside the eye, which can lead to progressive blindness. In America, a series of trials were carried out in which glaucoma patients were treated with THC-based drugs. As a result, fluid pressure in the eye dropped by more than a third.

Cannabis-based drugs have also been found to be useful in the treatment of cancer. One of the most distressing side-effects of the drugs used in the treatment of cancer is that they often cause nausea and vomiting. This is a major problem both for the patient and for the doctor. In some cases the side-effects can be so severe that the patient suffers from vomiting or retching every few minutes for twelve to twenty-four hours a day. Occasionally the patient finds this so intolerable that he would rather have no treatment at all than face the persistent feeling of sickness. Although the 1979 *Physicians' Desk Reference* lists more than thirty drugs which are meant to prevent feelings of sickness, very few of these drugs have proved successful in suppressing the nausea caused by the anti-cancer medications.

In the last year or two there have been a number of research articles in the medical journals suggesting that cannabis is a very effective treatment for these side-effects. For some years, doctors in the United States have known of cancer patients who were also regular cannabis smokers and who reported that cannabis seemed to reduce the nausea and vomiting associated with the cancer treatment. Recent medical research confirms that cigarettes or capsules containing THC produced a remarkable reduction in the side-effects from the primary treatment. In one study, THC reduced the incidence of nausea and vomiting from 72 per cent to a mere 6 per cent. In another investigation, more than two-thirds of a group of patients who had not benefited from conventional anti-emetic drugs improved when given THC.

If cannabis does live up to expectations as a treatment for glaucoma and as an aid to the treatment of cancer, this will add a further complication to the discussion about the drug. For a long time it has been convenient for those authorities who wished to prohibit any use of the drug to deny that it has any beneficial effects at all. Despite the positive uses of the drug that have been reported in respectable medical journals, as recently as 1979 the American Food and Drug Administration, and the Department of Health, Education and Welfare, were still denying that cannabis was of any medical value. It is encouraging, however, to note that at the time of writing this book twenty-four states have permitted the medical use of cannabis and its active ingredient THC.

## The evidence

I am well aware that some readers will take exception to things that I have written in this book. Nowhere is this likely to be more obvious than in the present chapter on cannabis. So for those who are interested, I include a brief research commentary.

First of all, let me say that questions about the effects of a particular drug cannot be answered satisfactorily on the basis of any single experiment. In order to understand such questions we need to look at a whole series of experiments. There are hundreds of psychological factors that can interfere with an experiment to produce an unreliable result. If the same experiment were repeated by another researcher, a quite different result could easily by obtained. The chances of error decrease when the researcher has greater control over the conditions of his experiment. In drug research, the experimenter often has comparatively little control, but it is unfortunately true that a good deal of drug research has been made even weaker by the use of badly designed experiments.

Because of this, there will be many occasions when different experiments produce what seem to be directly conflicting results. The newspapers, which are always eager for some new sensation, seize upon any scientific report that has shock value, and as a result the general public is told only of the more lurid research findings: yet these are often the least reliable of all. Another factor that complicates matters is that the medical and scientific journals will usually only publish positive results – that is, results which show that Drug X causes certain effects. For various reasons the journals are uninterested in research which fails to demonstrate any effect. This means that if a hundred apparently identical experiments are carried out but only one of them suggests that cannabis may cause brain damage, that paper will almost certainly get published and receive wide coverage in the media; the other ninety-nine will probably be rejected and forgotten.

The article published in *The Lancet* by Campbell and his

associates is a case in point. The experiment is full of design faults and its conclusions are extremely suspect. Further research has not confirmed its results. Yet its shock value was enough to fire it into the headlines. Even today, people are still referring to it as proof that cannabis causes brain damage.

Since there are literally thousands upon thousands of scientific and medical reports dealing with cannabis, it would be both tedious and confusing for the reader to attempt to evaluate and summarise even the most important research studies. As a compromise, it is informative to look at the conclusions of the various expert committees that have wrestled with this problem.

Before the 1960s there was virtually no controlled experimental research on cannabis. The available evidence was based mainly upon rather haphazard observational methods. One of the best early summaries of this evidence is the seven-volume report that the Indian Hemp Drugs Commission submitted to the British Government in 1894. More than one thousand witnesses were called before the commission, and, as today, all manner of conflicting opinions emerged. With respect to the possible physical harm caused by cannabis, the commission concluded:

The most striking feature of the medical evidence is perhaps the large number of practitioners of long experience who have seen no evidence of any connection between hemp drugs and disease, and when witnesses who speak to these ill effects from its moderate use are cross-examined, it is found that (a) their opinions are based on popular ideas on the subject; (b) they have not discriminated between the effects of moderate and excessive use of the drugs; (c) they have accepted the diseases as being induced by hemp drugs because the patients confessed to the habit; and (d) the fact has been overlooked that the smoking of hemp drugs is recognized as a remedial agent in asthma and bronchitis . . . the evidence shows the moderate use of ganja or charas not to be appreciably harmful, while in the case of moderate bhang drinking the evidence shows the habit to be quite harmless.

The commission did, however, suggest that long-term or

excessive cannabis smoking may well be associated with disorders such as bronchial irritation, to which cigarette smokers are prone.

During the late 1930s, the United States was in the grip of anti-cannabis fever. The American newspapers competed with each other in the race to publish more and more lurid headlines. As with public officials at other times and in other places, most politicians passively accepted the cannabis myths and used them for their own ends. One of the few people to hesitate before this wave of hysteria was Fiorello LaGuardia, the mayor of New York City, who asked the New York Academy of Medicine to prepare a scientific report on the issue.

The LaGuardia Committee, consisting of thirty-one eminent doctors, psychologists, chemists, pharmacologists and sociologists, published its findings in 1944. Like the report of the Indian Hemp Drugs Commission, it was limited by the weaknesses inherent in much of the evidence available at that time. Nonetheless, the report represents a reasonable attempt to evaluate the evidence for and against the drug. It concluded that cannabis is not addictive in the medical sense of the term and that it did not lead to the use of drugs such as morphine or cocaine; it had no effect on the user's underlying personality and was not a cause of crime or juvenile delinquency. Finally, it commented that the current publicity about its catastrophic effects was completely without foundation.

In 1966, the Wootton Committee was set up to advise the British Government about cannabis. Its report, submitted in 1968, found no evidence that it led to crime or aggressive behaviour, nor that it produced psychotic states in otherwise normal users.

Having reviewed all the material available to us we find ourselves in agreement with the conclusions reached by the Indian Hemp Drugs Commission . . . and the [LaGuardia Report], that the long-term consumption of cannabis in moderate doses has no harmful effects.

The next major investigation was authorised in America by Richard Nixon, and the Shafer Report, entitled *Marihuana, A*

*Signal of Misunderstanding*, was submitted to Congress in 1972. It stated that there is no reliable evidence that cannabis causes genetic defects in man; from a public health viewpoint, the effects of cannabis in the body are of little significance and have little or no permanent effect; no objective evidence of brain damage has been shown (in direct contrast to alcohol). Cannabis causes no psychological deterioration, either intellectual or in terms of motivation; it does not produce physical dependence and 'the overwhelming majority' of cannabis users do not progress to other drugs. The report notes that 'marihuana's relative potential for harm to the vast majority of individual users and its actual impact on society does not justify a social policy designed to seek out and firmly punish those who use it'. This was especially true in view of the manifest failure of the law to prevent an estimated 24 million Americans trying the drug and 8 million of them continuing to use it.

At about the same time, the Le Dain Commission reported its findings to the Canadian Government. The Le Dain Report is a model of balanced and reasonable thinking and is well worth reading in full. Its conclusions are, as before, that cannabis is non-addictive, its short-term effects on the body are of little clinical significance and it carries no real dangers even in an overdose. The commission took very seriously the suggestion that cannabis might cause lung damage, but found no evidence to support this view. As a postscript to the usual attempts to frighten young people away from drugs, the commission advised:

It is a grave error to indulge in deliberate distortion or exaggeration concerning the alleged dangers of a particular drug, or to base a programme of drug education upon a strategy of fear. It is no use playing 'chicken' with young people; in nine cases out of ten they will accept the challenge.

The abrupt and hostile dismissal that the Wootton Report received from the British Government is similar to the official response that has greeted the publication of each of these reports. Their conclusions and recommendations have generally either been ignored because they failed to confirm the comfortable prejudices of the politicians, or else used as a way of catching votes. Prior to the 1979 Canadian federal election, all three major parties agreed that cannabis penalties should be reduced and that criminal records for cannabis offences should be eliminated. After the election, however, there was no sign of action from the new government, and it looks as though the issue is to be put back on the shelf.

The sad and disillusioned comments of the Royal Commission into the Non-Medical Use of Drugs (South Australia, 1978) provide a fitting end to this commentary:

The regulation of the non-medical use of cannabis has been the subject of many official inquiries. These inquiries have reached strikingly uniform conclusions on the effects of cannabis use, both on the user and the community as a whole. The failure of legislators . . . to accept these conclusions suggests that legislative responses are affected more by the perceived social status of users and the values and perhaps prejudices of powerful groups in the community, than by a careful evaluation of the pharmacological, medical and sociological evidence.

# 8

## THE HALLUCINOGENS

Everything connected with the hallucinogenic drugs has aroused intense controversy. There is not even agreement about what they should be called. At different times they have been classified as psychedelics, psychotomimetics, psychodysleptics and hallucinogens.

'Psychedelic' is derived from the Greek words for mind (*psyche*) and visible (*-delos*), and it was coined by the psychiatrist Humphrey Osmond in a correspondence with Aldous Huxley in 1956. Certainly it captured much of Huxley's enthusiasm for his mescaline experiences, and it was later taken up in the 1960s by Timothy Leary and the psychedelic movement of the American hippies who regarded it as synonymous with 'mind expanding'.

'Psychotomimetic' and 'psychodysleptic' carry entirely the opposite connotations. 'Psychotomimetic' means that the drug has effects which resemble those of the psychotic illnesses such as schizophrenia – and by implication, therefore, that they are undesirable. Whether or not LSD-induced states of mind do resemble the psychoses is discussed later in the chapter. The term itself is rejected not only because of its negative connotations, but also because it is such an ugly word. 'Psychodysleptic' is equally negative and equally ugly: this means 'mind disrupting'.

There are other unfamiliar names for this category of drugs. The term coined by Louis Lewin, 'Phantastica', has a pleasant ring to it and conveys a good deal of the quality of the drug effects. Another was suggested by Moreau – 'Oneirogenic' (causing dreams). Again this is reasonably accurate, but both these terms must be rejected because of their unfamiliarity.

The final term, hallucinogenic, is misleading. These drugs do not generally cause true hallucinations in which the person becomes immersed in a world of unreality. The effects are more accurately described as perceptual distortions than as hallucinations, though the effects of these drugs also extend beyond perception. Changes in thought, mood and personality integration are all important effects, which are not really included in the term hallucinogenic. What is worse, some of the drugs in this category – such as MDA and MMDA – tend to produce changes in self-awareness, and in mood and intellectual functioning, without any sensory distortions at all. However, despite its inaccuracies, 'hallucinogenic' is the term most commonly used, and even Dr Osmond who coined the term 'psychedelic' eventually adopted it. There is also some historical justification for using this word rather than its alternatives, since the mental voyages of sorcerers have been described as hallucinogenic.

Before the advent of the twentieth-century synthetic alkaloids, most of the hallucinogenic drugs were derived from plants. Many of these plants have been used for magical and religious purposes (see Chapter 3). Some of these naturally-occurring drugs are still used occasionally (e.g. psilocybin); others are often mentioned but not often taken (e.g. mescaline). Finally, some of the hallucinogenic drugs are seldom if ever used nowadays (belladonna, henbane, fly agaric). This chapter is concerned mainly with the drugs that are used (or discussed) most frequently.


## Mescaline

Mescaline is one of the alkaloids of the peyote cactus which grows in Mexico. Peyote has played an important part in the religious traditions of Mexico for centuries. Mescaline first became known to science as a result of the interest of a young German pharmacologist, Louis Lewin. During the time he spent in America in 1886, he obtained some specimens of the cactus from which mescaline was subsequently extracted. 'No other plant brings about such marvellous functional modifications of the brain,' he wrote. Those who took the drug experienced 'pleasures of a special kind. Even if these sensations merely take the form of sensorial phantasms, or of an extreme concentration of the inner life, they are of such a special nature and so superior to reality, so unimaginable . . . it is easy to understand why the Indians of old time venerated this plant as a god.'

Oddly enough, Lewin himself experienced no such visions after taking the drug. It merely made him feel sick. Other famous men of the day were more fortunate in their experiences. Havelock Ellis, who took mescaline after reading reports of it in the *British Medical Journal*, found the visions that it produced entrancing. Colours seemed indescribably vivid and delightful. At the same time, it made him feel both physically healthy and intellectually acute. Much later, Aldous Huxley found the drug equally attractive.

In terms of its current availability and usage, mescaline is a rare drug. Although reports of the drug are fairly common among illicit drug users, what is called mescaline almost always turns out to be LSD – possibly adulterated with amphetamines. Among the hallucinogens seized and analysed by the London police, very few have contained any mescaline.

## Psilocybin

Psilocybin is another hallucinogenic alkaloid which is derived from a plant, though in this case from a mushroom instead of a cactus. To the Aztecs, the mushroom was sacred: they called it *teonanacatl* which translates as 'flesh of the gods'. There are several different varieties of the psilocybin mushroom. Most are insignificant tawny-brown toadstools which seldom grow to a height of more than one or two inches. One of the common varieties is otherwise called the 'Liberty Cap' because the shape of the head of the mushroom resembles that of the hats worn during the French Revolution. These are a widespread species throughout Europe and America and grow on grasslands and pastures during the autumn months. An average hallucinogenic dose of psilocybin would appear to be in the region of 20 – 60mg.,

134

though in its pure form the drug is seldom found on the black market. Samples of drugs called psilocybin, like mescaline, usually turn out to be adulterated forms of LSD.

## MDA and MMDA

These semi-synthetic drugs are produced by a modification of the psychoactive ingredients in nutmeg and mace. Nutmeg and mace both come from the same tree, *Myristica fragrans*. This is native to the East Indies, and produces a fruit about two inches in diameter. The seed is a dark brown or purple colour. This is the nutmeg. The outer covering is the mace. Both have been known as psychoactive drugs for thousands of years, though nowadays they are seldom used as a drug of choice. MDA and MMDA resemble the hallucinogens in many respects, though in others they are closer to central nervous system stimulants such as cocaine and the amphetamines.

## DMT

DMT has a similar background. It is the active agent in many Central and South American snuffs such as those that Columbus described being used by the natives of Hispaniola. It is a major constituent of the Virola tree bark. In its effects, it is like LSD. But whereas the LSD experience has been described as a long, strange journey, that of DMT has been compared to the experience of being shot out of a cannon. Its hallucinatory effects are intense, but short-lived, reaching a peak in five to twenty minutes, and ending after about half an hour. Because of this it has been called 'the businessman's trip'.

## LSD

The most widely used and the best-known hallucinogenic drug is LSD (lysergic acid diethylamide). This is one of the most potent drugs known to man. Whereas other drugs are measured in milligrams (thousandths of a gram), doses of

135

LSD are measured in micrograms – millionths of a gram. Doses as small as 20 micrograms produce effects similar to cannabis intoxication, but when it is taken for its full hallucinatory effects, doses of between 50 and 250 micrograms are more usual. Weight for weight, LSD is about five thousand times more powerful than mescaline and two hundred times more potent than psilocybin. As a further measure of its potency, only about 1 per cent of the tiny amount originally taken reaches the brain. It is difficult to know how much LSD would constitute a lethal overdose. One estimate puts it at about 2mg./kg., or about 150,000 micrograms for the average man.

The drug was discovered in 1943 by Dr Albert Hofmann at Sandoz Laboratories in Switzerland. (Hofmann also synthesised psilocybin from the Liberty Cap mushroom.) One afternoon, while working on derivatives of ergot, he felt rather strange, and believing himself to be ill, went home. He lay down, and as he closed his eyes, he saw fantastic visions and vividly coloured kaleidoscopic patterns. After about two hours these symptoms disappeared.

Some days later, Dr Hofmann took what he considered to be a small dose of one of the drugs that he had been working on, to see if it was responsible for the symptoms of the previous week. The small dose was one quarter of one milligram. In almost any other drug this would be unlikely to produce any effect at all. By the standards of LSD, however, 250 micrograms is a substantial dose, and Dr Hofmann was about to embark on a long and strange trip.

My field of vision wavered and was distorted like the image in a curved mirror . . . like the reflection in an agitated sheet of water . . . with my eyes closed, colourful and changing fantastic images invaded my mind continuously. It was especially remarkable how all sounds . . . were transposed into visual sensations, so that with each tone and noise a corresponding coloured image, changing in form and colour like a kaleidoscope was produced.

Synasthesia is one of the more curious perceptual effects that LSD users sometimes report. It is an unusual but fascinating effect in which the senses seem to get mixed up. As a result the person has the experience of 'seeing' music or of 'hearing' colours.

The next day, Dr Hofmann felt tired but otherwise completely well. Indeed, he felt so well that he describes feeling as if the world were 'newly created'. Hofmann's description of his experiences is a model of careful objective reporting. It is all the more fascinating in that it represents the first ever account of the LSD experience. We now know that any drug experience is powerfully influenced by the taker's expectations about how the drug might affect him. In Hofmann's case, the experience was untainted by any such ideas. His description picks out the three characteristic effects of the drug: the psychological changes in mood and thought processes, the physical changes, and most especially, the perceptual changes.

Visual perception is strikingly altered by the drug. One of the first signs of the drug taking effect is that the grey field that is seen with the eyes closed starts to become lighter. Later, this field becomes patterned with coloured lights. The patterns are usually described as kaleidoscopic, geometric or 'like a Persian carpet'. With increasing intoxication, the patterns become progressively less symmetrical and more complex. When the eyes are opened, ordinary objects seem to glow as if they were illuminated from within. Colours seem to be deeper and more intense, and not infrequently quite mundane objects seem to assume tremendous symbolic significance. At the peak of the drug experience, pseudo-hallucinations occur in which the person's visual perceptions are comparatively independent of the outside world. True hallucinations, however, are rare, though they do sometimes occur. Generally they are linked to high doses of the drug, though some individuals may be more sensitive to LSD than others. Unlike the visual pseudo-hallucinations, in which the person is aware that his experiences are drug-induced, true hallucinations usually carry no such insight. The person mistakes his hallucinations for reality itself.

Thought processes are also altered by the drug. Thinking becomes non-logical, and often it has a strong magical quality to it. The person may believe that he can read the thoughts of other people or that he is able to transmit his own thoughts. Several people have been convinced that they could fly, and one or two unfortunate cases have occurred in which they actually tried to put their beliefs into practice. This delusional idea has even led to deaths.

These incidents were well publicised at the time, and the idea that LSD caused people to jump from windows under the impression that they could fly became a part of the assorted myths and misconceptions of drug taking. I have only seen one such case. This woman was referred to a drug unit by a consultant psychiatrist who had identified a case of 'LSD psychosis' on the basis of the flying incident. However, the role played by LSD in the incident is uncertain. It is quite likely that the attempt to fly owed more to the woman's unusual personality than to any drug effect. For instance, she continued to believe that she could fly long after the effects of the drug had worn off. But she also claimed to see the Virgin Mary outside her window, heard voices, regularly took all her clothes off 'so that I could be like the angels', and was seriously negligent about her personal hygiene. In the end, it was decided that she was suffering from a schizophrenic disorder which had developed independently of her use of drugs.

However, as with true hallucinations, serious delusional ideas of this sort are rare. What is more typical is that the user may have pseudo-delusional thoughts – incorrect or irrational ideas, but with some insight into their strangeness. Although the user may believe that he is having profound or brilliant ideas, any attempt to express them usually reveals only banal or fragmented thoughts.

LSD has some of its most striking effects on the personality of the user. During the peak of the LSD experience, the individual begins to lose his sense of personal identity. He seems to lose that pervasive sense of being oneself that characterises our everyday experience. During the earlier stages of LSD intoxication the user is usually capable of erecting various psychological defences to guard against this, but as the effects increase in strength they tend to overwhelm the defences. As a result, the person moves from a sense of independent personal identity to feeling at one with the universe. Different people react to this in different ways. Some become euphoric or joyful, and regard the experience as a sort of mystical or religious revelation. Others are terrified by the apparent loss of their comfortable feelings of secure selfhood. These major alterations in personality integration resemble either the transcendental or the psychotic experience. They are the heaven and hell of which Huxley wrote.

Although no one had experienced the effects of LSD before Hofmann, there had been numerous historical instances of people developing bizarre mental disturbances after eating flour contaminated by ergot. This purple fungus is a veritable chemical factory, and for centuries during wet summers, this parasitic growth spoiled the rye crops from Spain through to Russia. Whether because of greed, ignorance or hunger, the spoiled flour was often eaten, with spectacular and distressing results. 'St Anthony's Fire' was characterised by visual disturbances in which the sufferer seemed to see a shimmering light surrounding things, making them look as though they were on fire. Consequently, it seemed as though people were being consumed by the fire. This impression was confirmed by the blackened fingers and toes that were another result of the poisoning (in fact, this was gangrene). Ergotism also led to mental disturbances, hallucinations and madness, and there are several well-documented descriptions of such epidemics during the Middle Ages. The derivatives of ergot now play a more domesticated role in the treatment of migraine headaches and to assist delivery in childbirth.

Ever since its discovery, LSD has polarised attitudes and generated hysteria. Every conceivable claim has been made about it: that it causes insanity and irreversible brain damage, that it leads to profound spiritual enlightenment, that it causes genetic damage and that it is a powerful aid to artistic creativity. In fact, LSD seems to produce very few *physiological* changes other than dilated pupils, increased muscle tension and a slight incoordination. Despite the powerful effects that LSD has upon consciousness it has been found to have surprisingly little effect upon the electrical activity of the brain. Several studies have been unable to detect any changes in subjects even after they had taken substantial doses of hallucinogenic drugs (up to 400 microgrammes of LSD and 1,000 milligrams of mescaline). The only changes that have been detected seem to indicate that these drugs produce a slight desynchronisation of brain rhythms similar to that produced by stimulant drugs. This desynchronisation has no particular relevance to psychiatric disturbances and is probably of no clinical significance. Considering the impressive range of psychological effects that the drug produces, its physiological correlates are fairly unremarkable.

## LSD and the search for mind control

For many of our political leaders, the most seductive dream of all remains that of controlling the mind itself. For centuries there have been crude but comparatively efficient methods by which this dream might be pursued. The Holy Inquisition made a long and loving study of the theory and practice of such techniques. The discovery of LSD reawakened the ancient dream – and with it, the fear that others might achieve the means of chemical conversion and use them against us.

Albert Hofmann has recently described how the US Army repeatedly approached him with the request that he take a more active part in their research programmes. Much of this early 'research' was organised by the CIA during the 1950s and 1960s. The specialists (if the word encompasses such incompetence) concerned with LSD at that time worked in one of the many subdivisions of the agency. The euphemistically named Technical Services Staff (TSS) were interested in the application of biological and chemical material to spying, and within the TSS was the little-known Chemical Division which specialised in the use of chemicals against specific individuals. Using chemicals rather than magic, the Chemical Division was concerned with such problems as whether LSD could be used to turn Russians into loyal Americans. Or (appalling thought) would the beliefs of the loyal American collapse before the chemical might of Soviet LSD? Rumours filtered through military intelligence that the Russians had made a deal with the Swiss pharmaceutical firm, Sandoz Laboratories, to obtain enough LSD for 50 million doses. Then another intelligence report suggested that Sandoz were trying to sell 10 kilos of LSD (enough for about 100 million doses) on the open market. Both reports were false, but they were sufficient to provoke the CIA to approach Sandoz with a deal of their own. Despite the fact that Sandoz had only manufactured 40 grams (about one and a half ounces) of the drug during the previous ten years, they agreed to sell 100 grams of LSD to the US Government every week for an indefinite period. Back home in America, CIA men took LSD. It was given to army recruits, and to mental hospital inmates. And it was given to people who had no idea that they had taken any drug, sometimes with tragic consequences. With the publication in 1975 of the report of the Rockefeller Commission, the public learned that the CIA's inept tinkering with LSD had led to the deaths of two men after they had been given the drug without their awareness.

There were other unforeseen consequences of the CIA's incompetence. So much LSD had been distributed throughout the United States that the youth of America had become aware of the non-military uses of the new drug. The LSD research project at Timothy Leary's university had been funded by the CIA. By a supreme twist of irony, the CIA's search for a mind-control drug had led it into the role of pusher. By the mid-1960's, a whole counter-culture had evolved, centred upon the West Coast of America. LSD had ceased to be simply a drug. It had become symbolic of a way of life, and Richard Nixon's hatred and contempt for 'college punks' and hippies led to talk of introducing the death penalty for possession offences.

## Of chromosomes and hallucinogens

Few scientific questions have been so obscured by the

emotional over-involvement of scientists as this issue of whether or not certain drugs can cause genetic damage in those who use them. The same question has been raised about every one of the illicit drugs, but most especially about LSD. As in other areas of science, when emotions run high the standards of scientific enquiry are allowed to fall. The investigator knows in advance what he wants to find. Consequently the quality of experimental research in this area has often been abysmal. It has left a blot upon the entire study of cellular and chromosomal function.

The spectre of genetic damage first attached itself to LSD in 1967 after an article appeared in the journal *Science*. This reported that when human blood cells were exposed to LSD, the cells showed some chromosome breakage. Within a matter of days, this disturbing but otherwise rather vague and ambiguous finding had been translated by newspapers and television into an incontrovertible 'fact'. Parallels were drawn with the thalidomide disaster, and unpleasantly sensational reports appeared linking articles about LSD with pictures of deformed children. The impact of these pitiful photographs was sufficiently powerful to override any reasoned objections at the time.

Yet in scientific terms, the original article was so weak that none of this panic could possibly have been justified. The only explanation as to why it provoked an anti-drug crusade of such intensity is that the public, and more especially the media, needed this sort of campaign. The *Science* article relied heavily upon observations made on a 51-year-old schizophrenic patient who had been given LSD on fifteen occasions while in hospital. But he had also regularly been given two tranquillising drugs, Librium and chlorpromazine. These are among the most commonly used drugs in psychiatry, and both are now known to cause chromosomal breakage.

If any weight can be attached to single-case studies of the sort that originally set off the chromosome panic (and this is in itself rather doubtful), it is worth mentioning the analysis that was made using Timothy Leary as the subject. Despite the fact that

Leary had taken LSD in spectacular amounts and on repeated occasions, no evidence was found to suggest abnormally high levels of chromosomal breakage.

But before going any further into this particular issue, it is necessary to remind oneself that even the experts are in considerable doubt about such basic issues as what actually counts as chromosomal breakage, and how we should interpret the significance of any breakages that are identified on the microscope slide. To the layman, chromosomal breakage certainly sounds more sinister than it really is. Chromosomal breaks have been observed in the cells of many perfectly normal individuals. The argument turns on the question of whether such breaks occur more often in LSD users. None of the sensational reports have even bothered to tell their readers that many other quite mundane substances have also been linked with chromosomal breakage – including caffeine, aspirin, antibiotics and even water unless it has been twice distilled. It is notable that the incidence of chromosomal breaks among people who have used adulterated black-market drugs is more than three times as high as among those who have taken pharmacologically pure LSD.

Now that more research (and better research) has been done on this question, it is beginning to seem increasingly unlikely that LSD causes chromosomal aberrations. The few reports that suggest the drug does cause damage of this sort have exposed cells to massive concentrations of LSD and for unrealistically long periods of time. Even so, they have failed to prove that the resulting damage is any greater than that produced by many commonly used substances. One study found that aspirin and LSD led to comparable levels of chromosomal breakage; in another study, one of the largest experimental investigations of chromosomal damage in LSD users, the authors found no evidence that LSD caused any change in the level of chromosomal abnormalities. During the course of this investigation, five out of the fifty subjects gave birth to seven normal, healthy infants (4 boys and 3 girls).

## Hallucinogenic drugs and psychological medicine

Many people know that LSD (and some of the other hallucinogenic drugs) have been used in psychiatry. Few realise quite how extensively they have been used. Between 1950 and the mid-1960s more than 1,000 articles were published dealing with more than 40,000 patients. Historically, medical interest in the psychiatric application of such drugs probably dates back to Moreau's work with cannabis. In his treatise *Hashish and Mental Illness* (1845), Moreau asserted that 'There is not a single elementary manifestation of mental illness that cannot be found in the mental changes caused by hashish', from simple manic excitement to frenzied delirium.

In the late nineteenth and early twentieth centuries, mescaline was regarded as a chemical model of the psychotic disorders and was occasionally prescribed for the treatment of certain psychosomatic complaints. But it was not until the discovery of LSD that a real interest developed in the therapeutic application of such drugs.

One of the initial hopes of LSD (as of cannabis and mescaline) was that it might provide a chemical model of unusual states of consciousness. For the physician, the most immediate interest was in the relevance of such drugs to schizophrenia. If we could discover how LSD affected the brain, the hope was that we would then be able to apply that knowledge to the treatment of the psychotic disorders.

Today, this hope has almost completely vanished. Despite the many similarities between the experiences of the LSD-intoxicated individual and the schizophrenic, there are also many significant differences. Unlike the schizophrenic, whose hallucinations are usually auditory, the person on LSD tends to have perceptual distortions or visual hallucinations, and LSD-induced mood states tend towards the emotional extremes rather than the more usual schizophrenic apathy. These and other differences led many researchers to question the value of LSD intoxication as a model of schizophrenia, though the main reason why research into this topic fell out of favour may have

144

more to do with the fact that such research was largely unproductive. Certainly no naturally-occurring chemical has been discovered that might explain the development of the psychoses, as was originally hoped.

LSD made more impact upon psychiatry as an aid to therapy. Many people who have taken LSD have reported that their lives have been changed for the better as a result. In one study, normal subjects were given a single high dose of LSD and mescaline. Several months later, more than three-quarters of them stated that they were happier, less anxious, more able to love other people and more able to understand themselves. Seventy-eight per cent described it as the greatest thing that had ever happened to them. It was hoped that LSD might have similar beneficial effects upon people suffering from various psychological difficulties. Some therapists relied on a single administration of a large dose to induce dramatic changes in the patient's view of himself. In some ways, it was meant to resemble a mystical experience or the process of religious conversion. Although this form of therapy rested on very doubtful theoretical foundations, it had been linked to the work of a psychologist, Abraham Maslow, on peak experiences.

Peak experiences are moments of pure, positive happiness when the individual is free from all his normal doubts, anxieties and tensions, when he loses his sense of self-consciousness. Maslow regarded peak experiences as being therapeutically beneficial in the sense that they led to a symptomatic improvement in people who suffered from various forms of psychological disorder, and more generally, in that they had a positive influence upon people's lives. Many people who have taken LSD have described it in precisely these terms. LSD was also used in psychiatry through the repeated administration of smaller doses of the drug in conjunction with psycho-analytically-orientated psychotherapies. By the middle of the 1960s, there were eighteen treatment centres in Europe which used LSD in this way.

In practice, various combinations of drug administration and psychotherapy evolved. These were used to treat virtually every

145

form of disorder to which the psychiatrist is exposed; anxiety disorders, depression, sexual problems, alcoholism, schizophrenia, and even drug addiction were treated this way. LSD was also used with dying patients.

Aldous Huxley was so profoundly impressed by his spiritual experiences after taking mescaline that he asked to be given the drug as he was dying. His wife gave him two doses of mescaline during the day and as he lay in bed he said little but gazed at his wife with an expression of love and happiness. His wife wrote of his death, 'is his way of dying to remain for us, and only for us, a relief and a consolation, or should others also benefit from it? Aren't we all nobly born and entitled to nobly dying?'

Several research studies have looked at the uses of LSD in this context. The final months of life for someone dying of cancer are usually marked by depression, psychological isolation, anxiety and pain. Even the efforts of doctors and nurses to keep the person alive can contribute towards the patient's unhappiness. LSD was originally given to cancer patients to discover if it relieved their pain. Although it had some success in this respect, its psychological effects were of far greater significance. These were explored in some detail at the Spring Grove Hospital in Maryland during the 1960s by Dr Pahnke, who was a doctor of divinity as well as a psychiatrist.

Of the patients who were given LSD, none were harmed even though some were physically in poor condition at the beginning of the trial. About a third of them were unmoved by the experience, and a third reported some benefit. More interestingly, the remainder appear to have experienced dramatic gains after taking LSD. As a result of what Dr Pahnke describes as a 'psychedelic mystical experience', these patients became more able to tolerate their physical pain: psychologically they showed an increase in their peace of mind and a decrease in their anxiety and depression. But most striking of all was the change in their attitudes towards death. After the LSD experience, they showed less fear of death.

Many of these investigations that were carried out into the therapeutic uses of LSD can be criticised from a scientific point of view, and few should be regarded in any way as conclusive. However, all available surveys suggest that the use of LSD in therapy is not especially dangerous, and although most of the early expectations about the therapeutic potential of the hallucinogenic drugs remain unfulfilled, it is surprising to find that these drugs are almost never used in psychological medicine today. There is no longer even an experimental interest in them. The reasons for this have more to do with the irrationality of human psychology than any process of scientific or medical evaluation. The LSD crusades (both for and against the drug) have made it all but impossible to hold a rational discussion about the possible benefits associated with these drugs.

## Ecstasy: MDMA

'The drug takes away all your neuroses. It takes away the fear response. There is an overwhelming feeling of peace. . . . You feel open, clear, loving. I can't imagine anyone being angry under its influence, or feeling selfish or mean, or even defensive. You have a lot of insights into yourself, real insights, that stay with you after the experience is over.'

This is not a 1960s statement about LSD. It is from the *New York Magazine*, 1985, and it is about 'ecstasy', a recent arrival on the drug scene which has revived many issues from the LSD saga.

Actually, ecstasy is not a new drug. It was first synthesised and patented in Germany in 1914 and was developed as an appetite suppressant, though it was never marketed. It is synthesised from molecular components of methylamphetamine and either safrole from sassafras or nutmeg. It is otherwise known as MDMA and is similar in its chemical structure to MDA though the two drugs have different effects.

Ecstasy is a difficult drug to categorise. Like LSD it leads to changes in states of consciousness but unlike LSD it does not produce hallucinogenic effects, nor does it usually lead to any disturbances in the person's grasp of reality. The changes in consciousness that occur after taking ecstasy tend to be more associated with emotional states. Many users find that the experience is very sensual.

Doses are generally in the range of 75-150 mg and the effects start within about half an hour of taking the drug by mouth. The peak effects tend to occur over the next hour or so, and then fade over the next two hours. In the same way that arguments about LSD were polarised, views about ecstasy have also tended to present it either as a sort of miracle drug which has vast psychotherapeutic potential or simply as one more drug of abuse.

The drug has been used in psychotherapy for purposes that have somewhat lyrically been described as 'the untying of psychic knots'. It has been given with some success to patients with long-term or terminal illnesses such as cancer, to help them come to terms with their impending death and to help them communicate their feelings to family and friends. In marital therapy it has helped to break down long-standing destructive barriers between husbands and wives. Those therapists who have used it claim that ecstasy has low abuse potential when used at clinical doses and under supervision.

Despite the promise contained in its name, even ecstasy has been unpleasant for some users. Anxiety, heart palpitations, and in a few cases, paranoid delusions have been reported. As with 'bad trips' on LSD, talkdown methods have generally been sufficient to deal with these adverse effects. The drug also produces increases in blood pressure and anyone with high blood pressure or heart problems would be well advised not to use it, as would people with a history of diabetes or fits.

# 9

## ARCHETYPAL DRUGS OF ABUSE

### I. Heroin and the opiates

Morphine (named after Morpheus, the god of dreams), was first derived from opium in 1803. In 1843, Alexander Woodin invented the hypodermic needle, thereby laying the necessary foundation for the drug addiction that is often thought to be such a typically twentieth-century problem. The history of opiate addiction stretches back over thousands of years, but it is only very recently that the problem has assumed its current form.

Interestingly, wars have played a central part in the historical development of the current problem. Both the Crimean War (1851–6) and the American Civil War (1861–5) contributed towards the development of opiate abuse. But whereas the Crimean War made little lasting impact on Europe, the Civil War left a permanent impression upon America. The troops had free access to morphine and opium which they carried so that they could give some relief to their wounded colleagues during the fighting. The Surgeon General, in his contemporary *Medical and Surgical History of the War of the Rebellion*, commented: 'Opium . . . was used almost universally in all cases of severe wounds and was found particularly useful in penetrating wounds of the chest. . . . When used with discretion, there can be no question of its great utility.'

The front-line soldier, famed for his brutality and licentiousness, is less often credited with a remarkably inventive turn of mind. It is, perhaps, hardly surprising that he found other uses for his drugs. Whether administered for the relief of pain or for other less official purposes, opiate addiction grew to such proportions that it became variously known as 'the soldiers' sickness' and 'the army disease'. At this time the drug was

149

legally available in America, and after the war many physicians encouraged soldier-addicts to buy their own hypodermic syringes so that they could continue to inject themselves with opiates.

It is always difficult to put any reliable figure on the incidence of drug addiction. One estimate relating to the period between the end of the Civil War and the Harrison Act of 1914 puts the number of American opiate addicts at a staggering 200,000. Another estimate suggests a minimum of 264,000 addicts by 1920. Whatever the precise numbers, by this time the problem had assumed alarming proportions. In 1921, the Chief Medical Officer of New York City noted that Americans were consuming twelve times as much opium as any other people in the world. More than 750,000 lb were being imported every year, even though legitimate medical uses of the drug accounted for only 70,000 lb.

1898 saw a further significant development. A new drug which had first been synthesised at St Mary's Hospital, London, was introduced. This new preparation was widely held to be both safe and non-addictive. The new miracle drug was used in the treatment of morphine addiction. It was given a name which reflected the high expectations that everyone held about it – heroin (from 'hero', meaning someone of superhuman strength, someone favoured by the gods). As with so many other miracle drugs, the miracle turned out to be sadly tarnished. The drug certainly helped morphine addicts to stop taking morphine. With some speed, they switched to heroin addiction. It is surprising that there should have been so few initial reservations about the value of heroin in the treatment of morphine addiction, since heroin is derived from morphine. (Its pharmacological name is diacetylmorphine.)

The next major event took place during the Second World War. A new opiate-type drug was synthesised by German chemists. Originally named Dolophine in honour of Adolf Hitler, the new drug was uncovered after the war by an intelligence group of the US Department of Commerce during an investigation of the Axis pharmaceutical industry. This drug, methadone, was later to play an important role in the search for a medical cure for drug addiction.

These, then, are the three main opiates. Among their lesser-known cousins are pethidine and dipipanone (Diconal). Although the different opiates differ somewhat in their relative strength and in their overall duration of effect, they have broadly the same effects. Each produces an initial stimulation of the central nervous system followed by a more marked depressant effect. This shows itself in drowsiness, changes in mood and mental clouding.

In their legitimate role, the opiates are mainly used to relieve pain, though it is not clear how much this pain-relieving property owes to physiological and how much to psychological effects. A standard experimental technique that is used to measure the effects of drugs on pain is to apply a small heat stimulus to the skin. The temperature can be gradually increased until the subject reports that it is painful. After taking morphine, the pain threshold is only slightly altered. If these drugs were used only for their physiological effects, they would be of little use as analgesics. Their advantage as pain relievers is that although the person can still feel the pain, he is no longer afraid of it – and it is this fear and anxiety that is associated with pain which causes so much distress. Rather than blocking out the pain directly, heroin and morphine relieve the anxieties which the pain causes. Opiates also affect the gastro-intestinal system; they cause constipation and have been used to treat diarrhoea.

For many years, heroin addiction was almost exclusively associated with the act of injecting the drug into a vein. Intravenous injection gives an almost instantaneous effect – the *rush* or *flash* – which is much prized by the drug taker. The intensity of the rush is something difficult to describe: the nearest analogy for the non-user seems to be that of sexual orgasm. The dramatic initial effect is extremely pleasurable to many (though not all) first-time users. However, it soon dies away, to be replaced by the drug 'high', which is usually described as a feeling of calm, detached and dreamy relaxation. This pattern of intravenous use is still very common among heroin addicts, but since the late 1970s another pattern of use has emerged, heroin smoking, or 'chasing the dragon'.

Chasing the dragon usually involves heating the heroin on a piece of tinfoil and inhaling the fumes through a small tube. Smoking heroin in this way gives an effect which is just as rapid but generally less intense than injecting it. The act of inhaling the drug, however, *seems* far less dangerous than pushing a needle into a vein, and for this reason, it has proved to be a seductive pathway into heroin use for many people.

Some heroin smokers falsely believe that the drug is not addictive if used in this way, but chasing the dragon regularly leads to psychological and to physical dependence. As the user becomes more dependent upon smoking heroin, and the costs of using it regularly begin to mount, the temptation to switch to injecting also increases. Injecting represents a more economical use of a given quantity of heroin. This decision to switch from smoking to injecting is almost inevitably a sign that the person is drifting into more severe problems with their habit.

It is doubly unfortunate that chasing the dragon appeared on the scene at the same time as the drug became more easily available. Greatly increased quantitites of heroin began to be smuggled into Western Europe during the late 1970s and early 1980s. Heroin is currently more widely available in Britain, and used by more people, than ever before. Its cost (allowing for inflation) has dropped by almost half since 1978. Using heroin is no longer a bizarre and dangerous habit confined to a small number of junkies in central London. The drug and those who use it are spread throughout the country and throughout all sections of society, and the casualties of heroin are becoming more obvious. At one time, few people in Britain knew anyone who had ever seen a heroin addict. Now, too many people know a friend or family member who has or has had a heroin problem.

The opiates have had a powerful influence upon our attempts to understand drug dependence. Indeed, opiate addiction has served as a yardstick by which other forms of drug dependence have been measured. The two most characteristic features of physical addiction to drugs both apply to the opiates: the development of tolerance to the drug effects, and the withdrawal syndrome.

## Tolerance

Tolerance shows itself in the need to increase the dose of the drug to obtain the effects that were previously obtained with a lower dose. For the first-time user, or when it is used medically, an effective dose of heroin would be in the region of 5-10 mg., and for the non-tolerant user a dose of 200 mg. would probably be fatal, though non-addicts have survived overdoses in excess of 350 mg. As the regular user increases his tolerance, he can take ever-increasing doses of the drug. The highest daily dose of heroin that I have known is 900 mg. This was the daily dose of a Canadian man who had been a heroin addict for more than forty years. He had reduced his intake of drugs to this level from more than 1,600 mg., and when he first attended one of the London drug clinics there was some doubt among the staff as to whether he could really be using such a large amount. Because of this he was asked to inject his drugs under supervision. After his first injection of 160 mg. of heroin he said he felt 'less fidgety' and went off to have lunch. During a four-hour period he injected himself seven times with a total of 1,000 mg. of heroin and 600 mg. of cocaine. Even this is by no means a record. There have been reports of addicts using astronomical doses of heroin, and there seems to be no known limit to the amount of opiates that the body is capable of tolerating.

Tolerance to some effects of the opiates occurs after even a single dose of the drug; other effects are partially resistant to tolerance: and yet other effects are almost completely resistant to the development of tolerance. Most textbooks of pharmacology and most addicts are in agreement that the euphoria produced by opiates disappears fairly rapidly with repeated use of the drug. At one time it was thought that all opiate addicts would inevitably take larger and larger doses of drugs in order to compensate for this tolerance to the euphoria of the initial injection. This does not always happen. Many addicts stabilise their daily intake of drugs at a particular level, and provided that they are able to obtain a regular supply, seem to be happy to go on using that amount. Because of this, the tendency to increase the amount of drugs used is better thought of as satisfying some sort of psychological need rather than merely as a reflection of physical needs.

## The withdrawal syndrome

Above everything else, this is the most distinctive feature of physical addiction: it is certainly the most visible and the most dramatic manifestation, and it has had a profound influence on almost every theory that has been put forward to explain drug addiction. Despite this, few people have understood the nature of the opiate withdrawal syndrome, and the myths surrounding it could fill a whole book. A few of these are discussed in Chapter 11.

The withdrawal syndrome begins to show itself within hours of the drug effects wearing off. During the early stages, the addict may feel drowsy and be subject to frequent bouts of yawning. After about twenty-four hours he becomes anxious and apprehensive: he is restless and finds it difficult either to sleep or to rest comfortably. Glandular secretions increase; the eyes and nose run, and salivation and sweating are increased. As the process develops, the bones, muscles and joints ache, and the addict may also suffer from vomiting and diarrhoea. Stomach cramps are another common symptom at this stage.

Two phrases of junkie slang are derived from the symptoms of withdrawal. *Cold turkey* refers to the appearance of the skin. The sweating, hot and cold flushes, and piloerection (gooseflesh) can make the skin look very much like that of a cold turkey. As a response to drug deprivation, there is often a slight tremor in the limbs with occasional twitches of the legs. This produces a sudden kicking movement, hence *kicking the habit*. Among the more esoteric withdrawal symptoms that have been reported are involuntary ejaculation in the male and spontaneous orgasms in the female addict. With the exception of these curious symptoms, opiate withdrawal is comparable to a bad dose of influenza.

The acute phase of withdrawal lasts for a period of several days. However, during the 1930s and 1940s some doctors who were treating opiate addicts began to suspect that the withdrawal effects lasted very much longer. Since then, researchers have confirmed that it can take months for the body to return to a completely normal level of functioning. In an experiment where volunteers took a small dose of heroin on three consecutive days, there was evidence of sleep disturbance for up to two months. This study involved normal, non-addicted subjects. In studies with addicts, physiological abnormalities have been found as long as six months after the drugs have been withdrawn, though these are generally detectable only with sophisticated measuring equipment.

## The dangers of heroin

Few people have any doubt that heroin is a killer drug. After all, the newspapers never tire of bringing us new examples of 'drug deaths'. In the same way, the medical journals report the range of diseases 'caused' by heroin addiction, of which liver disease and blood poisoning are the two most common. Yet the facts of the matter are quite different. Rather than being a particularly dangerous drug, heroin itself is comparatively safe; it is safer, for instance, than alcohol. One of the few adverse effects of addiction to heroin and the opiates (apart from constipation) is that they reduce the user's sexual capacity. In the male, this usually shows itself as impotence. In the female addict, the drugs interfere with her menstrual cycle. Sometimes the periods become irregular; often they stop altogether. In both sexes, opiates reduce the sexual drive, the level of sexual activity and the user's enjoyment of sex. Strangely, the effects of the drug during the early, experimental phase, may increase the level and the pleasure of sexual activity. I have even seen cases where men have become addicted to opiates after taking them in the first place to treat their impotence. But after a short period in which the user gains some benefit from the drug, there almost inevitably follows a period of sexual suppression. This is probably due to the drug's effect on the body's biochemistry, and as a direct drug-related effect it usually disappears after the person has stopped taking opiates.

The dangers of heroin addiction owe far more to the psychology of the addict and the ways in which addicts use the drug, than to any property inherent in the drug itself. Yet for most people, this conclusion seems to run contrary to the vast weight of evidence. How can such an assertion be supported? The death rate among opiate addicts, for instance, is much higher than that of the general population. Several estimates have suggested that addicts may be twenty times more likely to die than comparable groups of non-addicts. In order to understand why this happens we must again look at the psychology of the addict. Many addicts show a remarkable lack of concern for, if not deliberate disregard of, their own physical welfare. A surprisingly large number of addicts openly express their wish to die, and much of their behaviour reflects this. The analogy between opiate addiction and death has been a recurrent theme of the addict literature. Jean Cocteau, himself an opium addict, wrote in his *Diary of a Cure*, 'Death separates completely our heavy waters from our light waters. Opium separates them a little.'

It is important not to lose sight of the fact that the injection procedure is a separate feature of drug taking from the direct drug effects themselves. Many complications of drug taking can

156

be traced to the injection rather than to the drug. Addicts often use unsterile or even downright dirty equipment to inject themselves. This deplorable habit can lead to septicemia (blood poisoning) and to such other infections as endocarditis (infection of the heart valves) and hepatitis (jaundice). Each of these infections seriously weakens the sufferer's health, and can even lead to death. But none are directly caused by the drug itself. They are consequences of the dangerous and ill-advised ways in which the addict takes drugs. (It is a tragic irony of drug dependence that the same anti-drug campaigns which made it harder for young people to obtain needles and syringes have increased these dangers by encouraging addicts to re-use and to share their equipment.)

There are other complications associated with persistent injection into a vein, especially when done clumsily. The formation of scar tissue and other vein damage can eventually lead addicts into the position where they find it increasingly difficult to discover any further sites to inject themselves. When this happens, a minority may reconsider the wisdom of continuing their use of drugs. Some others adopt alternative routes of administration, perhaps by injecting into muscle tissue. Least sensible of all are those addicts who continue to search for more and more hazardous injection sites. Some of the more bizarre and dangerous examples that I have seen include injecting drugs into veins in the breast, ankles, fingers (I have known several cases of addicts needing amputation of a finger), and even the jugular vein. Some addicts resort to injecting themselves in the femoral vein in the groin. This can be dangerous through the increased risk of blood clots forming at this site. These could either cut off blood supply to the leg, or even break away and be transported to the brain with disastrous consequences. There is the further danger that the injection could easily penetrate the femoral artery by mistake.

The most alarming recent development here, is the appearance of the infection leading to AIDS (acquired immune deficiency syndrome). This was first recognised in Spring 1981, and since that time AIDS has spread rapidly. The first people to be affected were mainly homosexual men and intravenous drug takers.

AIDS is caused by a virus, and the virus (sometimes called HIV or HTLV III) is spread through blood products, semen or vaginal secretions. In almost all cases the virus has been transmitted in one of three ways: these are by sharing blood or blood-contaminated instruments, for instance syringes and needles, through heterosexual or homosexual intercourse, or from a pregnant woman to her foetus.

HIV infection can have several consequences. Some people show no symptoms: some become slightly unwell, often with swollen glands. Some develop a number of symptoms with varying degrees of disability. Most serious of all are those cases in which people go on to develop the syndrome known as AIDS that often includes pneumonia and a rare form of cancer. AIDS is almost always fatal. Probably all who carry the virus are infectious to others.

Every drug taker who shares needles or syringes is at risk, even from the very first injection. There are also risks attached to sharing spoons or other pieces of equipment that have been used to prepare injections. One of the first parts of Britain to be badly affected was Edinburgh where a 1986 survey of injectors found that more than half of them had HIV infection, a rate higher than in any previous European study, and similar to that reported in New York City. The Edinburgh problem has been attributed almost entirely to heroin injectors sharing equipment because of the difficulties in obtaining needles and syringes locally.

In view of the fact that many injectors are heterosexually active with people outside the narrow world of drug misuse, HIV infection will not remain confined within this group. The infection can be sexually transmitted from male injectors to their partners (whether male or female). There are also cases in which the infection has been sexually transmitted from women to men. If, or perhaps, more pessimistically, one should say *when* the infection is established in the general population it will spread in the same 'epidemic' fashion as other sexually transmitted diseases. At present there is no preventive vaccination nor any cure.

*The mysterious case of the heroin overdose*

The most publicised form of drug-related death, of course, is the overdose. Until the recent increase in the numbers of young people addicted to opiates, there were relatively few fatal overdoses. By the 1970s this had changed and thousands of deaths, particularly in New York, were being attributed to drug overdose. This is a most peculiar development, for several reasons.

In the first place, the quality of street heroin in New York is extremely poor. The amount of heroin is rarely more than 10 per cent, and one analysis of a range of street drugs taken from Brooklyn dealers revealed a heroin content of only one part in a thousand. This analysis found sixteen different adulterants, of which quinine was the most common. In London the quality of street heroin is somewhat better, with a heroin content of about 50 per cent, though this still leaves the addict using a mixture with half of its ingredients unknown.

Between the late 1960s and the mid-1970s, the most widely available heroin in Britain was 'Chinese' heroin. This came from a variety of South-East Asian sources and was sold in two forms, *Rice* and *Elephant*. Rice owed its name to its appearance; it was light-coloured and granular. The other form was called Elephant after the picture of an elephant that appeared on the large packets of heroin that were smuggled into the country. Elephant was a mid-brown in colour and was the stronger of the two. Oddly enough, many addicts described Chinese heroin as stronger and superior in the quality of its effects to English heroin, even though Chinese usually contained only about one-third of the amount of heroin in the pharmaceutically pure English heroin. The reasons for this strange preference may have something to do with the adulterants used in Chinese heroin, or, more probably, the preference may be yet another example of the potency of attitudes, beliefs and other psychological factors in determining a person's response to drugs.

Chinese heroin virtually disappeared from the streets in the late 1970s after a number of successful police raids. Its place was immediately filled by 'Iranian' heroin, and, at the time of writing the first edition of this book, most of the street heroin available in Britain was Iranian. Iranian heroin was a dark-brown powder. Pharmacologically, it was a fairly crude preparation, probably because of some fault or faults in the preliminary process of cleaning up the morphine.

At the time of preparing this second edition of *Living with Drugs*, almost all of the illicit heroin available on the streets of Britain comes from Pakistan (or from adjacent areas). On average the drug is about 70 per cent pure at the point of import. When sold on the street its purity has dropped to about 50 per cent with a range of about 30-60 per cent.

Like the Chinese and Iranian heroin that preceded it, Pakistani heroin is cut with various adulterants. In British street heroin, unlike American, quinine is seldom used as an adulterant. Instead, the user may be privileged to pay for heroin which has been cut with anything from bicarbonate of soda and sugar powder to brick dust and talcum power. Even strychnine has been used. (In small doses, strychnine acts as a stimulant. In larger doses it is a poison.) Street heroin has recently been found to contain other sedative drugs such as barbiturates. This may persuade the users that they are being sold a good quality product, but it increases the risks both of overdosing and of certain medical complications such as abscesses if the drug is injected.

One theory about narcotics overdoses is that they are really caused by the impurities in the street drugs. Quinine, for instance, can cause death in a way that matches up almost exactly with the symptoms described in cases of heroin overdose. Another theory, and one to which many addicts subscribe, suggests that overdoses are the result of unexpectedly pure samples of the drug. Although not impossible, this is unlikely. Packets of heroin found near to the bodies of dead addicts have been analysed and found to contain heroin of the same strength and sort as ordinary packets. In any case, if street heroin were of such unpredictable strength, the non-tolerant experimenter would be most at risk. In fact, it is usually the experienced, long-term addict who dies in this way.

Another theory sees alcohol (or, more precisely, the joint effect of alcohol and the opiates) as the real villain of the piece. Even an ordinary, safe therapeutic dose of an opiate such as morphine or heroin can be fatal when administered to someone who has already been drinking. Many deaths might have been avoided in the past, and more could be avoided in the future, if addicts were clearly warned of this danger. What masquerades as a heroin overdose may actually be due to the interaction of alcohol and heroin. The two drugs do not mix. (The same is true of heroin and the barbiturates, both of which are injected by addicts.)

## II. Cocaine

Sigmund Freud, the founder of psychoanalysis, and, for better or worse, probably the most influential psychologist in the twentieth century, had a considerable personal involvement with drugs. He was always an extremely heavy smoker, consuming twenty cigars a day. Indeed, his tobacco intake was so great that in 1894 he suffered from an attack of what was diagnosed as 'nicotine poisoning', and there can be little doubt that he was dependent on tobacco. In his letters to Wilhelm Fliess, he describes his efforts to reduce or give up the habit. These all failed, and he comments that he would rather have the pleasure of smoking even at the risk of his health, than lead 'a long and miserable life' without it.

Freud also became very interested in cocaine after reading about the way Peruvian Indians chewed coca leaves to increase their endurance and their capacity for work. He himself was troubled with what he referred to as 'nervous exhaustion', and decided to try cocaine as a remedy. He tried the drug both orally and by injection, and found that it gave him a quite remarkable sense of wellbeing. He gave it to his friends; he sent some to his fiancée; he gave it to his sisters and to his patients. He wrote

161

several articles in praise of it, describing 'the exhilaration and lasting euphoria which in no way differs from the normal euphoria of a healthy person'. He also wrote that 'this result is enjoyed without any of the unpleasant after effects that follow exhilaration brought about by alcohol'. In a letter to his fiancée, he described one of his articles as 'a song of praise to this magical drug'. After using cocaine for three years, Freud gave it up without any difficulty (in direct contrast to his dependence upon tobacco). His friend Ernst von Fleischl, on the other hand, had developed such a taste for the drug that he felt himself to be hopelessly dependent upon it.

At this time, there was general agreement among the medical profession that cocaine was a most valuable drug. Freud had called it an instrument of almost unbelievable curative power, and an editorial in *The Lancet* (1885) commented:

The therapeutical uses of cocaine are so numerous that the value of this wonderful remedy seems only beginning to be appreciated. Almost daily we hear of some disease or combination of symptoms in which it has been tried for the first time and has answered beyond expectation.

One sickly young man who was given cocaine at this time was Robert Louis Stevenson. Stevenson hardly enjoyed a single day's relief from illness during his entire life and spent much of his time confined to the sick-bed. After taking cocaine for his respiratory condition, Stevenson seems to have shown a quite remarkable response to the drug. He wrote 60,000 words of his novel *The Strange Case of Dr Jekyll and Mr Hyde* within six days. It is not clear precisely what role cocaine played in this. It is probable that the mental and physical energy released in him by the drug enabled him to do the actual writing, but it is equally likely that its effects inspired the theme of the book itself – that of a man completely transformed by a strange potion.

Conan Doyle's creation, Sherlock Holmes, was another regular user of the wonder drug. In *The Sign of Four*, Holmes describes his 'seven per cent solution' as being 'transcendingly stimulating and clarifying to the mind'. At the end of the book,

Dr Watson comments that it seems unfair that everyone except Holmes should have received some credit for solving the case; he asks,

'What remains for you?'
'For me,' said Sherlock Holmes, 'there still remains the cocaine bottle.'
And he stretched his long, white hand up for it.

Cocaine was sold in cigarettes, in soft drinks, in nose sprays, in chewing gum and various patent medicines. 100 per cent pure cocaine could be freely bought over the counter from the local chemist. It was also commercially available in wine which was first introduced to the public in the 1860s and was produced by Angelo Mariani. Mariani's goods became so well established that Pope Leo XIII is said to have been 'supported in his ascetic retirement by a preparation of Mariani's coca', and later he presented Mariani with a gold medal, citing him as a benefactor of humanity.

In 1885, America saw the introduction of another interesting preparation which eventually came to symbolise the American way of life itself. This contained extracts of the Africa Kola nut (caffeine) as well as cocaine; hence its name, Coca Cola. The cocaine was taken out of the drink in 1906, and by 1909 the American Bureau of Food and Drugs was able to initiate a legal action against the company producing the drink. It was alleged that the name was likely to mislead the customer because it contained no Coca and very little Kola.

Coca comes from a flowering shrub which is indigenous to the eastern slopes of the Andes and can be found from the southern tip of Chile to the northernmost part of the range. For centuries coca has played a central part in the life of the Peruvian Indians who use it to increase their physical strength and endurance, and to lessen fatigue. Coca increases heart rate, arterial pressure and the number of breaths per minute. All these effects are useful for the special requirements of high-altitude living. Typically, coca leaves are chewed together with a little lime powder made from crushed shells. The lime helps to

163

extract the cocaine and its related alkaloids from the leaves. Obviously there are wide variations in the daily intake of cocaine, but it is probable that an average amount is in the region of 350–400 mg. This constitutes a sizeable dose of the drug.

Despite the invasion of the Incas and the Spaniards, both of whom tried to suppress the use of cocaine, the Andes Indians have never stopped using it. Various estimates suggest that the region still contains between 8 and 15 million users. In Bolivia, cocaine is currently one of the mainstays of an extremely shaky economy. The distribution of the drug is largely in the control of the army, and in 1980, just prior to the military coup that overthrew the government, an aircraft belonging to a general was reported to have been discovered with 1,500 lb of 90 per cent pure cocaine on board.

There is some doubt as to who first isolated cocaine. This seems to have occurred during the middle of the nineteenth century. By 1883, German army physicians were giving the drug to Bavarian soldiers during the autumn manoeuvres. The effects were similar to those reported by the Andean Indians – increased levels of physical energy and reduced fatigue. The value of the drug as a local anaesthetic was also demonstrated at this time.

Cocaine is regularly and mistakenly described as a narcotic, a term which has no precise meaning but is usually applied to the opiates, such as heroin and morphine. Cocaine has next to nothing in common with the opiates except that in Britain it shares the same legal status as those drugs. Heroin, morphine and the other opiates are classified together with cocaine under Schedule 2(1) of the 1973 Misuse of Drugs Act, and it is possible that this legal quirk encouraged people to assume that cocaine is the same sort of drug as the opiates.

There has always been disagreement about whether cocaine is or is not an addictive drug. This argument is not worth pursuing since it is based upon one of the central misunderstandings which this book aims to correct, namely that addictiveness is an intrinsic property of the drug itself. Cocaine is not physically addictive in the same way as heroin or alcohol. The important feature of cocaine is that it can produce what many people regard as a powerfully attractive experience. The drug is a central nervous system stimulant and the first site of action is the cortex. Among its effects, users describe euphoria, laughter, talkativeness and excitement. Along with many other pills and potions it also has a reputation as an aphrodisiac.

At low doses there is an increase in activity levels and bodily movements are well coordinated. At high doses, the excessive stimulation of lower centres of the brain leads to tremors and convulsive movements. Overdoses produce anxiety, depression, headache, confusion and fainting; occasionally they lead to convulsions and respiratory arrest due to over-stimulation of the lower brain. It is very difficult to say what constitutes an overdose of cocaine because of the wide range of individual differences in sensitivity to the drug. A few individuals are so sensitive to its effects that even a small amount can produce the symptoms of an overdose. Shortly after cocaine was introduced as a local anaesthetic it was found to produce dangerous toxic reactions in some patients. It is not clear why some people should show what seems to be a sort of allergic reaction to the drug.

When the majority of cocaine users took the drug by sniffing small doses of it, it tended to produce comparatively few adverse effects. In recent years there has been a clear trend towards using purer forms of the drug, higher doses, and techniques of administration that lead to a more rapid onset of action. One illustration of this is 'freebasing', a phenomenon that has been around for some years but which has become more popular.

Freebase cocaine is a different chemical product to cocaine. Street cocaine, which is usually cocaine hydrochloride, is chemically treated to remove the hydrochloric acid and is dissolved in a solvent such as ether, from which a purified cocaine base in crystal form (freebase) is obtained. This is then smoked, and causes a more potent 'rush' and a more powerful high than ordinary cocaine. As a result, freebase is more likely to produce a psychological dependence in its users.

Another comparatively recent (and unsettling) change in patterns of cocaine use involves the smoking of cocaine paste, a practice which originated in the drug-using communities of South America, but has since spread to other countries. In some respects, smoking cocaine paste is a less technologically sophisticated version of freebasing.

Cocaine paste is the first extraction product in the process of refining cocaine from coca leaves. The leaves are mashed up and mixed with such chemicals as sulphuric acid and paraffin. Laboratory analyses have shown that paste can have a cocaine content ranging between 40 and 90 per cent. Unfortunately cocaine paste also tends to contain traces of all the chemicals that have been used to process the leaves and these can cause serious damage to the lungs.

Yet another recent variety of the cocaine preparations is known as 'crack'. This is the gift to mankind of a Los Angeles basement chemist who discovered a way to transform a gram of cocaine into half a dozen little 'rocks' by combining it with baking soda. The resulting product could be smoked, and, therefore, produced a quicker, more intense onset of the drug experience than sniffing ordinary cocaine.

The effects of smoking paste, 'crack' or freebase cocaine resemble those of intravenous cocaine injection. The blood concentration rises as fast if not faster causing a sudden 'rush' of pleasure. This pleasant effect soon subsides to be followed usually by a 'down' of depression, irritability and craving.

One of the more common types of problem associated with cocaine is that some users find themselves locked into a compulsive need to take the drug, and find that their psychological dependence upon the drug is very difficult to handle. This problem is often associated with cocaine 'binges' in which the users take the drug continuously over a period of days until either the supply is exhausted or they are. The binge usually ends with the person falling into a disturbed sleep.

A telephone information service for cocaine users established in the United States in 1983 received more than a third of a million calls in its first year. A random survey of callers revealed that they were spending an average of $637 per week on the drug. Most of them said they would use more if the price went down. Most of them said they used sedative drugs to help them calm down after using cocaine, and the majority described such adverse effects as sinus headaches, nasal problems such as cracked, ulcerated or bleeding nasal membranes, or sexual problems such as impotence. More than two-thirds of them complained of insomnia, anxiety, depression, irritability and difficulties in concentrating, and a quarter said they had had fits or loss of consciousness.

Continuous consumption of high doses of cocaine carries its own special dangers. The user may become irrational and start to develop feelings of persecution; in extreme cases, he may develop a toxic psychosis. Another curious side-effect of immoderate use that is sometimes seen revels in the title of 'formication'. The word can usually be relied upon to get a laugh, but for the victims, the symptoms are no laughing matter. They have the delusion that ants or insects are crawling about on or under their skin. In their distress the victims may pick at their skin and produce open wounds in an attempt to free themselves from this imaginary infestation. Such catastrophic reactions, however, are comparatively rare, and cocaine is currently much in vogue as a recreational drug in certain artistic and intellectual circles. The drug has retained its élitist aura (which is reflected in its black-market price), and cocaine spoons and various related drug paraphernalia are available from some of the most expensive shops in the capital cities of Europe and America.

### III. The amphetamines

The amphetamines* are another central nervous system

* There are also a few non-amphetamine stimulants included in this discussion, notably Ritalin (methylphenidate) and Kethamed (pemoline). Although these drugs are chemically distinct from the amphetamines, their effects and the ways in which they are used are for all intents and purposes identical.

stimulant. Their most common oral forms are dexedrine and benzedrine. Methedrine is also available as an injectible preparation. Amphetamines were first introduced in the form of a benzedrine inhaler as a treatment for asthma, but, as with virtually every other drug described in this book, there was an immediate rush to extend their therapeutic applications, and amphetamines were promoted as a treatment for such diverse medical conditions as schizophrenia and migraine, alcoholism and epilepsy.

In the Second World War, amphetamines were widely used. The German army found them 'very useful in modern battle conditions when used in mass attacks'. Presumably others found them equally useful: 72 million tablets were distributed to the British armed forces, and the Japanese were reported to use even greater amounts of the drug. In the decade after the war, the old war stocks of amphetamines were dumped on the open market in Japan. As a result, there was an unprecedented increase in the use of these drugs – mainly methedrine, and often in an injectible form. The use of amphetamines seems to have reached a peak in Japan around 1954 when up to a million people were estimated to be using these drugs. It is not clear what are the current military attitudes towards amphetamines, but as recently as the end of the 1960s the US army was consuming millions of amphetamine tablets (mainly dexedrine). The military values of amphetamine are obvious enough. It creates a temporary increase in energy, in alertness and in confidence.

It is not generally known that Adolf Hitler regularly used drugs. Many of these were taken to relieve his various physical symptoms (for he was not a well man), but others were taken without any proper medical rationale. In 1938, his physician began to give him occasional intravenous injections of Eukadol and Eupaverinum for abdominal pain. These synthetic opiates have the same sort of effects as morphine. It is unlikely that Hitler became addicted to them if they were administered on only an occasional basis. Throughout the war Hitler also took barbiturates for his insomnia: again there is no evidence that he used these except as a night sedative, though this pattern of daily use may well have established both a physical and psychological dependence upon them. It is possible that his insomnia and his need for sedatives were themselves caused by other drugs.

From about 1941 Hitler received daily morning injections of what seems to have been methedrine. By 1943 he needed more than just the one injection – sometimes as many as five a day. Witnesses at the time described how these made Hitler instantly alert and talkative. In addition to the injections, Hitler also took methedrine tablets. Such prolonged and progressive use of amphetamines takes its toll, and it has even been suggested that Hitler's unrealistic optimism and his fixed, rigid thinking during the battle of Stalingrad and on subsequent occasions may have been due to the adverse effects of his amphetamine abuse. This sort of speculation is interesting but inconclusive, though the irrationality, outbursts of rage, obsessional thinking and persecutory ideas that Hitler showed at that time are known symptoms of excessive use of amphetamines.

Hitler may have been a uniquely horrible political leader, but the prospects of any powerful figure acting under the influence of such drugs is not reassuring. During the brief fiasco of the 1956 Suez War, the British Prime Minister Anthony Eden has described how he was 'living on benzedrine'.

It is not only the armed forces that have seen the potential of these drugs. As a source of artificial energy, they are not without their appeal to athletes. Some sports, such as cycling, have gained quite a reputation for their involvement with stimulants, but it is clear that the performance of athletes in many different sports can be improved by amphetamines. Swimmers, runners and weight-throwers all perform better on amphetamines than on a placebo; and this enhancement occurs both when the athlete is rested and when he is tired. Weight-throwers showed the most gain in performance after taking stimulants – between 3 and 4 per cent.

Medically, it is far from clear what value the amphetamines have. Most of the original claims for their therapeutic powers

169

have been discredited. They are still occasionally used in the treatment of obesity because of their appetite-suppressant effects, though other, safer alternatives are now available. Something like 20 million people in the United States are obese, so there is no shortage of potential customers for such drugs. However, it is very doubtful whether obesity can be effectively treated by drugs of this sort. The causes of obesity are usually social and psychological, and it is these factors that need to be dealt with if the patient is to lose weight successfully. In view of the potential hazards of prolonged amphetamine use, it would be unwise to keep any patient on these drugs for more than a short period of time.

One of the most peculiar uses of the amphetamines (and Ritalin) is in the treatment of hyperactive children. Although it is a stimulant, amphetamine has a paradoxical calming effect on such children. Many hyperactive children who have been treated in this way show a marked reduction in their restlessness, coupled with an improvement in their ability to concentrate. Some children maintain their improvement even after the drug has been withdrawn. However, there are problems. In the first place, somewhere between 10 and 40 per cent of hyperactive children show no improvement when given amphetamine. More worrying, perhaps, is the potential for misusing drugs to control difficult children. Hyperactivity (hyperkinesis) is far from being a unitary or properly understood phenomenon, and the label is often wrongly applied. It would be mistaken to regard any disruptive child as necessarily being hyperkinetic. Nonetheless, it is tempting and convenient to dismiss unacceptable behaviour as 'sick' and to treat what is really a social and psychological problem as if it were a medical one.

All the ambiguities inherent in the concept of addiction come to the fore in any discussion of the amphetamines. Some authorities are convinced that amphetamines are definitely not addictive. Others are equally certain that they are physically addictive, and that statements to the contrary are dangerously inaccurate.

What is certain is that some people are so impressed by the elation produced by amphetamines that they feel a powerful need to go on using them. And with prolonged use, some individuals take progressively larger doses of amphetamines. However, this does not necessarily reflect the tolerance-producing properties of the drug itself. In the strict sense of the term, tolerance to the stimulant effects of the drug does not occur. Patients with narcolepsy (a rare disorder in which the sufferer suddenly falls asleep) can be maintained for years on a fixed dose of amphetamines. In terms of their response to stimulants, the difference between the speed-freak and the patient with narcolepsy can be found in the reasons why they take the drug. The psychological needs of chronic amphetamine abusers which led them to become dependent upon the drug in the first place, make them increasingly dissatisfied with the effects from a given dose. So they take more. In so far as tolerance occurs with the amphetamines, it reflects the body's capacity to cope with the progressive increases that are taken to achieve some psychological reward. It is not an inevitable process. Certainly not all amphetamine users escalate their dose, as might be expected if a true tolerance were present.

Similarly, when the regular user stops taking amphetamines he experiences a sort of withdrawal syndrome. This is a rebound effect, and is characterised by the opposite responses to those produced by the drug. The person becomes sleepy, lethargic and depressed. Again, it is not clear whether this is evidence of physical addiction to the drug or merely of the body's reaction against a prolonged chemical over-stimulation that has suddenly been removed. The argument about whether the amphetamines are *really* addictive is actually a semantic rather than a medical issue.

There is no longer any doubt that the amphetamines can produce one of the more dramatic examples of the hazards of drug taking. With prolonged heavy use, or after a sudden increase in the dose, the user may develop persecutory symptoms which resemble those of paranoid schizophrenia.

For many years, cases of amphetamine psychosis were mistakenly diagnosed as schizophrenia. It was not until the publication of Philip Connell's research monograph on the topic in 1958 that this toxic state was properly identified. Most commonly, sufferers believe that others are trying to harm them in some way; occasionally they have visual or tactile hallucinations. These delusions are often accompanied by intense fear.

Amphetamine psychosis seems to be a true toxic reaction which can develop in individuals whose personality does not predispose them to such feelings. No special treatment is needed. If a person is kept drug-free the psychotic state can be expected to disappear within a matter of days.

## IV. The barbiturates

The barbiturates, otherwise appropriately known as barbs (or occasionally, and even more appropriately, as gorilla pills), are probably the most dangerous of all the drugs discussed in this book. They depress activity in the central nervous system, and in small doses they act like tranquillisers to relieve anxiety and tension. In larger doses their depressant action causes drowsiness, laziness and sleep. Until the discovery of the barbiturates, alcohol, opium and belladonna were the only soporific drugs available to doctors and it is in this role of sleep-inducing drugs (hypnotics) that the barbiturates are most often prescribed.

The first barbiturate was produced in 1903 under the trade name Veronal (named after a Munich waitress); in 1912 it was followed by Luminal. Since then, more than 2,500 derivatives of barbituric acid have been synthesised. Tuinal, Seconal, Amytal, and Nembutal are among the more common barbiturates currently available. Since 1954 more than 350 tons of the barbiturates have been manufactured in the United States *every year*. During 1968, more than 17 million prescriptions were issued for over 1,000 million tablets of these drugs in England and Wales. Since then, there has been a considerable reduction in the overall levels of prescribing for barbiturates, partly as a result of the introduction of better alternative drugs, and partly because of the increased awareness by doctors of the dangers associated with barbiturates.

Very soon after the introduction of the barbiturates, cases of fatal poisoning began to be recorded. These drugs have been widely used as a means of committing suicide, and for many years barbiturate poisoning has been a major cause of death. In 1965, barbiturate overdoses accounted for half of all cases admitted to the Edinburgh poisoning treatment centre. In America, barbiturates are still the drugs most commonly mentioned in coroners' reports into drug-related deaths.

With the development of physical tolerance to barbiturates, the user is tempted to take higher doses. There are special dangers involved in this, since the proportional difference between the effective dose and the lethal dose *decreases* as the dose level goes up. Because of this, the chronic high-dose user is particularly vulnerable to the risks of overdosing.

Despite their toxicity, the barbiturates have been dispensed on a massive scale as a remedy for sleeplessness. But although they once seemed to be highly efficient sleep-inducing drugs, there is increasing doubt even about their value in this role. Some people experience a definite hangover the morning after, and some of the long-acting barbiturates (such as phenobarbitone) have more serious dangers since the user might be quite obviously intoxicated and drowsy the next day.

Most sleeping tablets produce marked changes in the type of sleep the person gets. Sleep consists of several different stages, and one of the most important of these is the lighter level of sleep during which we have dreams. Everyone goes through this stage of dreaming-sleep. When people say that they never dream, they are really saying that they never remember their dreams. Most barbiturates reduce the amount of dreaming-sleep that occurs during the night, and this is a worrying sign that normal sleep is not occurring. Some experiments have found that when deprived of this stage of sleep, people become more irritable and suspicious, and occasionally they show signs

173

of emotional disturbance. When someone stops taking barbiturates as sleeping tablets, there is an immediate rebound increase in dreaming, as if the body needed to make up for being deprived of this part of sleep.

In any case, the initial advantages of sleeping tablets often wear off. When people first start taking barbiturates to help them sleep, the drugs usually work well and they fall asleep quite quickly. But with continued use, the drug seems to lose its effectiveness and they begin to take just as long to fall asleep as they did before they took the drug. If they continue taking the drug or even increase the dose, they risk becoming addicted to it. On the other hand, the real problems are likely to begin when they stop taking it. The period immediately afterwards is marked by considerable difficulty in sleeping, disturbed sleep, many body movements and nightmares.

During the 1960s a new, non-barbiturate sleeping tablet was being promoted as a safer alternative to the barbiturates. It was not until about 1970 that the medical authorities began to suspect what the sophisticated drug-taker had known for some time: that the new drug was just as attractive as the barbiturates in terms of its intoxicating effects. This drug, Mandrax (otherwise available as Quaalude and Dormutil), had almost exactly the same effects as the barbiturates; it was misused in the same ways; and its withdrawal effects were so similar to those of the barbiturates that for most purposes it can be regarded as the same sort of drug. Its attractions were so considerable that within a few years of its appearance, a 'Mandrax problem' was being described in America, Britain, Japan, France, Germany and many other countries around the world.

Barbiturates act in many ways just like alcohol. In small doses they remove anxiety; at high doses they produce slurred speech and encourage displays of heightened emotional behaviour. Whether this emotion turns out to be of the maudlin or aggressive variety, will depend upon the user and the circumstances. Pharmacologically, the barbiturates are another way to get drunk, and it is hardly surprising that they should have lent themselves so readily to abuse. As with alcohol, excessive use of barbiturates causes a hangover the next day: and, as with alcohol, prolonged use of barbiturates establishes a physical dependence on the drug, complete with a full-blown withdrawal syndrome. Their resemblance to alcohol is sufficiently close for the two sorts of drug to combine in their effects. Anyone who takes barbiturates after drinking a large amount of alcohol puts himself at risk of overdosing, and many suicides have been due to the combined effects of both drugs.

Because there have been such vast quantities of barbiturate drugs available, they have been used by a large proportion of the population, and there is little doubt that many people who are leading perfectly ordinary 'normal' lives are both psychologically and physically addicted to the barbiturates they take under the label of sleeping pills. Despite their addiction, they would be outraged by any suggestion that they were drug addicts. At the other end of some social scale of drug involvement are those deviant and disorganised barbs addicts who present such an obviously unacceptable face of drug taking.

The casualty departments of London hospitals close to the West End see a steady procession of barbs addicts in various stages of overdose. Although some overdoses are accidental, most belong to a peculiar category halfway between accidental and suicidal. Certainly a sizeable number of the overdose cases are regular customers of the emergency services and many are known to the ambulancemen by name. They are not, however, much appreciated. Some cases are simply a nuisance, staggering about being drunkenly abusive. Others have passed beyond that stage and are comatose. Of this latter group, many will recover, discharge themselves and return on some future occasion (or even later on the same day). A few will join the pathetic and anonymous statistics for drug-related deaths.

The risks of overdose are greater among barbs users than among other drug users and, obviously, they are greater for the addict who is seeking oblivion than for those who take the drug under medical instructions or with some degree of restraint.

But there are other, special dangers associated with the injection of barbiturates. This is one of the most hazardous of all forms of drug abuse. Some addicts argue that they have been forced to use barbiturates because they have been unable to get hold of the heroin they really need. In fact, a considerable number of drug takers prefer the effects of the barbiturates, and will choose them in preference to the opiate drugs.

Most of the barbiturates used by addicts are chemically unsuitable for injection. They form an acidic mixture which can cause inflammation if it is not injected properly into a vein. Also, most barbiturates dissolve very poorly in water, especially since the street addict often grinds up chalk-based tablets which were manufactured for oral use only. As a result, many barbiturate abusers inject themselves with an unsterile acid containing lumps of chalk, and abscesses are a frequent medical complication of this most ill-advised form of drug taking. Such abscesses are smelly, nasty, unpleasant for the nursing staff to treat, and generally leave a disfiguring scar. Occasionally they set up complications which require surgery. This danger is increased by another side-effect of the barbiturates. These drugs reduce blood flow, and as a result, users may develop blisters and ulcerations of the skin. This is often caused by users being overcome by their injection of barbs and lying heavily on some part of their body in a semi-conscious condition. By cutting off their blood circulation in this way, several addicts have had to have limbs amputated, and some have even died as a result.

Even the process of withdrawing the barbiturate addict from his drugs is more complicated than for most of the other drugs of dependence. The barbiturate withdrawal syndrome is a serious condition, and unlike heroin withdrawal, which is comparatively trivial, it can have fatal consequences. The first symptoms of withdrawal are usually restlessness and anxiety coupled with irritability and insomnia. Body temperature rises slowly, sometimes reaching levels as high as 105°F in the most advanced stages of withdrawal. The pulse rate goes up and the person begins to feel a muscular stiffness. This may be followed by vomiting, delirium and convulsions, and occasionally, if untreated, by coma and death. These symptoms can be alleviated by using a gradual withdrawal schedule in which the person is given progressively smaller doses of phenobarbital (a long-acting barbiturate which is seldom chosen by addicts). Nonetheless, barbiturate withdrawal remains a serious medical problem, and even at the end of the most gradual withdrawal, the person may still have fits.

# 10

## THE CONTROL OF DRUGS

One of the most comprehensive and systematic works dealing with the relationship between the individual and the society that he lives in is John Stuart Mill's essay *On Liberty*. It was Mill's thesis that individual liberty was the primary principle which should govern relations between the individual and society, and that there were large and important areas of human conduct which should be beyond the control of the state. Mill was worried by the tendency of the state, like some malign octopus, to take over more and more of the individual's freedom of action.

The disposition of mankind, whether as rulers or as fellow citizens, to impose their own opinions and inclinations as a rule of conduct on others is so energetically supported by some of the best and by some of the worst feelings incident to human nature that it is hardly ever kept under restraint by anything but want of power; and as the power is not declining, but growing, unless a strong barrier of moral conviction can be raised against the mischief, we must expect, in the present circumstances of the world, to see it increase.

Mill felt that,

The only purpose for which power can be rightfully exercised over any member of a civilised community, against his will, is to prevent harm to others. His own good, either physical or moral, is not a sufficient warrant.

Things have changed since Mill's essay was first published in 1859. As he feared, the state has increased the extent of its influence and control over the individual. Some of the legislation and government intervention has sought to promote economic security or material welfare or racial equality; and while some might find fault with this, most of us would not. On the other hand, there are more doubtful areas in which the state has tried to exert its influence over individuals in matters affecting their moral welfare, such as sexual practices, pornography, obscenity and, of course, the use of drugs.

## Prohibition

There are few points of general agreement with respect to the control of drugs. But one thing which should no longer be in doubt is that laws do not stop the use of drugs.

The earliest record of prohibitionist thought can probably be credited to an Egyptian priest who in 2000 BC wrote: 'I, thy superior, forbid thee to go to the taverns. Thou art degraded like the beasts.' By the sixteenth century, a German prince was offering financial rewards to anyone who gave information leading to the conviction of coffee drinkers; and a century later, the Czar of Russia executed anyone found in possession of tobacco.

In Britain during the Great War, Lloyd George laid the basis for the British system of 'opening hours'. Lloyd George felt that one of the most serious obstacles to increasing the output of munitions was heavy drinking by the workforce. The factory owners who made so much profit out of the war were in complete agreement with this opinion. The Ship Building Employers Federation asked for the closure of all public houses and clubs in the area of any munitions factory. The King himself offered to give up alcoholic drink if it would provide an example to the workers. This gesture, which became known as 'The King's Pledge', was not a success, partly, one feels, because of a conspicuous unwillingness on the part of certain politicians and other public figures to adopt such extreme measures. After trying various other ideas, Lloyd George produced the Defence of the Realm Act. This drastically reduced the availability of alcohol, and introduced the British system of opening hours.

Whether as a result of this or of other factors, there was an immediate and dramatic change in the nation's drinking habits during the war. Between 1914 and 1918, the consumption of spirits was reduced by half, and that of beer was cut even more drastically from 1,200 million gallons to 460 million gallons. Drunkenness convictions were reduced by almost 80 per cent and death from liver cirrhosis dropped by more than 60 per cent. For various reasons, these changes seemed to occur mainly in the large towns and cities; the new licensing regulations had little effect on country areas. It is also apparent that what effects the new laws did have, were short-lived. Within a year or two, the initial effects seem to have been swamped by other more important changes that were taking place at the time. Quite apart from the massive social disruption that was a result of the war and the post-war economic depression, there was already a clear national trend towards reduced consumption of alcohol prior to the war.

This British system of control was primarily geared to restricting the overall levels of alcohol consumption. It does not prevent (indeed it may even encourage) 'binge drinking' during the licensing hours. As closing time approaches in the British pub, it is fairly typical to find an increased tempo of drinking and an increased number of drunks, with all that that entails.

The most dramatic efforts to control alcohol, however, have attempted to prevent any use of it. Finland and Norway have both tried this approach. Both subsequently abandoned it when it failed. But the best-known example of prohibition occurred in America between 1920 and 1933. During this period, America provided a convincing demonstration of what can go wrong with efforts to legislate drug taking out of existence.

Among the pressure groups which worked to achieve the Act of Prohibition were the temperance societies. Variously appalled both by drinking as a form of pleasure in its own right and by the wide range of social ills that they attributed to the effects of drink, they were firmly convinced that alcohol itself was sinful; and they were determined to enforce their beliefs on the rest of American society. To this end, they applied their considerable political influence.

As in Britain, part of the rationale behind the American legislation was also linked to the war effort. The Anti-Saloon

League declared alcohol to be 'un-American, pro-German, youth corrupting, and treasonable'. The Eighteenth Amendment (otherwise known as the War Prohibition Law) was introduced partly to prevent the alcoholic subversion of the war effort, though by the time it was introduced the war had been over for a year.

It attempted to remove alcohol from the American culture without providing any alternative form of satisfaction. The legislators were strong in their moral certainty that alcohol was a bad thing, but weak in their psychology. Drug taking should not be regarded merely as some trivial fault in human behaviour that can be easily corrected. Those whose business it is to pass our laws are deluding themselves if they believe that a law can achieve things that people themselves cannot.

The weight of public opinion was not behind Prohibition. Throughout the country, illicit alcohol was produced and distributed to meet the popular demand. It has been estimated that, during a one-year period, the citizens of America consumed 200 million gallons of malt liquor and 118 million gallons of wine. By 1930 more than half a million Americans had been arrested for drink offences and sentenced to a total of more than 33,000 years imprisonment. More than a quarter of a million stills were confiscated, but the bootleg liquor continued to flow. The black market that was necessary for the manufacture and supply of illegal alcohol encouraged the involvement of organised crime: there were more than 700 gangland assassinations during Prohibition. At the same time, many public officials showed an obvious disregard for the prohibition law. Respected public figures, including many politicians in Washington, routinely broke the alcohol laws. Al Capone commented on this state of affairs:

I make my money by supplying a public demand. If I break the law, my customers, who number hundreds of the best people in Chicago, are as guilty as I am. The only difference between us is that I sell and they buy. Everybody calls me a racketeer. I call myself a businessman. When I sell liquor, it's bootlegging. When my patrons serve it on a silver tray on Lake Shore Drive, it's hospitality.

As with other attempts to prohibit a particular drug, the black-market alternatives are frequently of poor quality. Some of the illegal alcohol that was manufactured may have been as good as the original product; some of it can only be regarded as poisonous. Thirty-five thousand people died from drinking illicit alcohol, and many more were permanently incapacitated. Such was the deterrent effect of Prohibition that in Chicago, deaths from alcoholism rose by 600 per cent during that period.

Prohibition is still with us. It no longer applies to alcohol in Western society, but to drugs; and most people accept this as a completely natural and desirable state of affairs. As with the prohibition of alcohol, the laws prohibiting drugs were passed not so much on the basis of reasoned argument or scientific evidence, but more often as the result of some moral crusade. It is not so long since heroin, LSD, cannabis and the amphetamines were all legally available. In America, heroin and the opiates were outlawed at the same time as alcohol.

At the end of the nineteenth century, American newspapers 'discovered' a new scandal. Lurid tales of crime and debauchery emerged, all centred on the sinister Oriental menace of the opium den. Anti-Chinese feeling, which has been endemic in America throughout much of its history, was translated into a fear and hatred of one of the most characteristic habits of this group, opium smoking. Feeling at this time reached a peak of hysteria culminating in the Harrison Act. This made it impossible for the hundreds of thousands of opiates addicts in America to go on obtaining their drugs by legal means. The people who were dependent upon opiates were appalled. They wrote to the Treasury Department in their thousands asking for 'registration permits' but no such permits were available. In 1918, a number of clinics were opened to treat the addicts. Within a year the government had forced them all to close down. The addict was forced to become a criminal and to associate with criminals if he wanted to go on using drugs. As a result, the myth that all addicts were criminals became a self-fulfilling prophecy: the laws had made it a criminal offence simply to be a heroin addict.

The British system was less harsh. Throughout most of the nineteenth century, opiates had been freely available, and there is little evidence that this led to any dramatic increase in either the amount of the drug that was consumed or the narcotic death rate. As laws were introduced to restrict the availability of specific preparations of these drugs, the public switched to other, unrestricted, forms. The influence of the recently passed Harrison Act, and the increasing pressure applied by the medical profession to limit this form of self-medication, furthered the trend toward legal control. If any final impetus was needed, it conveniently appeared in the form of scare stories about the use of morphine and cocaine by Allied troops. (This was during the most severe period of the Great War.) The use of cocaine by soldiers on leave in the West End of London was rumoured to have reached alarming proportions. Respectable London stores (including Harrods) had been fined for selling morphine and cocaine to the troops: one store advertised them as a 'useful present for friends at the front'.

These and other incidents were inflated by fears about the potential threat that such drugs might pose to national security, and they too were prohibited under the Defence of the Realm Act. In *The Lancet*, Sir William Collins confidently but mistakenly predicted that the new laws would eliminate the use of these drugs.

Prohibition does not work. It does not work whether it is alcohol, tobacco, cannabis or heroin that is being forbidden. But worse than that, it is too often forgotten that any law has certain social costs which must be endured by society. The most serious of these is that the drug prohibition laws encourage and maintain a black-market economy and a criminal subculture. Prohibition may actually increase the likelihood that those who continue to take drugs will be damaged by them, either as a result of the impurities and adulterants that are sold with street drugs, or because the user who has suffered physical or psychological harm is afraid to seek help because of the illegality of drug taking. Anti-drug laws may lead otherwise law-abiding citizens into direct confrontation with the police as a result of which they may suffer considerable social harm. Many students who have been caught experimenting with drugs have been expelled from universities and people have been dismissed from their jobs after a drug conviction. Nor are the police themselves left untouched by the prohibition laws. There have been various cases over the past few years in which members of police drug-squads have been convicted on corruption charges after accepting bribes and even re-selling confiscated black-market drugs. Society pays a heavy price for retaining these laws, yet there is a surprising reluctance to take account of these costs.

The drug prohibition laws have already established cocaine as a central part of Florida's economy. An estimated 60–80 per cent of all the cocaine that enters the US enters through Miami: this may be more than 20 metric tons of the drug. Although this may have increased the growth rate in the standard of living by up to 5 per cent per year, the social costs, as with alcohol prohibition, include some of the worst gangland battles for many years. Local police have described their attempts to enforce cocaine prohibition laws as impossible. Whenever there is a gangland killing, or some similarly shocking episode hits the headlines, the predictable reaction is to blame the drug. In fact this crime and violence is a direct product of the prohibition laws. The organised criminal is involved because he can make huge amounts of money out of the black market. It is immaterial to him whether he deals in diamonds, paintings, illegal immigrants, heroin or alcohol.

The Icelandic laws against alcohol are among the most strict in the Western world. The sale of beer is forbidden and alcohol is only available from State shops under very restricted conditions and at an extremely high price. There are no pubs or bars and alcohol can only be drunk publicly in restaurants. The familiar result of all this is that there is a thriving black market. Most drinkers use spirits rather than wines or beer, and unlike the regular daily consumption of alcohol that is often found in wine-producing countries like France, the pattern of heavy drinking typically involves episodes of drunkenness followed by periods of sobriety. As a system of control it is associated with one of the highest rates of alcoholism in Europe.

A different social cost of the prohibition laws lies in the waste of social resources that is involved. The Mexican Government is currently directing 70 per cent of its Federal Law Enforcement Budget into a campaign against the opiates, even though narcotics-related offences account for only 7 per cent of the criminal prosecutions in the country. The most significant result of this is that the purity of street heroin in Mexico has dropped from 40 per cent in 1976 to a mere 3 per cent. The Mexican addict is now paying more for his heroin and injecting a more impure solution into his veins.

But if prohibition of the opiates does not prevent people from using heroin, as a law it is not disregarded by any significant proportion of the population. Only a comparatively small number of people use such drugs. The laws prohibiting cannabis, however, are more questionable.

## Cannabis: the new prohibition

The laws that prohibit the use of drugs have not usually been conspicuously based on scientific evidence or even on rational thought. The Eighteenth Amendment was carried onto the statute books largely as a result of the political pressure exerted by temperance societies; the laws against narcotics owed much to xenophobia (in America) and to fears about the threat to national security (in Britain). The laws against cannabis are of equally doubtful parentage.

The British laws against cannabis are almost entirely a product of the Geneva International Convention of 1925. More specifically they owe a great deal to an emotional outburst by the Egyptian delegate in the discussions preceding the conference. This led to cannabis being included among the opiates and addictive drugs needing control. The British delegates were content to legislate against cannabis through their lack of interest in a drug that was hardly ever used in Europe at that time, and the Act was ratified by Parliament almost without comment.

Unlike Britain, which adopted its anti-cannabis laws more or less by default, there was no such disinterest behind the American laws. Paradoxically, the prohibition of alcohol had stimulated interest in cannabis as an alternative drug. In New York City, 'tea pads' appeared. These smoking parlours were similar to opium dens, and sold cannabis very cheaply either for consumption on the premises or to take away. Such places were tolerated by the city in much the same way as the speakeasies, the illicit drinking houses, and during the early 1930s New York City alone had about five hundred of them. However, the use of cannabis was not particularly widespread, and following the legalisation of alcohol in 1933 it might well have gradually faded back into obscurity had it not been for the reawakening of interest inspired by Commissioner Anslinger.

In 1932, Harry J. Anslinger was appointed commissioner in the Federal Bureau of Narcotics. Cannabis held an intense fascination for Anslinger who was committed to the extinction of this 'lethal weed', and in his enthusiastic zeal he promoted the most misleading and ridiculous drug myths, some of which are detailed in the next chapter. But whether they were myths or not, these stories made a powerful impact both on the general public and on the legislators.

Medical authorities at the time were less impressed by the value of a further act of prohibition. One medical expert who spoke against the new bill pointed out that the case against cannabis was not based on any satisfactory scientific or medical evidence, but rested upon a few, mostly sensational, newspaper stories. And not only was the case against cannabis very weak, but there was no reason to believe that a new law would work. An editorial in the *Journal of the American Medical Association* at the time (1937, Vol. 108) commented:

The best efforts of an efficient bureau of narcotics, supplemented by the efforts of an equally efficient bureau of customs, have failed to stop the unlawful flow of opium and coca leaves and their compounds and derivatives . . . What reason is there, then, for believing that any better results can be obtained by direct federal efforts to suppress a habit arising out of the misuse of such a drug as cannabis?

Other opposition was voiced by birdseed distributors who complained that canaries would not sing as well (or might even stop singing altogether!) if they were deprived of their diet of cannabis seed. Congress was sufficiently impressed by this argument to exclude sterilised cannabis seed from the bill. The opposition of the American Medical Association, on the other hand, was disregarded.

As soon as the new law had been passed, Anslinger extended his campaign against the drug. Even the medically authorised use of the drug was so energetically discouraged that it rapidly ceased altogether. Penalties against the drug increased in severity. Indeed, as recently as 1970, a first conviction for selling cannabis in Georgia could lead to a life sentence: a second conviction was punishable by death. In Louisiana, mere possession of the drug carried a minimum sentence of five years' hard labour, though the judge could sentence such vicious criminals to as much as fifteen years' hard labour at his discretion.

Despite the savagery of these laws, they did not stop people from using cannabis. In most Western countries, the current trend is towards a relaxation of penalties. Many of the American states now regard possession of cannabis as a trivial offence, comparable to a minor traffic violation. In Denmark, Italy, Norway, Sweden, Switzerland, West Germany and Yugoslavia, people who have been caught in possession of small amounts of cannabis are usually let off with a warning or a small fine. Britain remains one of the few European countries that still sends people to prison for up to five years merely for possessing cannabis; only Iceland and Spain still have more severe laws.

Irrespective of how harmful cannabis may (or may not) be, this new prohibition works no better than the Eighteenth Amendment. The prohibition of alcohol produced men like Al Capone. The prohibition of cannabis has already enticed organised criminals into this area and gun battles between them and the police have been seen in America, in Europe, and now in London.

Like it or not, the tendency to use drugs would appear to be an important part of the human condition, and it is one that will not be eliminated by external restraints. Physical, fiscal and statutory means have been used at various times and in connection with various different drugs. Sometimes they have discouraged some people from using a particular drug. But on other occasions, they have had unforeseen and undesirable consequences. Occasionally, they have failed in the most conspicuous way.

But whereas governments cannot prevent people from using certain drugs, they are capable of making it extremely convenient for people to use them. As laws of prohibition represented the least subtle means of preventing drug taking, so the Opium Wars stand as one of the least subtle examples of the promotion of drug taking.

## The Opium Wars

During the eighteenth century, England was in the grip of what the newspapers would fondly call a 'drugs epidemic'. The consumption of tea had increased by more than twenty times during the century, and the British Government was worried about the strain imposed upon the economy by this drug which was imported mainly from China. If the Chinese had been prepared to buy British manufactured textiles there could have been an exchange of commodities between the two countries. Unfortunately, trade with foreign powers had been restricted by the Chinese Government. In any case, the only commodity for which there was any demand was opium. Supposedly, this could only be imported under licence, but because of the demand for the drug, opium was smuggled into China in some quantity.

Although it is generally assumed that opium smoking has always been part of the Chinese cultural tradition, it seems to have been introduced to China as late as the end of the seventeenth century. The commercial interest behind this was the East India Company who cynically suggested that opium was 'a pernicious article of luxury, which ought not to be

188

permitted except for the purposes of foreign commerce'. So successful was this commercial enterprise that by the end of the eighteenth century the regular use of opium was an established part of the Chinese way of life, with perhaps as many as 10 per cent of the population using the drug; in some provinces the majority of the population seems to have been addicted. The unfortunate social effects of the drug became more widespread and the abuses associated with it more unacceptable to the Chinese authorities. Opium smoking was rife among the Chinese soldiery. Out of a thousand troops sent to put down a rebellion in the province of Canton, the commanding officer was forced to reject two hundred as unfit for service. When the rebels defeated the imperial forces, opium was blamed. Every part of Chinese society was affected. Three of the Emperor's sons were addicts and the drug was again blamed for their deaths.

Prohibition had been completely unsuccessful, despite the fact that it was reinforced by flogging, exile, imprisonment, and finally death. In the end, the Emperor sent Imperial Commissioner Lin to Canton to suppress the illicit traffic in opium. After making various appeals to the British, including a letter which was sent to Queen Victoria (but was never delivered), Lin confiscated and destroyed almost 2,500,000 lb of British opium. It was mixed with lime and salt, dissolved in water and flushed into the sea.

Angered by this affront to British dignity no less than by the considerable loss of revenue involved, Lord Palmerston and the Government decided that China must be compelled to pay compensation for enforcing its own laws against smuggled drugs. It was also to be compelled to extend the British right to import opium. A naval force of sixteen warships backed up by 7,000 troops was sent to enforce this arrangement, which it duly did. Imperial policy, however, remained the same in its attempt to enforce the ineffective laws against opium smuggling. In 1856, more than ten years after Commissioner Lin's confiscation of opium in Canton, the new emperor sent another commissioner to resume Lin's policies. As a result the *Arrow* was seized. The *Arrow* was a Chinese-owned smuggling ship which had been registered as a British vessel in Hong Kong. Again Palmerston sent out the gunboats. The commissioner's official residence was shelled, and a British expeditionary force occupied Peking and burned down the Emperor's Summer Palace. As before, the military contest was one-sided, and as part of the settlement China was compelled to accept unlimited imports of opium on payment of a duty. Afterwards, there was a massive increase both in the amounts of opium imported into China and in the corresponding economic benefits to the British Government.

So successful was the opium trade that in many Asian countries, good agricultural land was turned over to the cultivation of the poppy instead of food crops. Whole communities became dependent upon the production of opium, and the local warlords found it a reliable source of revenue. During the Japanese occupation of these territories in the 1930s and 1940s, opium was used to provide revenue for the occupation forces and morphine factories were set up. Throughout Asia there are many communities that rely upon the opium crop for their survival. The same is true in a number of Middle Eastern countries where the poppy is the staple of village life. Its oil is a base for cooking; its leaves can be used to make a salad, its seeds to enrich the bread, and the pods to feed cattle. And there remains the gum itself which can be sold to many interested parties. Once the poppy has become an established crop, it is very difficult to eradicate it. Once the opium is available, the temptations for the drug smugglers are enormous. The Opium Wars were a comparatively trivial incident in history, but their consequences are still very much with us.

## Alternative methods of control

Somewhere between total prohibition (which is ineffective), and the promotion of drugs by the state (which is undesirable), there remain a number of less dramatic alternatives.

Undoubtedly there is a need for better information to be made available about drugs and their effects. A better-informed public might use drugs more sensibly and suffer less harm from them as a result. However, it would be naive to imagine that to provide the public with such information would necessarily lead to any dramatic decrease in drug use. Indeed, it is possible that unrealistic fears about drugs actually serve as a deterrent to drug use.

The early abolitionists believed that teaching children 'the evils of alcohol' would lead to abstinence, but it didn't. Since anti-drug propaganda does not prevent the use of drugs, there is little reason to expect impartial drug information to do so. Psychologists have found little evidence that knowledge and behaviour are directly related. A person may know that riding a fast motor-cycle is extremely dangerous and still continue to do so; equally, knowing that air travel is one of the safest forms of transport does not stop many people from being terrified of flying.

A good deal of drug education has been an anxiety-stricken enterprise which has tried to 'innoculate' children with 'preventative' information that will keep them safe from drugs. This approach has not worked. All too often it has failed because the educational material has purveyed an alarming but completely unrealistic picture of drugs and drug taking. The 'facts' have simply not been true, and they have not deterred children from experimenting with drugs. Most of the studies that have looked at the effects of drug education have found that it makes little impression upon attitudes and has no consistent effect on subsequent behaviour. For years, health education programmes have emphasised the risks associated with cigarette smoking. Cigarette packets carry government health warnings. No one who smokes can have avoided exposure to this deluge of information, yet millions of people continue puffing away.

There is an urgent need to reassess what drug education can realistically be expected to achieve. It is vital that everyone realises that it cannot *eliminate* drug taking. What it could do, is to reduce the amount of harm that people suffer as a result of their drug taking. If the quality of information about drugs was better, and if it were more widely available, it might help people to use drugs more intelligently. If the relative hazards of the different drugs were fully appreciated, those who chose to take drugs might avoid the more obviously dangerous ones. Unfortunately, any attempt to direct drug education in the direction of reducing the rates of casualties among users inevitably provokes severe opposition from the prohibitionists who expect it to focus upon drug taking as a dangerous, unpleasant, and totally unacceptable activity.

Few of us are in favour of the individual systematically harming himself; it is, nonetheless, legally permissible to eat yourself to death, or indeed to smoke and drink yourself to death. Since the Suicide Act was passed, you can deliberately kill yourself by taking an overdose of legally available drugs or of a legally available poison. Yet we retain laws prohibiting the recreational use of certain drugs. These laws have comparatively little to do with the intrinsic dangers of the drugs involved (though this issue is always one of the first to be cited by proponents of the existing prohibition laws): for instance, the available evidence suggests that cannabis is a less harmful drug than alcohol, yet this provides little impetus towards changing the legal status of these drugs.

A more central principle in this issue is that of society seeking to protect the individual from the consequences of his own actions. This principle was first stated by Plato who argued that the State must save its citizens from the corruptions that are intrinsic to the masses: it is based upon a belief that the general public lack the intelligence, discipline and motivation to protect or even to know what is in their own interests. Unfortunately, drug taking may well be something from which people do not want to be saved.

Among the other factors behind the drug prohibition laws is the desire of certain sections of society to suppress anything that upsets or offends them. In recent years, this point of view has been vigorously expressed by Lord Devlin, who has argued that the law is a legitimate means of forcing the individual to adopt conventional moral codes of conduct. Devlin's argument turns on the point that anything which offends the community may justifiably be made against the law.

John Stuart Mill had anticipated each of these paternalist arguments and found them repugnant.

So monstrous a principle is far more dangerous than any single interference with liberty; it acknowledges no right to freedom whatever, except perhaps to that of holding opinions in secret, without ever disclosing them; for the moment an opinion which I consider noxious passes anyone's lips, it invades all the social rights attributed to me.

Nonetheless, Mill did consider an alternative – that although the State should permit such forms of behaviour as drug taking which might be against the best interests of the individual, it could also indirectly discourage such behaviour. One way of doing so is through taxation.

This system is already used for alcohol and tobacco, both of which have carried a high excise duty for so long that this is accepted as a fact of life. (The actual cost of a bottle of whisky is only about one fifth of its retail price.) For some years now, there has been a growing acceptance of the notion that the incidence of drug-related problems in society is closely related to the average consumption levels in that society. As a result there has developed a preference for tackling such problems by legislative controls. The comments of the advisory committee to the British Government in 1977 reflect a good deal of common sense in this matter:

We do not recommend, for example, that alcoholic drink should, by the increase of taxation, be priced out of the reach of many people. We consider that this step would unfairly penalise the vast majority of unaddicted drinkers, and do nothing to reduce the incidence of alcoholism amongst those who could still afford it, whilst tempting those who could not toward dangerous alternative sources of intoxication.

However, it is still not clear precisely how taxation does affect consumption. Detailed analyses show that whenever there has been an increase in the cost of alcohol or tobacco, there has been a short-term fall in consumption (or the rate of consumption has increased less sharply). There may be some connection between the price of a drug and consumption of it, but this relationship would appear to be rather weak.

In any case, there are problems involved in using taxation as a way of controlling the use of drugs which are currently only available from illicit sources. If these drugs were legally available, but taxed heavily enough to deter consumption, there would be an incentive to evade paying the tax by using the illegal channels of distribution that already exist.

Another way in which the State can attempt to influence the consumption of drugs is through advertising. It remains an intriguing but unanswered question whether advertising really does affect the amount of drugs that people take. The companies that advertise cigarettes and alcohol have argued that advertising does not turn non-users into users, but that its major purpose is to change brand preferences. The manufacturers would like us to believe this was true. The alcohol-control lobby would wish us to believe otherwise. In fact, there is little evidence one way or the other. No one knows to what extent cigarette and alcohol advertising contributes towards the consumption or abuse of these drugs.

One of the few occasions on which a government has prohibited the advertising of alcohol and tobacco occurred in British Columbia between 1971 and 1972. This was done in the hope that it would reduce smoking and drinking, especially among young people. The ban proved to be generally unpopular: six months after it was introduced almost two-thirds of the population was opposed to it, and after only twelve months the ban was lifted. The Addiction Research Foundation of Toronto, which examined the effects of the ban as it related to the consumption of alcohol, found no evidence that it led to any reduction in drinking. Ultimately, the control of drug taking always remains in the hands of the individual, and the best chance of achieving effective control lies in helping each person to make a responsible choice.

# 11

## JUNKIE MYTHS

### The slavery of the drug fiend

At the very heart of the twilight world of drug addiction is the archetypal junkie, a nebulous figure misunderstood both by drug takers and by others. To the straight world, the addict is variously seen as a depraved criminal and as a sick person in need of help; but the addict is often a fiction even to himself. The fascination of the addict attaches not to the person who is dependent upon drugs, but to his fabulous shadow.

One of the most powerful of the drug myths is that of the dope fiend. This has had a crucial influence upon our understanding of drug addiction. Its great popularity during the early years of this century owed much to the efforts of Commissioner Anslinger. The remarkable Harry J. Anslinger, former US Commissioner of Narcotics, has already appeared briefly in these pages. It is worth returning to him because he was such an influential force in establishing certain drug myths. In setting up the myth of the drug fiend, one of Anslinger's successful ploys was to attach to cannabis the thread of xenophobia that runs through the American cultural tradition. Not only was cannabis a foreign drug, but almost certainly it was an un-American drug. Mexicans and blacks smoked it. An article published in the *New York Times* (15 September 1933) described how Mexican drug peddlers had been seen distributing cigarettes containing marihuana to school children. Not surprisingly, foreigners were affected in a particularly awful way by this drug. A Colorado newspaper of the time commented obliquely, 'I wish I could show you what a small marihuana cigarette can do to one of our degenerate Spanish-speaking residents'. The reader is not shown, but is encouraged to muse upon, the worst sorts of atrocities. Violence, sexual frenzy and homosexuality are the most common themes that turn up in the discussions of the cannabis threat.

It was no accident that such stories came to be linked with cannabis. During a conference on the drug, a government official is on record as asking Commissioner Anslinger for details of how cannabis affected the user: 'Have you lots of cases on this? Horror stories – that's what we want'. Anslinger was happy to oblige with descriptions of the total moral and physical degradation produced by the drug. The smallest dose, he told his eager audience, was likely to cause fits of raving madness, sexual debauchery, violence and crime: it was one of the most dangerous drugs known to man. In his book *The Traffic in Narcotics* he spares none of the lurid details that were requested, offering several revolting case histories which describe in the sort of detail familiar to certain Sunday newspapers how cannabis had caused rape, violation of a seventeen-month-old baby, berserk violence, murder and even mutiny. As an example of the quality of this evidence, there is one case history that describes how a man shot two women and then committed suicide by 'slicing himself to bits about the abdomen, heart and throat'. Anslinger was convinced that this was directly caused by cannabis because 'law enforcement officers believed that G. was under the influence of marihuana at the time'. If that 'evidence' were not enough to convince the reader, he adds: 'It was the opinion of the doctor who saw G. just before he died that . . . the only thing . . . that would produce such a condition, to such a degree, is marihuana.' Some evidence!

The myth of the dope fiend clearly satisfied some profound need in the citizenry. It became more and more widely accepted. By the 1930s it was firmly established in popular literature. In *Bulldog Drummond at Bay* (1935) the villains are torturing a man to make him talk: after a whispered conversation, the deadly cannabis is produced and administered.

'That drug; what is that ghastly drug?' moaned the prisoner.
'Haven't they told you?' asked Veight. 'It is not a nice one, Waldron, and its result in time is to send you mad. It is . . . a Mexican drug

called Marihuana . . . It instils such fear into the mind of the taker that he ceases to be a man. He is mad with terror over nothing at all; his brain refuses to function; his willpower goes. And finally he finishes up in a suicide's grave or a lunatic asylum.'

In the years prior to the 1937 anti-cannabis legislation, Anslinger and his Bureau on Narcotics spearheaded the propaganda campaign linking the drug with various atrocities. Anslinger had read what he was pleased to refer to as 'a very unfortunate report released some years ago by the so-called LaGuardia committee. The Bureau immediately detected the superficiality and hollowness of its findings and denounced it.' Like so many drug myths, the notion of the dope fiend was immediately adopted as incontrovertible fact. In some strange way, it provided a psychological satisfaction too profound to give way easily in the face of more considered evidence, and it has proved remarkably resilient.

The myth of the dope fiend is still with us. Every so often it thrusts its way back into the public consciousness to mobilise our deepest fears and to provide a scapegoat for our anger and hatred. Anslinger did not restrict his mud-slinging to cannabis users. His righteous anger was exercised even more by those who indulged in the use of opiates. His book *The Traffic in Narcotics* (which might lay legitimate claim to the title of the worst book written about drugs) is packed with little gems. One of his 'acknowledged experts' on drugs is Judge Michelsen of San Francisco; 'the dope fiend in his every activity should be recognised and indexed for what he is . . . In the world of crime we find him standing in the front ranks of the most subversive and anti-social groups in the country.' Also quoted in the book is a more recent decision of the Supreme Court of the United States which described addiction in the following terms:

To be a confirmed drug addict is to be one of the walking dead . . . The teeth have rotted out, the appetite is lost, and the stomache and intestines don't function properly. The gall bladder becomes inflamed; eyes and skin turn a bilious yellow; and in some cases membranes of the nose turn a flaming red; the partition separating the nostrils is eaten away – breathing is difficult. Oxygen in the blood decreases; bronchitis and tuberculosis develop. Good traits of character disappear and bad ones emerge . . . Nerves snap; vicious twitching develops. Imaginary and fantastic fears blight the mind and sometimes complete insanity results. Often times too, death comes – much too early in life.

Most people would like to believe that this was an accurate and objective description of the consequences of drug addiction. It is not.

There are many individuals who have used heroin or other potentially addictive drugs (and this includes alcohol) throughout their lives without suffering any of the physical and mental damage described in this statement. I have seen several people who have been addicted to huge amounts of heroin for more than forty years, yet even this had produced none of the horrifying effects supposedly linked to drug addiction. Two addicts, both men in their sixties at the time of writing, had used heroin in large doses, sometimes as high as 1,600 mg. a day, since they were teenagers. By any normal standards, they were in reasonable mental and physical health: certainly they had suffered none of the appalling consequences listed above. Nor are these just two isolated cases.

Since the setting up of the London drug clinics, there has been a sizeable number of 'stable' addicts who have not been involved in crime, who have not involved themselves with the black-market drug scene, and whose physical health has been generally satisfactory; most have been regularly employed. Despite the fact that these addicts are in many respects the most 'normal' group within the addict population, they have been prescribed larger amounts of heroin than other more chaotic addicts. The drug itself does not cause the social and psychological, nor even the physical, deterioration that is so often attributed to it. The reasons for such deterioration must be sought in terms of the psychological characteristics of individual addicts and in the social meaning that drug taking has for them. Descriptions of addicts that merely reiterate Anslinger's stereotype of the 'parasitic', 'depraved', 'vicious', 'dangerous' drug fiend, are worse than useless. Not only do these descriptions present the most misleading of stereotypes, but they also construct an imaginary type with which the addict can identify. This is not as far-fetched as it may sound. The myth of the dope fiend is just as firmly entrenched in the junkie subculture as it is in straight society.

Indeed, addicts are often the most fervent believers in their own total and irreversible slavery to drugs. Jean Cocteau's book *Opium: The Diary of a Cure* is based on a set of notes written in 1929 and 1930; in it he writes how 'one always speaks of the slavery of opium'. This theme runs through most of the junkie literature. Few writers have put the position more forcefully than William Burroughs. In his book, *The Naked Lunch* (1968), he wrote:

Junk is the ideal product . . . the ultimate merchandise. No sales talk necessary. The client will crawl through a sewer and beg to buy . . . The junk merchant does not sell his product to the consumer, he sells the consumer to his product. He does not improve and simplify his merchandise. He degrades and simplifies the client.

Later in the same book he amplifies this point:

Beyond a certain frequency need knows absolutely no limit or control . . . lie, cheat, inform on your friends, steal, do anything to satisfy total need . . . Dope friends are sick people who cannot act other than they do.

On the first page of Leroy Street's autobiography *I was a Drug Addict* (1953) the author declares: 'I became a liar and a thief to support my habit . . . I plunged the depths of degradation.'

This theme occurs regularly in junkie conversation: such comments are both a celebration of, and an apology for, the junkie life. They excuse any fault on the grounds that as a helpless slave to his addiction the addict is not responsible for his own behaviour. It is a view of drug taking that combines the perverse satisfactions of martyrdom with a powerful rationalisation about why it is pointless to try to give up drugs. Such beliefs are both a justification and a trap. They give meaning and significance to the addict's life-style, but because they attribute such invincible power to the drug effects, they create a barrier to change. The world that the addict invents for himself hardens and imprisons him. Instead of freeing him from the demands of reality, the junkie identity has a nasty habit of turning into a cage that traps him, and from which escape seems only the most remote possibility.

## Withdrawal, the torment of the damned

The addict's exaggerated fear of withdrawal fulfils a similar role, offering a powerful justification for not coming off drugs. A good deal is made of 'the sickness' both by addicts and non-addicts. Indeed, a good deal too much is made of it. The idea that heroin withdrawal involves unbearable pain has proved to be a most convenient fiction for the media. It provides exactly the right sort of voyeuristic titillation for which the general public has shown itself to be so eager. *The Man with the Golden Arm* was one of the first films to linger over the agonies of withdrawal. More recently, *French Connection II* showed the tough-guy hero reduced to a grovelling animal as he tried to kick the habit that had been forced on him by the gangsters. John Lennon's record *Cold Turkey* is a celebration of the torments of withdrawal, culminating in Lennon's screams of pain and anguish. And in the magazine *New Society* (6 March 1980), an article, 'Cold Turkey in Harlem', tells the same story. An addict 'has endured the withdrawal tortures . . . and pulled through'. This is described as 'miraculous' and 'unbelievable'. The hyperbole of these accounts bears little resemblance to what might more realistically be compared to a dose of flu – certainly withdrawal can be unpleasant and distressing, but it fails by some considerable distance to match up to the myth.

Although the opiate withdrawal syndrome is one of the accepted criteria of physical addiction, it has a very large psychological component. For most addicts, withdrawal and craving are inextricably linked: each one produces the other. According to the principles of Pavlovian conditioning, if an addict regularly associates a particular place or event with his injection of drugs, that place or event will acquire some of the rewarding properties of the drug itself. As a result, things that are of no special significance to other people can provoke a powerful need for drugs in the addict. Craving and conditioned withdrawal symptoms can be triggered off by the sight of a regular scoring place such as Piccadilly Circus or Times Square, or by music that has strong drug-related memories for the addict. After giving up heroin, Anthony Sharples wrote;

In practice I had to avoid the company of other addicts, for their presence and conversation was . . . the strongest stimulus of all . . . Equally there were whole areas, geographical and social, financial and cultural, which overlapped with the junk community and which I had to avoid. (*The Scorpion's Tail*, 1975)

Conditioning processes can also have the opposite effect. When an addict is badly in need of a fix but has no drugs, he can obtain some relief from his craving by injecting water, or even by just pushing the needle into a vein. This event has come to provide a small part of the drug experience with which it has been so often associated.

For most forms of drug taking, the actual process of withdrawing from drugs presents few medical problems and can be managed easily and with the minimum of discomfort for the addict. Using a gradual in-patient withdrawal scheme, an addict can be withdrawn from any dose of any drug over a period of a few weeks. There are different problems for different drugs. Withdrawal from alcohol, for instance, carries some of the more serious medical risks, and it can be one of the most distressing withdrawal periods for the individual. In comparison, the opiate withdrawal syndrome can be reduced to minimal proportions by a carefully regulated withdrawal regime, yet almost all opiate addicts are terrified of withdrawal. This exaggerated fear makes more sense if it is reinterpreted as a fear of living without drugs. What terrifies the addict is not the symptoms of withdrawal, distressing though these may be, but the yawning emptiness beyond, the prospect of learning to live without a chemical crutch.

201

In this context, it is futile to look for objective causes of addiction, or to talk of whether or not the addict can *really* give up drugs. The attitudes, beliefs and expectations of the addict himself are of paramount importance. If the addict believes that he is totally helpless before the power of heroin or whatever drug it might be, then he is indeed helpless. But the origins of the helplessness lie in the psychology of the addict and not in some chemical property of the drug.

The clearest and most convincing evidence against the addict's need to remain addicted is that large numbers of people abandon their addictions through their own efforts. People can and do give up tea and coffee if they are convinced that it is important and necessary for them to do so; they give up cigarettes and alcohol; and they give up other supposedly more addictive drugs such as heroin. In her studies of American servicemen, Lee Robins found that although the use of drugs was rife in Vietnam, the numbers who became re-addicted to drugs on their return to America was extremely small.* Even among those who had been addicted to opiates (mainly heroin) in Vietnam, only 7 per cent became re-addicted after going home. More than nine out of every ten addicts were able to give up. Admittedly, the circumstances in which these studies took place are very unusual, but even among the ordinary street addicts, it is not generally known that many successfully give up drugs.

In 1969, Dr Gerry Stimson began a study of a representative group of heroin addicts attending the London drug clinics. Since then, these addicts have been followed up in great detail by a research team. After seven years, almost one-third were known to be no longer physically dependent upon opiates (or on any other drug), and were living in the community. Although much lower than Robins' remarkable figures, this 'recovery rate' is still impressive. It shows that drug addiction is far from the irreversible condition that has sometimes been assumed.

*The social significance of these studies is described in greater detail in Chapter 3.

## The serpent

Now the serpent was more subtil than any beast of the field which the Lord God had made. (Genesis 3: 1)

Clearly the serpent was too clever for Adam and Eve who were expelled from the Garden of Eden after succumbing to temptation.

One of the recurrent spectres of drug mythology is the pusher. Society is haunted by a stereotype of the pusher as a totally evil and unscrupulous figure, the serpent who corrupts the young and innocent by forcing drugs on to them: (He, of course, does not use drugs, being fully aware of their terrible powers.) Once his victims are enslaved by their addiction – which is presumed to occur immediately and irreversibly – he assumes command of their very existence, leading them into a life of crime, vice and degradation.

Although this picture bears virtually no resemblance to reality it is one of the most popular and enduring of all the drug myths. Its appeal is that it allays primeval fears about our own vulnerability. There is always a temptation to construct outside enemies as convenient objects for us to blame when things go wrong. When confronted by the threat of serious internal opposition, politicians have traditionally sought for, and even invented, some common external enemy to unite the faithful. In George Orwell's *1984* this fear of the danger outside has been elevated to one of the central pillars of state power. The same fear underlies one of the most widespread views of physical illness. This is based upon an idea that the world is full of hostile germs designed expressly to attack us (a fear that the deodorant and disinfectant manufacturers are careful that we should not overcome).

When faced by some threat to our cherished social and moral order, we look for the menacing stranger. When young people became dependent upon drugs, we want to blame the pusher, the demon that takes possession of their souls. Any explanation seems preferable to the prospect that the drug addictions may be due to properties of ourselves and of the social structures we believe so blameless. Addiction re-awakens that ancient dread reserved for the omniscient and utterly evil corrupter.

The idea that there was a drugs problem in Britain developed quite suddenly during the 1960s and it seems to have been provoked largely by a sudden change in the numbers of heroin and opiate addicts who were known to the Home Office. Throughout the earlier years of this century, the numbers had been uniformly low: there were 367 addicts in 1945 and 335 in 1955. Most were either therapeutic addicts who had become addicted to opiates while taking them for medical reasons, or else they were doctors and nurses whose access to drugs puts them at risk. During the 1950s the number of non-therapeutic addicts had remained extremely low, fewer than 100. But during the 1960s, the number of young people who were addicted to heroin suddenly began to increase at an alarming rate. In the four years prior to 1968 the number of non-therapeutic addicts known to the British Home Office quadrupled. From a mere 68 in 1958 it had reached almost 2,500 ten years later. At the time, these figures caused considerable alarm. Indeed the hysteria that greeted the new drug problem would not have been inappropriate if the Devil himself had appeared on the streets of London.

The inevitable search for a scapegoat soon bore fruit. Several popular newspapers made a great deal of capital out of this new sensation. Pushers were sighted everywhere. One apocryphal story told how pushers had been seen masquerading as icecream salesmen, lurking outside schools to entrap their innocent victims. Paradoxically, the child who is brought up to believe in the pusher is least well-prepared to cope with the actual offer of drugs. In reality, almost all drug dealing goes on between users. The attempt to draw some hard-and-fast line between users and pushers is based upon a misunderstanding of the drug subculture. The first time a person is offered drugs, this is most likely to involve a casual offer in a relaxed, social setting such as a party, and the offer is most likely to come either from a friend or from someone who is already known to the person. As a result, the offer is evaluated not in terms of the conventional morality tale about the evil pusher, but in terms of the current situation and the normal rules of social behaviour. Having been prepared to resist the inveiglings of a sinister stranger, the person is taken by surprise that he should be offered drugs in such a familiar and ordinary manner.

The myth of the pusher can also take on different guises. At the time, a new angle to the pusher scare was found in the behaviour of a small number of London doctors who were prescribing what appeared to be alarming amounts of heroin and cocaine for addicts. The Brain Committee's 1965 report to the British Government identified a small group of junkies' doctors as the major source of supply for the new addicts. During the intervening years, this story has been repeated so often as an explanation of how the heroin problem arose in Britain that its plausibility is very seldom re-examined.

Six doctors in particular were said to have acted irresponsibly. One of these was Lady Isabella Frankau who ran a private practice in Wimpole Street, one of the most fashionable and prestigious medical addresses in London. In order to keep her patients away from the black market, Dr Frankau was prepared to prescribe whatever they asked for. During 1962, she was said to have prescribed almost 600,000 tablets of heroin. On one occasion she prescribed 900 tablets of heroin to an addict and then, only three days later, she issued a further prescription for another 600 tablets 'to replace pills lost in an accident'. Two other doctors each issued a single prescription for 1,000 tablets. Stated in such bald terms, these figures suggest malpractice. However, without knowing how many addicts were being treated, nor how heavily addicted each patient was, the figures can be misleading. In the absence of this sort of information, it is impossible to make any exact interpretation of each doctor's prescribing habits. For instance, I know of addicts attending the junkies' doctors at that time who were heavily addicted to heroin and who needed more than 1,000 tablets of heroin each week. If this is taken into account, the Brain Committee's figures lose something of their initial shock value.

By 1967, two new doctors had emerged on the drug scene. One of them, Dr Petro, had no surgery but would meet addicts in pubs, or on stations in the London Underground, where he charged £3 for each prescription. After he was arrested for failing to keep proper records of the narcotics in his possession, hundreds of his addict patients turned to other agencies for help. Petro is remembered with genuine affection by some of the addicts he treated (and not merely because he provided them with a ready source of drugs). Eventually he was struck off the Medical Register, but even as a sad and broken old man, he was occasionally to be seen in the Underground station at Piccadilly Circus tending the sores of the addicts.

In fact there was never a single group of just six junkies' doctors. Although the number of doctors involved rarely fell below six or rose above twelve, the group was not always made up of the same people. It is too easy to vilify these doctors. Without doubt, some of them were corrupt and deliberately exploited the addicts for financial gain or for other more sinister purposes. One of them was later declared to be mad and was committed to an institution for the criminally insane. But others were compassionate and well-intentioned even if their actions now seem naive. Those who are so ready to condemn these doctors conveniently forget that most other general practitioners refused to have anything to do with drug addicts, and that there were no specialist drug dependence clinics in Britain until 1968.

## Addiction as sin and sickness

In view of the muddled thinking that surrounds the addictions, it is hardly surprising that there should be even greater confusion about how we should treat people who become addicted to drugs. This confusion is epitomised in the inimitable Commissioner Anslinger's view of the problem. On the one hand he wants to regard the person's dependence on drugs as an illness which can be cured by medical treatment; but at the same time, he cannot really bring himself to believe it.

After talking of the addicts as 'unfortunates' who need treatment, Anslinger reverts to contemptuous references to 'so-called patients' and their dreadful vice; and he cites with approval a report stating that 'addiction is simply a degrading, debasing habit . . . it is not necessary to consider this indulgence in any other light than an anti-social one'. In the end, Anslinger calls for a form of treatment which is indistinguishable from imprisonment. The addict must be hunted down, 'plucked out of the community and quarantined, forced to undergo a cure' (though he does not specify how this cure is to be achieved). The essence of Anslinger's idea of treatment is long-term, forcible control of the addict's behaviour; the addict must be deprived both of his freedom of movement and of his freedom of choice, 'the development and utilisation . . . of legal methods of restraining the personal liberty of the addict . . . is highly desirable'. Some addicts, Anslinger suggests, will need this control for the rest of their lives.

It is no great surprise that Anslinger, as Commissioner of Narcotics, should have thought that this was an appropriate way for society to respond to drug-taking. What is more alarming is to find an editorial in the *American Journal of Psychotherapy* (1972) not only agreeing with most of Anslinger's opinions, but proposing even more extreme solutions to the problem. Among its proposals was that any heroin addict with a criminal record pre-dating his addiction should be permanently imprisoned on a work-farm if he committed any other crime while addicted to drugs. Also suggested were the compulsory sterilisation of all opiate addicts, and the removal of children from the homes of any parent addicted to heroin. These extraordinary suggestions are based on the unsupported and erroneous assumption that addicts are by definition unable to bring up children properly: 'While this programme may sound cruel, it is far less so than to leave a child to the mercy of an addict.'

The essence of the dope fiend myth is the dehumanisation of the addict. He is no longer regarded as a person who has become

207

dependent upon drugs, but is reduced to a robot, lacking emotion and morality, whose only desire is to obtain drugs at any cost. Provided he is kept at this level, then the need to extend to him the usual human rights can easily be withheld; and what more basic human right than that to bring up one's own children?

The inevitable moral, physical and social decay that has so often been attributed to the use of drugs turns out to be another myth, a moral judgement masquerading as an impartial medical observation. One of the curiosities of the Wootton Committee's 1968 report to the British Government is the main appendix, written by Aubrey Lewis, Professor of Psychiatry at the University of London. Lewis was firmly of the opinion that continued use of cannabis leads to the individual's moral and social decay. This degradation was said to be shown by the way the addict becomes irritable and impulsive, by his self-neglect and inability to sustain any effort, by his refusal to accept responsibility for his family, by his homosexuality or other sexual abnormalities. 'His unkempt and prematurely aged appearance, inflamed eyes, tremor and malnutrition . . . make up a fairly characteristic picture.'

When doctors talk like this, it is time to withhold any easy credibility. In all discussions of drug taking there is a danger that moral attitudes may eclipse scientific judgement. It is not so long since masturbation was well-known to both the medical profession and the general public as the cause and the symptom of a variety of illnesses. Benjamin Rush, the father of American psychiatry, knew that solitary sex caused impotence, pain on urination, a lack of coordination, tuberculosis, indigestion, dizziness, epilepsy, loss of memory and many other disorders. In France, the great psychiatrist Esquirol stated that masturbation 'is recognised in all countries as a common cause of insanity'. From our smug contemporary omniscience we can laugh at this hopeless tangle of medical science and puritan morality. It was, however, not so funny for the victims of this error. In the mid-nineteenth century, the president of the Medical Society of London created a surgical procedure to remove the clitoris in order to prevent the female version of this disease. In 1891 the Royal College of Surgeons advocated amputation of the penis as a treatment for masturbation. The final accolade for this new disease was Sigmund Freud's recognition that masturbation is the 'primal addiction'; all others, whether to alcohol, morphine or tobacco, were merely a substitute and a replacement for it. This curious episode in the history of medicine is seldom mentioned in the medical and psychiatric textbooks, though it provides an instructive example of how behaviour that offends accepted morality may be mistaken for an objective medical disorder.

It is no more logical to suppose that drug addiction, any more than masturbation, should in itself cause the sorts of deterioration described. We no longer expect addiction to tobacco or coffee to cause these changes (though they were once widely believed to do so); why then should heroin or any other illegal drug have such magical effects? There is no reason, for instance, why a drug addict should not work productively. Sigmund Freud, who was a regular and enthusiastic user of cocaine, found that it enabled him to think more clearly and to work more intensely when he was under its influence.

Another successful medical addict was Dr William Stewart Halstead, one of the greatest American surgeons, and a founder of the prestigious Johns Hopkins Medical School. For most of his life Halstead never used less than 200 mg. of morphine a day (a large dose by today's standards), and on this he was able to work efficiently. Because of his morphine addiction, he was at first offered only a junior position in the hospital, but his work was so impressive that he was soon made senior surgeon, and as such went on to earn national and international renown. While on morphine he married the head nurse in the operating room at the Hopkins and they lived happily until Halstead's death at the age of seventy. There has always been a sizeable number of doctors and nurses who are addicted to drugs. A considerable number of them continue to work effectively without detection, leading otherwise ordinary lives.

Prior to the passage of the Harrison Act in 1914, the average

American addict had little or no involvement with the criminal world. He carried on his job, keeping his home and his family life much as anyone else. A study published in 1928 showed that out of 119 American morphine addicts 90 had good work records. The same was true of the British addict until as late as the 1960s. The contemporary picture of drug addiction as a chaotic and criminal activity is largely due to the different people who are now attracted to this subterranean world of drugs. Something like 80 per cent of the opiate addicts today have a record of criminal convictions (sometimes an extensive record, and sometimes for serious crimes). Yet it is unwarranted to jump to any simple conclusion that the addiction caused the criminal behaviour. Most addicts become involved in crime *before* they become addicted to drugs. The crime and the drug addiction both reflect a more general social deviancy factor that led the person to reject a more conventional life.

The moral view of addiction as a form of depravity is no longer as fashionable as it once was. It is now more acceptable to say that the addict is sick. But in itself, drug addiction is neither sickness nor moral depravity. Addictions are habits, and as such they may be regarded as being good or bad according to what they help us to do or what they interfere with our doing.

The idea that addiction was a sickness developed partly as an alternative to the punitive approach. For most of this century, the American opiate addict was left completely untreated, except by punishment and imprisonment. In this context, it seemed more humane to try to help the addict to escape his dependence upon drugs than simply to punish him. As a result, addiction was redefined as an illness. More humane it may have been, but in the end this view may be no more helpful, and it actually perpetuates many of the misconceptions that so bedevil our understanding of addiction. Dr Marie Nyswander, whose work was largely responsible for the establishment of the methadone maintenance clinics in America, begins her book on *The Drug Addict as a Patient*: 'Drug addiction is a distinct medical entity which ravages the patient, destroys the entire

210

fabric of his life.' In some respects, this view of addiction as a sickness may even be positively harmful. In so far as it perpetuates the myth that the drug addict is a passive and helpless victim of his addiction it contradicts any expectations that the addict can, through his own efforts, learn to live without drugs. Nyswander stated: 'As in every other major disease, the patient is helpless before its destructive inroads. Struggle as he may, the . . . inexorable process overwhelms him.'

Methadone maintenance is the epitome of the medical approach to heroin addiction, and it deserves special mention among the drug myths if for no other reason than the fact that it has now generated a multi-million-dollar industry to back it up. In 1975, the annual budget for the New York methadone maintenance treatment project alone was as high as 20 million dollars. Methadone maintenance embodies several of the more traditional misconceptions about addiction as well as fostering some new ones.

The search for a drug to cure drug addiction, for instance, is not new. Heroin was once thought to be a safe and non-addictive drug to be used in the treatment of morphine addiction; in its own time morphine had been used to treat cocaine addiction. Dr Halstead, after being dependent upon cocaine, 'cured' himself by taking morphine. On the other hand, in 1878 a Dr W. H. Bentley announced that cocaine could be used to cure morphine addiction. By the 1960s methadone had replaced them all as the new wonder-drug. Now this drug in its turn was being lauded as the definitive treatment for heroin addiction: yet again, the new drug was hailed by the medical profession as 'the safest narcotic drug yet produced'.

The rationale behind the use of methadone was that addiction to heroin or morphine was a medical disorder – a fault in the addict's metabolism induced by the repeated use of opiates. It was a disease much like diabetes; and just as the diabetic could be treated by the daily administration of insulin, so the heroin addict could be treated by the daily administration of methadone. Provided that the heroin addict was maintained on

211

his methadone, the proponents of this new treatment saw no reason why he should not lead an otherwise normal life. Yet this is the same mistake as that made by those who believe in the drug fiend myth.

The drug addict is not an evil, vicious and depraved monster; nor is he a perfectly normal person suffering from a metabolic disease. Addicts are individuals. Some are friendly, others are hostile; some are law-abiding, many are not. There is no such thing as a single addictive personality. Nor is there a single addict life-style. People become drug addicts for many reasons. A considerable number of people who become addicted to drugs have extensive problems in their personal and social lives; many were involved in crime prior to using drugs. There is no reason why such people should suddenly experience radical psychological and social changes merely because they have switched from heroin to methadone. Equally, some addicts become addicted to drugs, not because of their personal and social problems, but simply because of the availability of drugs. Their access to drugs put doctors and nurses at a much greater risk of addiction than the general population. In such cases, there is no necessary reason why their dependence upon drugs should cause such people to become the depraved, vicious criminals described by Anslinger and others.

As so often before in the history of medicine, the new treatment (methadone maintenance) gained immediate and uncritical acceptance by many doctors and politicians because it gave the illusion of solving the drug addiction problem. The supporters of this new treatment were soon proclaiming that its effectiveness had been proved beyond any doubt. One textbook of psychiatry cited success rates of between 70 and 90 per cent in the treatment of drug addiction. In view of the usual poor success rates for such treatments, these optimistic assessments were startling. Unfortunately, as with other instant solutions to the problem of addiction, methadone maintenance failed to live up to its promises. The early experiments were so badly designed that their results were inaccurate and misleading. Methadone did not turn criminal addicts into law-abiding

212

citizens; addicts on methadone did not abandon the junkie subculture for the straight world. What was claimed to be a treatment success often turned out to be no more than the transfer of the addict from one drug to another (from heroin to methadone). This represented the same sort of success as might be claimed if an alcoholic were given vodka instead of gin. And in some cases, it did not even prevent addicts from using black-market heroin in addition to their prescribed methadone. Few addicts were under any misapprehension about the new drug treatment. William Burroughs wrote: 'If the addicts lose their desire for heroin it is because the methadone dosage is stronger than the diluted heroin they receive from the pushers' (*The Soft Machine*, 1961).

It may sometimes be useful to prescribe maintenance drugs to addicts. If the addict is determined to go on using drugs, he will do so despite the most severe penalties. Under these circumstances, it seems more humane to prescribe chemically pure drugs than to force the addict to obtain a supply of impure, and sometimes contaminated, powders from the black market at a cost that encourages him to commit crimes to obtain them. But having said that, there is no more reason to prescribe methadone to heroin addicts than there is to give heroin to methadone addicts. In terms of their addictive appeal, the two drugs are virtually interchangeable. Methadone is no more a cure for heroin addiction than heroin was for morphine addiction. For the addict and the doctor alike, 'Methadone itself has turned out to be another illusion . . . providing a spurious belief that one was accomplishing something by not using heroin' (Anthony Sharples, *The Scorpion's Tail*, 1975).

# 12

## DOORS IN THE WALL

Mankind has always sought for doors in the wall of reality. In *The Doors of Perception,* Aldous Huxley wrote that 'Most men and women lead lives at the worst so painful, at the best so monotonous, poor and limited that the urge to escape, the longing to transcend themselves if only for a few moments, is and always has been one of the principal appetites of the soul.' Whether or not Huxley is correct in this pessimistic analysis of the reasons why people need such diversions, the longing for escape remains, and the ways in which different people have sought their own doors in the wall are infinitely varied. Drugs may be the most conspicuous way of producing altered states of consciousness, but they are far from being the only way. There are many other activities which do not involve drugs at all that produce powerful changes in the individual's state of consciousness. Art, literature, music, fantasy, dancing, religion, sport and holidays can all serve as escape routes from the ordinariness of reality, and some of these will be discussed later in this chapter. But there are still a few remaining drugs that deserve mention. Man's longing for altered states of consciousness has led him to try all manner of strange potions, a positive A to Z of chemical oddities, from Angel Dust to ZNA.

One of the most recent developments is the appearance of the 'designer drugs'. Designer drugs are synthetic versions of commonly misused drugs: they are manufactured illegally, often in kitchen laboratories. Because they have been made by producing subtle changes in the molecular structure of drug types, they have often evaded the drugs laws (at least in the United States). Some of the designer drugs have been of truly awesome potency. Some have carried equally awesome health risks.

In 1980 the first wave of problems linked to designer drugs

turned up on the West Coast of America. A new 'synthetic heroin' was leading to fatal overdoses. The drug turned out to be an analog of fentanyl, a powerful, short-acting, opiate-type drug. It has since been estimated that there are about 1400 analog combinations in this family group – easy to synthesise, highly potent, and more likely to produce fatal overdoses than heroin.

In 1982 another designer drug based upon pethidine (again an opiate-type drug) appeared in California. Because of a basic error in the manufacturing process of the new drug (known for short as M3P), many users developed an incurable syndrome similar to Parkinson's Disease. Symptoms included severe damage to the brain and central nervous system with almost complete paralysis. In some users, the side-effects were so rapid that they were found paralysed with the needle still in their arms. Many other users suffered severe but less immediate forms of damage to their nervous systems with arthritis-like symptoms including stiffness, tremors and seizures appearing two to ten days after use.

Designer drugs are now available in all manner of shapes and forms but mainly they have heroin-like sedative effects, or hallucinogenic effects. Probably the best advice to users is to be extremely wary of them. Drugs have always been dangerous enough in the first place. The use of untried and illegally manufactured drugs raises the existing risks to a new and unpredicatable level.

The history of drug taking sometimes appears to be little more than a catalogue of statements that this or that drug is the most dangerous known to man. The latest to receive this title is Angel Dust (a veterinary anaesthetic otherwise known as PCP or phencyclidine). In 1978 it was described by a coroner as the most devastating drug available in the United States, and by a congressman as 'a threat to national security'. It is certainly surrounded by a gruesome reputation. There are reports which tell such stories as how one user extracted all his teeth with a pair of pliers or another shot his best friend while intoxicated on the drug. Some of these stories are true but many seem to be apocryphal. By their very nature, such bizarre accounts are readily repeated and embellished with repetition. Although the drug was first synthesised in 1926 it was not until the mid-1950s that its value as an anaesthetic began to be investigated. The early animal studies seemed promising; it produced anaesthesia without loss of consciousness (a considerable advantage in some surgical operations). But the later work with humans showed that it had many unwanted side-effects. Some patients became agitated, others experienced severe disorientation, delirium and hallucinations, and further clinical investigations were abandoned.

Angel Dust seems to have made its debut as a street drug in San Francisco during the hippie era, but it quickly developed a bad name because of its unpleasant side-effects and came to be used less frequently. Its reappearance as a 'problem' during the late 1970s prompted a federal investigation of the drug. One of the best recent studies of it concluded that Angel Dust was used mainly by white adolescents looking for excitement to counter their feelings of boredom, and that most users had a fairly sophisticated understanding of the drug and its effects. Almost all of them recognised the risks involved in using such a powerful drug and developed ways of minimising these risks. Despite the public image of Angel Dust causing berserk violence, this seemed to be a rare occurrence. The picture that emerged was largely one of early adolescent experimentation with drugs. At about the age of sixteen most users found other satisfactions and other ways of demonstrating their bravery and competence. In this, Angel Dust resembles another problem that is currently causing much concern in Britain – glue sniffing.

Various substances originally intended for non-drug purposes have been used as drugs. Among them are certain industrial solvents, cleaning fluids, nail polish removers, petrol and glue. It is precisely when faced by such forms of drug taking that the deficiencies of any substance-based definition of drugs become most obvious: in these cases it is clear that what defines a psychoactive drug are the uses to which it is put.

The first synthetic psychedelic or hallucinogenic drug to have any impact on Europe and America was probably nitrous oxide (otherwise known as laughing gas). This was discovered in the eighteenth century by Joseph Priestley, and has a long association with famous men. Humphry Davy carried out a thorough and enthusiastic exploration of its effects about which he wrote at great length, and Coleridge described it as 'the most unmingled pleasure' that he had ever experienced; others who used it were Josiah Wedgwood and Peter Roget. It was nitrous oxide that first seems to have persuaded William James of the consciousness-expanding potential of drugs. For more than half a century after its discovery it remained an esoteric diversion for the cultural élite until it was applied to dentistry during the 1840s. It is still used legitimately as an anaesthetic gas, and although it is not available as a street drug it is said to be used for the occasional amusement of medical and dental staff.

In some respects, ether has a similar history, having been used on both sides of the Atlantic as an occasional inebriant for many years after its discovery. After a doctors' gathering at Epsom in 1880 the ground was reported to have been littered with empty bottles of Champagne and phials of ether. By the turn of the century ether had descended the social scale and its use as a cheap intoxicant was causing concern throughout Europe from Ireland to St Petersburg. In some countries it rivalled alcohol in its popularity as a drug, despite the fact that it is nauseating to the palate and difficult to swallow or to keep down. Its period of greatest popularity in the US was during the Prohibition era when it was added to soft drinks.

Glue sniffing is a more recent phenomenon. (The phrase 'glue sniffing' is generally used to refer to the inhalation of a variety of different solvents.) Although its origins are not clear, the first reported sighting seems to have occurred during the 1950s in California. It instantly received full television and newspaper coverage and was soon a widespread practice. The hysteria and over-reaction that greeted the identification of glue sniffing seems to have done more to popularise it than to deter young people from experimenting with it. Glue sniffing is typically a pastime of early adolescence, and is usually abandoned as alcohol or other more attractive alternatives become available. Those who become most seriously involved with glue sniffing tend to be isolated, psychologically disturbed individuals. Users have described visual distortions (colours changing, cracks appearing in walls), feelings of disorientation in time and space, and delusions of being strong and invulnerable. Sometimes there are unpleasant effects such as feelings of dizziness and nausea which soon subside as the effects wear off. The period of intoxication may last from five minutes to half an hour. The more objective signs of glue sniffing are a 'chemical' smell on the breath, slurred speech and a red facial rash; heavy users may lose weight through lack of appetite.

The various substances that are sniffed for intoxication contain organic (carbon-based) solvents, which to a greater or lesser extent vaporise at normal temperatures – like alcohol. Inhaling petrol fumes produces effects similar to those of glue, though the lead and other additives of petrol make this a more hazardous venture. Aerosols containing metallic paints have also been used in this way. Again there are considerable risks involved in the inhalation of vapours carrying copper, zinc and tin particles since the toxic effects of these metals are known to include circulatory problems and damage to the kidneys and liver. The propellant gas in aerosols is refrigerated, and if it is sprayed directly into the mouth it can cause the larynx to go into spasm, blocking off the air supply to the lungs and causing asphyxiation. Among the other organic solvents that have been inhaled to produce intoxication are nail polish remover, antifreeze, chloroform, paint thinners, lighter fuel and cleaning fluids. It is important to be aware of the differences between these substances, since each carries different risks. Glue sniffing is probably the least dangerous because its vapours do not contain the complicated chlorine and fluorine compounds in some other products and it is free from lead and other metals.

The shelves of the pharmacist produce some of the most fruitful ares of exploration for the person seeking new sources of intoxication. Although the heyday of the patent medicine is now long past, there were once hundreds of pharmaceutical preparations offering various combinations of heroin, morphine, chloroform and alcohol. Few remain. One of them is Chlorodyne – a potent syrup of opium, chloroform and alcohol. In Britain this can still be bought over the counter of the local chemist and it is advertised as a treatment for coughs, colds, diarrhoea, colic and bronchitis. It is known to most addicts as a last resort to avoid withdrawal sickness, though there is a small minority of users who seem to prefer Chlorodyne as their drug of choice. Codeine-based cough syrups also have a small number of devotees. The effects of these drugs are broadly similar to those of most opiates. Chlorodyne seems to have added complications caused mainly by the chloroform. Asthma medicines are also occasionally used to produce some sort of altered psychological state. Isolated cases of people using asthma inhalers to get high have appeared in medical journals, and the abuse of ephedrine tablets is a more widely recognised phenomenon. Ephedrine has stimulant effects broadly similar to those of the amphetamines, though it can also cause tremor, palpitations of the heart, anxiety and nausea.

Many of these preparations are readily available and the impossibility of bringing under control all substances that can be used for their psychoactive effects should be clear from the way in which petrol, paint and glue can be used for such purposes. Other familiar domestic substances that have been adopted for intoxicating purposes are the spices nutmeg and mace (see also Chapter 8). These contain psychoactive chemicals that are structurally similar to the amphetamines and mescaline. Those who have taken large doses of nutmeg or mace have reported a wide range of reactions, from euphoria and elation to anxiety, agitation and panic. Nutmeg intoxication also seems to carry a powerful hangover with weakness and aching joints. Because of the unsatisfactory nature of the experience induced by these drugs, they have typically been used only by people who are denied access to other psychoactive drugs: for instance, nutmeg abuse has been reported among prisoners. At the beginning of this century there was serious concern about the possible adverse effects of nutmeg. Doses of up to 5 mg. (about the equivalent of one nutmeg) were said to cause stomach pains, vomiting, delirium and acute anxiety attacks, these symptoms usually disappearing after about twenty-four hours, though there have also been reports of fatal cases of nutmeg poisoning. The first experimental investigation of nutmeg reported that it could cause fatty degeneration of the liver and kidney damage, though the amount required to produce such effects is probably way above what would ever be normally consumed. Nutmeg poisoning is rarely seen, but it has been reported as a consequence of attempting to use the drug to induce an abortion. This use of nutmeg is both unreliable and hazardous.

During the hippie era there emerged a popular rumour that dried banana skins could be smoked to achieve a cannabis-like state of intoxication. Federal authorities declared this to be a hoax, though there may have been a basis for the effect. Banana peel contains serotonin, a substance which is converted by heat to bufotenine, and bufotenine has effects similar to those produced by hallucinogenic drugs. However, the mild, drowsy mental state reported after inhaling banana smoke does not sound like the more powerful toxic effects of bufotenine and is more likely to be a product of the hopes and expectations of the user. The fact that it soon fell out of favour is perhaps the most telling evidence that it produced no satisfactory results. Other even more bizarre concoctions are reputed to have been used. A mixture of aspirins and Coca Cola has occasionally been used by adolescents too young to have access to the adult mysteries of alcohol and other drugs, though any pleasurable effects must be ascribed to the placebo effect or to the social rewards that go with it. At most it might produce dizziness and a sensation of ringing in the ears, but the amount of aspirin required to produce such minimal effects would be dangerously near to an overdose. At the end of this collection of oddities, again used only rarely and by those lacking access to better alternatives, is ZNA, another refugee from the kitchen. ZNA is a mixture of dill and monosodium glutamate which is smoked for its alleged hallucinogenic effects.

There is a vast number of chemicals intended to put us to sleep, wake us up, calm us down, increase our concentration, intoxicate us, or stimulate perceptual alterations and hallucinations. When we take into consideration those substances intended for other purposes but used as drugs, the range is truly enormous. However, a casual visitor from another planet could be forgiven for believing that our propensity for drug taking was even greater than it is. He could hardly fail to notice that vast numbers of people are avid consumers of a certain white crystalline substance. They take it several times every day without fail, often in amounts large enough to have physically damaging effects, and when temporarily deprived of it they seek out new supplies and become upset if none are available; when asked to give it up they become agitated, and offer such rationalisations as that they need it because it gives them energy. For the dependent heavy-dose user, few things could be more distressing than to be deprived of their 'fix'. (One of the surest ways of identifying drug dependence is through the craving that the user shows when he cannot obtain his drug.)

Sugar is a quite extraordinary substance. People buy and consume huge amounts of refined sugar (sucrose), yet there is absolutely no physiological need for it. For the average American, it may contribute up to one fifth of the total calories in his diet. Coca Cola (that most American of products) and most other soft drinks contain large amounts of sugar; about one-quarter of all the sugar consumed in the United States reaches American stomachs in this form. Such drinks are virtually the staple food of school children, and a casual inspection of the ingredients listed on the tins of food available in any supermarket will confirm how entrenched this need for sugar really is.

Some readers (especially the sugar-junkies) may be tempted to dismiss this analogy as far-fetched. After all, they might argue, sugar differs from drugs in one crucial respect – it does not harm your health in the same way that drugs do. Quite apart from the contentious issue that not all forms of drug taking do damage the health of the user, there is an increasing amount of medical research which has identified damage to health associated with sugar. Virtually everyone now accepts that sugar contributes massively to dental decay. In Britain, where the average person may consume as much as 120 lb of sugar a year, more than one-third of the adult population have had every single tooth extracted. A letter to the *British Dental Journal* (Vol. 150, 1981) described the case of a sweet addict, a thirteen-year-old boy whose need for sweets was so great that he would faint if deprived of them. Not surprisingly, the boy's teeth were in a terrible condition, and his dentist put him on a maintenance regime of sugar-substitute sweets and drinks (much like drug maintenance for opiate addicts), during which no new dental decay appeared.

Sugar is also related to more serious diseases. Coronary thrombosis, one of the greatest killers in America, is the result of a complex interaction of different factors, but sugar certainly plays a contributory role as a cause of heart disease. As the consumption of sugar goes up, so does the incidence of coronary heart disease. Even among people who are physically active and who do not smoke cigarettes (inactivity and smoking have both been implicated as contributory factors in heart disease), those who consume large amounts of sugar run a high risk of suffering a coronary thrombosis.

Experiments have also shown that a sugar-rich diet can alter the body's secretion of hormones, produce an enlarged and fatty liver and enlarged kidneys, and result in a shorter life-span. If these results were obtained in experiments with any illegal drug, they would certainly be used to justify the most severe forms of retribution against those unfortunate enough to be caught in possession of such a dangerous substance.

Eating habits can be just as compulsive as any drug addiction, just as physically and psychologically destructive to the individual, and just as difficult to give up. Almost invariably it is the sweet and starchy foods that are irresistibly attractive to compulsive eaters. It is significant that the phrases that have been used by doctors to describe compulsive eaters and obese patients are often the same ones used for drug addicts: they are difficult, they reject the patient role, they don't want to change, they lie to the doctor, they don't keep appointments. And the techniques that have been used to control and treat obesity are as bizarre as those that have been applied to the drug addictions. People have even gone to such extreme lengths as to have their jaws wired together, or to undergo surgery to by-pass the small intestine and the stomach in order to lose weight. It is ironical that whereas the illicit possession of amphetamines can lead to a compulsory high-carbohydrate prison diet, these drugs were once the most popular medically-sanctioned treatment for obesity.

Just as some people use alcohol, heroin or Valium for the psychological reassurance they promise, so others relieve their nagging feelings of anxiety, guilt, insecurity and unworthiness by filling themselves with food. But as if in answer to some archetypal memory of the days when gluttony was a sin, for many binge-eaters their over-indulgence merely intensifies the very feelings that they sought to forget through their eating. If the exchange of morality for medicine has given us obesity where once we had gluttony, we also have anorexia where we once had fasting. Fasting was primarily a method of self-purification, a penance, but its psychological effects are not merely symbolic. It produces many alterations in the body's biochemistry and physiology, and there is no doubt that it can produce a light-headed euphoric state of mind.

A quite different sort of deprivation involves reducing the level (or, more precisely, reducing the variability) of sensory stimulation. This can also produce interesting psychological effects. Whether or not these changes in consciousness are regarded as pleasurable depends upon the conditions in which they take place, upon the personality of the person who experiences them, and on what they mean to that person. For some people the experience of sensory deprivation is unpleasant. Conditions involving reduced levels of sensory stimulation have long been used as a punishment (as in solitary confinement), and more recently they have been systematically used as part of 'brain washing' procedures (for instance, during the Korean War). One series of experiments that were carried out into sensory deprivation involved volunteers lying quietly on beds in light-proof, sound-proof rooms. A few people find these conditions extremely unpleasant and ask to be let out fairly quickly; others are able to endure them for quite long periods (in one experiment the average time was thirty-nine hours); and a further group seem to be able to tolerate and even enjoy more extended periods of sensory deprivation.

Most of the people who have taken part in sensory deprivation experiments had elaborate and vivid day-dreams, and their capacity for rational, logical thinking was somewhat impaired. More strikingly, almost everyone reported unusual visual experiences. Often these were merely perceptions of simple geometric patterns, but some people 'saw' more complex patterns and a few saw complex scenes similar to a cartoon film. Auditory hallucinations were rare, though there were a few isolated reports of such phenomena. The most enthusiastic accounts of the experience have been given by John Lilly, a medical researcher and psychoanalyst who conducted a series of trials using a more profound technique of sensory deprivation in which the subject floats motionless in a tank of water heated to body temperature, in a darkened room, wearing a breathing mask.

Lilly spoke of his initial experiences in terms of heightened awareness and increased sensory experiences in the absence of external stimulation, and denied that sensory deprivation need be either stressful or aversive. He suggested that such responses were due to the negative expectations of the experimenter and subjects, and emphasised the beneficial and enjoyable aspects of the experience. After ten hours or so in the immersion tank, he described moving into 'dream-like states, trance-like states, mystical states', and had hallucinatory experiences in which he saw and heard other people. On later occasions Lilly took LSD while in the immersion tank, and his book *The Centre of the Cyclone* provides a full account of his strange experiences and his attempts to explain them. Other people have also been powerfully convinced that some significant qualitative change in their perceptions of reality occurred while in the immersion tank, and have described feelings of mellowness, total relaxation and being in harmony with the universe.

There are more prosaic claims that immersion can facilitate creative thinking, relaxation and reflection, and can help to alleviate pain. Immersion tanks are now commercially available in the United States where it is possible to hire time in them, or even, as hundreds of people have done, to build your own. As with almost every other device that people can use to alter their states of consciousness, the immersion tank has provoked the standard warnings, among them that it can precipitate a psychotic breakdown in unstable users and that it has led to the breakdown of marriages.

It is far from clear how to interpret the validity of any of these claims, though it is interesting that extreme solitude and isolation have played a part in many important religious revelations. The founders of four of the world's greatest religions, Moses, Jesus, Mohammed and the Buddha, all achieved insight that led to their ministry while isolated in the wilderness. Many thousands of mystics have maintained that transcendental experiences are best sought in solitude – whether in the highest mountains, jungles, the desert, or within an enclosed order, and the emphasis upon stimulus reduction is common to many of the practices of yoga, Zen, Tao, Sufism and Christian monasticism. All forms of meditation shut out the external world to a greater or lesser extent.

Music and rhythmic stimulation undoubtedly have the power to produce altered states of consciousness. Music has been used successfully as a substitute for anaesthetic drugs in certain operations, notably in dental extractions, and music therapy and dance therapy have both been used in psychiatric hospitals to help change mood and emotional states. Rhythmic repetition has been used for many centuries to produce trance-like states, for instance, by the Dervishes and certain Hindu groups as well as by Christian sects such as the Shakers and the Holy Rollers. It can also be used as an aid to more reflective states of mind: there is a form of 'Moving Meditation' which involves repetitive body movements. The effectiveness of this technique is thought to be due largely to the soothing, monotonous quality of the repetition, but other techniques, chanting and singing hymns, for instance, if persisted with for long periods, can produce a feeling of light-headedness through the alteration of oxygen levels in the blood.

Many children know that over-breathing (hyperventilation) can induce such states. It was a playground game among ten-year-olds when I was at school, and it is documented in Andrew Weil's book *The Natural Mind*. There can be few children who have not been delighted by the altered mental states produced by whirling themselves around (or, better still, getting an adult to spin them round) until they fall to the floor in a dizzy, giggling euphoria. Somewhat later in life, as adolescents, they may seek the same effect from listening to deafeningly loud rock music while nodding their heads or jumping up and down to the beat. And at a time when marathon running is enjoying a certain vogue, it is intriguing that long-distance runners sometimes find that the physiological changes and the repetitive, rhythmic stimulation of running produce a trance-like 'high'.

There are other routes to altered states of consciousness which involve changes in the body's internally-produced chemicals. Sex is the most obvious of these. It should be no secret that sex can be intensely pleasurable nor that it can be used like a drug; the analogy between orgasm and intravenous injection has been drawn many times. A good deal of sexual activity, particularly of the single-handed variety, involves elaborate fantasies which both help to intensify the experience and to distance it from ordinary states of reality. Sexual fantasy often conjures up perverse or forbidden versions of sex which increase the sense of excitement through the complex emotional mixture of pleasure and fear that they provoke.

Like all human emotions, fear is more complicated than it might seem. In terms of our subjective experience, it seems unmistakably different from excitement and euphoria, but they are closely related; they share the same components of physiological arousal, and psychologically, too, the line dividing fear from excitement is hard to define. It depends upon the social circumstances in which the arousing event occurs and on what the event means to the person experiencing it. Fear is not always an unpleasant feeling, as is shown by the popularity of fairground rides, horror stories and films. Provided that it does not go beyond a certain level, most people can enjoy being frightened, though it must be said that this level varies widely depending upon the personality of the individual. For some, the thrill of the detective novel is enough. Others need a more pronounced element of danger to get their internal jolt of adrenaline.

Crime can provide this thrill. Petty theft such as shoplifting is more often stimulated by the need for the rush of adrenaline that accompanies the act than by simple economic necessity, and gambling too holds out a similar promise of risk and excitement. Both can produce an addiction as pronounced and as destructive as any drug. Skiing, hang-gliding, rock climbing, free-fall parachuting and pot-holing all provide opportunities for risk, fear and excitement, and all are capable of producing the same single-minded devotion that the addict reserves for his drugs.

Among that peculiar brand of person aiming for the world speed record on skis, attitudes towards speed are indistinguishable from those towards drugs. The 'sport' involves ski-ing down a 45 degree track of polished ice. Skiers wear shiny rubberised suits and bizarre fishhead helmets to reduce wind resistance. After setting the women's record of 187.5 k.p.h. (117 m.p.h.) Stella Sylvester said 'It's like a balloon bursting. It's like sex, only more peaceful.' Another woman, after a 112 m.p.h. descent said 'You do three runs a day, and you're walking on air for a week. I'm hooked.' Between runs, the world record holder, Franz Weber, also ski dives: 'I'm not suicidal . . . but it extends my boundaries of fear.'

In its most extreme form, mountain climbing combines

danger with perceptual changes due to sensory deprivation, metabolic changes due to food deprivation, and the rigours of extreme cold and oxygen starvation. When climbing the south-east ridge of Dunagiri in the Himalayas, Joe Tasker had the hallucination that another group of climbers was watching him and criticising the slowness of his progress. Such hallucinations are not uncommon. Tasker described having had three or four such experiences, and another climber, Alan Rouse, described how on the ascent of the north face of Nuptse, at nearly 26,000 feet, he had the illusion of leaving his body and watching himself climbing. Neither Tasker nor Rouse felt that these experiences were frightening, though neither found them in any way exciting. After being buried by an avalanche close to the summit of K2 (the world's second highest mountain) Joe Tasker says that after he had escaped, he felt as if he were high on a drug; he felt privileged to be alive, and his impression of everything seemed to be intensified. Such states of euphoria were rare. Even reaching the summit of a mountain was often something of an anti-climax. Any feelings of euphoria were lessened by the extreme tiredness and weakness produced by the climb and by the climber's need to maintain his focus of concentration upon the details of the climb itself. Tasker said that he could not allow himself to relax enough to enjoy any such indulgence until he had completed the climb. The thrill is produced not by the danger but by controlling it.*

James Hunt, the 1976 World Champion Formula One racing driver, spoke to me of maintaining this delicate balancing act on the edge of disaster where the overriding need is for control and mastery. The penalties of taking undue liberties while racing a Formula One car are both obvious and severe. But the capacity for coping with danger does not rule out an inclination towards

*The tragic footnote to this story is that Joe Tasker and Alan Rouse subsequently died on the world's two highest mountains. Joe Tasker's final climb ended in Tibet on the North-East Ridge of Everest. He and Peter Boardman, another British climber, were last seen climbing above 26,800 feet at 9 p.m. on 17 May 1982. Their bodies were never found. Alan Rouse was the first Briton to climb K2, the mountain on which he died. He was last seen alive on 10 August 1986 at Camp 4 (at 26,000 feet). He is presumed to have died of severe mountain sickness.

such sources of exhilaration. The late Patrick Depailler seems to have had a pronounced taste for dangerous pursuits, having injured himself badly in a motor-cycle crash and later a hang-gliding accident before he was killed in a practice session at the Hockenheim circuit in 1980.

In contrast to the volatile Depailler, James Hunt seems a most equable person, yet after retiring from Formula One racing, Hunt seriously injured his knee while skiiing ('I always ski too fast'). During the earlier stages of his racing career he admitted that he would often be physically sick prior to a race and that 'there is a definite kick involved in frightening yourself'. Hunt felt that being under stress had a positive effect upon his driving ('To me the surge of adrenaline felt like pressure to do better').

Some indication of the intensity of the stress of Formula One racing can be gauged from the measures taken during the Monaco Grand Prix of the heart rate of one of the drivers (Didier Pironi). Pironi's resting pulse rate is between 60 and 70 beats per minute. This rose to 125 as he arrived in the pit lane but dropped to 73 as he sat in the car. During the race itself, which lasted for almost two hours, it rarely fell below 190 and shot up to a peak of 207 when his car touched another while overtaking. Pironi's Ferrari finished the race in fourth place.

There are other darker and more obscure avenues by which men have approached danger and excitement. Men are attracted to warfare for many reasons, and for most of the survivors the experience leaves a vile and sour taste. For a few, war is detestable but has a fascination that goes to work on them. Nor is this to be dismissed merely as pandering to the needs of sadistic killers. The ranks of the war junkies also include a sizeable number of non-combatants, one of the most extravagant of them being Tim Page, a young Englishman who drifted into the role of war photographer in Vietnam because 'he would go places for pictures that very few other photographers were going'.* Page was wounded on several

*Cited in Michael Herr's excellent book about the Vietnam War.

occasions, the first time by shrapnel in the legs and stomach, the second time, again by shrapnel in the head, back and arms. Later a boat in which he was travelling was blown out of the water by US aircraft under the misapprehension that it was a Viet Cong vessel: Page sustained more than two hundred individual wounds and floated in the water for hours before being rescued. He left Vietnam for a while but was drawn back after the disasters of the Tet Offensive in 1968. Finally, 'a helicopter in which he was riding was ordered to land to pick up some wounded men. Page and a sergeant ran out to help, the sergeant stepped on a mine which blew his legs off and sent a two-inch piece of shrapnel through Page's forehead and into the base of his brain.' The doctors predicted that he would be permanently paralysed down his left side.

While convalescing, he received a letter from a publisher asking him to prepare some work for a book to be called *Through with War*, and which would be intended to take the glamour out of war. For Page the idea was preposterous; 'Page couldn't get over it, "Take the glamour out of war! I mean, how the bloody hell can you do *that*? . . . It's like trying to take the glamour out of sex . . . " [Page] was speechless. ' . . . it just *can't be done!*' In the same way that drugs speak to the innermost needs of the drug addict, so for the terminal adrenaline addict war whispers things that echo loudly within him and the whisper proves irresistibly fascinating.

The desire to experience some altered state of consciousness seems to be an intrinsic part of the human condition, and the persistence that people have shown in pursuit of this goal is as remarkable as the diversity of ways in which they have sought such altered states. This same diversity is shown in the range of different types of drug taking. Whether taken alone or in company, for relaxation or stimulation, to satisfy some personal need or to comply with social pressures, we are surrounded by drugs, some more visible than others – the cups of coffee and tea, the glasses of beer, wine and whisky, the cigarettes, the snorts of cocaine, the joints, the tablets of acid, the fixes of heroin, and the ubiquitous tranquillisers and sleeping pills. It may be that every drug-induced state has its counterpart in a state of mind arrived at without drugs, but drug taking still remains one of the easiest and most immediate ways of altering psychological states; for some people the ease and immediacy with which drugs achieve their effects proves particularly seductive. So long as there are drug takers there will be drug casualties. No form of drug taking is without its dangers, but the quest to eliminate drug taking has proved to be the search for a chimera. Drug taking is here to stay and one way or another we must all learn to live with drugs.

# SELECTED BIBLIOGRAPHY

The following books are useful general sources of information about drugs and drug taking.

Brecher, E. M. *The Consumers Union Report on Licit and Illicit Drugs.* New York: Consumers Union, 1972.

Goode, E. *Drugs in American Society.* New York: Knopf, 1972.

Inglis, B. *The Forbidden Game.* London: Hodder & Stoughton, 1975.

Johnston, J. F. W. *The Chemistry of Common Life.* London: Blackwood, 1879.

Lewin, L. *Phantastica, Narcotic and Stimulating Drugs.* London: Kegan Paul, Trench, Trubner, 1931.

Malcolm, A. I. *The Pursuit of Intoxication.* Toronto: ARF, 1971.

Schultes, R. E. and Hofmann, A. *Plants of the Gods.* London: Hutchinson, 1979.

The remainder of the references provide a more detailed background to some of the issues raised in this book.

Anslinger, H. J. and Tompkins, W. F. *The Traffic in Narcotics.* New York: Funk & Wagnalls, 1953.

Ashley, R. *Cocaine: Its History, Uses and Effects.* New York: St Martin's Press, 1975.

Beattie, R. T. Nutmeg as a psychoactive agent. *British Journal of Addiction,* 63 (1968), 105-109.

Becker, H. Becoming a marihuana user. *American Journal of Sociology,* 59 (1953), 235-242.

Beecher, H. K. The powerful placebo. *Journal of the American Medical Association,* 159 (1955), 1602-1606.

Berridge, V. Opium in the Fens in Nineteenth-century England. *Journal of the History of Medicine and Allied Sciences,* 34 (1979), 293-313.

Brain Committee Report. *Drug Addiction: Second Report of the Interdepartmental Committee.* London: HMSO, 1965.

Burroughs, W. *The Naked Lunch.* London: Corgi, 1969.

Cameron, H. M. and McGoogan, E. A prospective study of 1152

hospital autopsies. I and II. *Journal of Pathology*, 133 (1981), 273-283 and 285-300.

Carter, W. (ed.). *Cannabis in Costa Rica*. Philadelphia: ISHI, 1980.

Cederlöf, R., Friberg, L. and Lundman, T. *The Interactions of Smoking, Environment and Heredity*. Stockholm: Gotab, 1977.

Claridge, G. *Drugs and Human Behaviour*. London: Allen Lane, 1970.

Cocteau, J. *Opium: The Diary of a Cure*. London: Owen, 1957.

Cohen, M. M., Hirschhorn, K. and Frosch, W. A. In vivo and in vitro chromosomal damage induced by LSD-25. *New England Journal of Medicine*, 277 (1967), 1043-1049.

Cohen, M. M. and Marinello, M. J. Chromosomal damage on human leukocytes induced by lysergic acid diethylamide. *Science*, 155 (1967), 1417-1419.

Cohen, S. and Taylor, L. *Escape Attempts*. London: Allen Lane, 1976.

Connell, K. H. Ether drinking in Ulster. *Quarterly Journal of Studies on Alcohol*, 26 (1965), 629-653.

Connell, P. H. *Amphetamine Psychosis*. London: Oxford University Press, 1958.

Corti, C. *A History of Smoking*. New York: Harcourt Brace, 1932.

Crowley, A. *Diary of a Drug Fiend*. London: Collins, 1922.

Davies, D. L. Normal drinking in recovered alcohol addicts. *Quarterly Journal of Studies on Alcohol*, 23 (1962), 94-104.

Dishotsky, N. I., Loughman, W. D., Mogar, R. E. and Lipscomb, W. R. LSD and genetic damage. *Science*, 172 (1971), 431-440.

Doll, R. The age distribution of cancer: implications for models of carcinogenesis. *Journal of the Royal Statistical Society*, 134 (1971), 133-155.

Doll, R. and Peto, R. Mortality in relation to smoking: twenty years' observations on male British doctors. *British Medical Journal*, 2 (1976), 1525-1536.

Du Toit, B. M. *Drugs, Rituals and Altered States of Consciousness*. Rotterdam: Balkema, 1977.

Edwards, G. British policies on opiate addiction. *British Journal of Psychiatry*, 134 (1979), 1-13.

Edwards, G. and Grant, M. *Alcoholism, New Knowledge and New Response*. London: Croom Helm, 1977.

Erickson, P. *Cannabis Criminals: The Social Effects of Punishment on Drug Users*. Toronto: ARF, 1981.

Ewing, J. A. and Rouse, B. A. *Drinking: Alcohol in American Society*.

Chicago: Nelson-Hall, 1978.

Eysenck, H. J. *The Biological Basis of Personality*. Springfield, Illinois: Charles C. Thomas, 1967.

Farkas, C. Caffeine intake and potential effect on health of a segment of Northern Canadian indigenous people. *International Journal of the Addictions*, 14 (1979), 27-43.

Feldman, H. W., Agar, M. H. and Beschner, G. M. *Angel Dust*. Lexington: Lexington Books, 1979.

Fields, A. and Tararin, P. Opium in China. *British Journal of Addiction*, 64 (1970), 371-382.

Fisher, R. A. *Smoking. The Cancer Controversy*. Edinburgh: Oliver & Boyd, 1959.

Fletcher, D. *The Amazing Story of Repeal*. Chicago: Willett, Clark & Co., 1940.

Frankenhaeuser, M., Post, B., Hagdal, R. and Wrangsjoe, B. Effects of a depressant drug as modified by experimentally-induced expectation. *Perceptual and Motor Skills*, 18 (1964), 513-522.

Furst, P. T. *Flesh of the Gods. The Ritual Use of Hallucinogens*. New York: Praeger, 1972.

Gay, G., Sheppard, C. and Inaba, D. An old girl: flyin' low, dyin' slow, blinded by snow: cocaine in perspective. *International Journal of the Addictions*, 8 (1973), 1027-1042.

Gertler, R., Ferneau, E. and Raynes, A. Attitudes towards death and dying on a drug addiction unit. *International Journal of the Addictions*, 8 (1973), 265-272.

Goldstein, A., Kaizer, S. and Whitby, O. Psychotropic effects of caffeine in man. IV. Quantitative and qualitative differences associated with habituation to coffee. *Clinical Pharmacology and Therapeutics*, 10 (1969), 489-497.

Gossop, M. R. A review of the evidence for methadone maintenance as a treatment for narcotic addiction. *Lancet*, 1 (1978), 812-815.

Graham, J. D. P. *Cannabis Now*. Aylesbury: H.M. & M. Publishers, 1977.

Gregory, R. J., Gregory, J. E. and Peck, J. G. Kava and prohibition in Tanna, Vanuata. *British Journal of Addiction*, 76 (1981), 299-313.

Grinspoon, L. and Bakalar, J. B. *Psychedelic Drugs Reconsidered*. New York: Basic Books, 1979.

Grinspoon, L. and Hedblom, P. *The Speed Culture*. Cambridge, Mass.: Harvard University Press, 1975.

Herr, M. *Dispatches*. London: Pan Books, 1979.

## Selected Bibliography

Hirayama, T. Non-smoking wives of heavy smokers have a higher risk of lung cancer: a study from Japan. *British Medical Journal*, 282 (1981), 183-185.

Huxley, A. *The Devils of Loudun*. London: Chatto & Windus, 1961.

Huxley, A. *The Doors of Perception* and *Heaven and Hell*. Harmondsworth: Penguin, 1969.

Indian Hemp Drugs Commission. Report. Simla: Government Printing Office, 1894.

James, W. *Varieties of Religious Experience*. London: Longmans, 1942.

Jellinek, E. M. *The Disease Concept of Alcoholism*. New Haven, Conn.: College & University Press, 1960.

Jones, R. T. Marihuana-induced 'high': influence of expectation, setting and previous drug experience. *Pharmacological Review*, 23 (1971), 359-369.

*Journal of the American Medical Association*, 159 (1955), 780. Placebos (Editorial).

*Journal of the American Medical Association*, 216 (1971), 1701-10. Cannabis and educational performance (Medical News).

Keller, M. The great Jewish drink mystery. *British Journal of Addiction*, 64 (1970), 287-296.

Kingsley, C. *Alton Locke*. London: Dent, reprinted 1970.

Kissin, B. and Begleiter, H. (eds). *The Biology of Alcoholism*. New York: Plenum, Vol. 1, Biochemistry, 1971; Vol. 2, Physiology and Behaviour, 1972; Vol. 3, Clinical Pathology, 1974; Vol. 4, Social Aspects, 1976.

Kumar, R., Cooke, E. C., Lader, M. H. and Russell, M. A. H. Is tobacco smoking a form of nicotine dependence? In R. E. Thornton (ed.), *Smoking Behaviour*. Edinburgh: Churchill Livingstone, 1978.

Lader, M. H. Benzodiazepines – the opium of the masses? *Neuroscience*, 3 (1978), 159-165.

LaGuardia Committee. *The Marihuana Problem in the City of New York: Sociological, Medical, Psychological and Pharmacological Studies*. Lancaster, Penn.: Jacques Cattell, 1944.

*The Lancet*, 21 April 1973, 867. Unreasonable profit (Editorial).

*The Lancet*, 21 April 1973, 876. Chlordiazepoxide and diazepam prices (Editorial).

*The Lancet*, 12 May 1973, 1069. Price of Tranquillisers (Editorial).

*The Lancet*, 19 May 1973, 1101-2. Benzodiazepines: use, overuse, misuse, abuse? (Editorial).

*The Lancet*, 14 July 1973, 108. Price of tranquillisers (Editorial).

Le Dain Report. *Interim Report of the Canadian Government Commission of Inquiry*. Harmondsworth: Penguin, 1971.

Le Dain Report. *Cannabis. A Report of the Commission of Inquiry into the Non-Medical Use of Drugs*. Ottawa: Information Canada, 1972.

Lennard, H. L., Epstein, L. J., Bernstein, A. and Ransom, D. C. *Mystification and Drug Misuse*. San Francisco: Jossey-Bass, 1971.

Lewis, S. A., Oswald, I., Evans, J. I., Akindele, M. O. and Tompsett, S. L. Heroin and sleep. *Electroencephalography and Clinical Neurophysiology*, 28 (1970), 374-381.

Lilly, J. C. *The Centre of the Cyclone*. New York: Julian Press, 1972.

Logan, F. (ed.). *Cannabis: Options for Control*. Sunbury, Middlesex: Quartermaine House, 1979.

Mapes, R. (ed.). *Prescribing Practice and Drug Usage*. London: Croom Helm, 1980.

Marks, J. *The Search for the 'Manchurian Candidate'*. London: Allen Lane, 1979.

Masters, R. E. L. and Houston, J. *The Varieties of Psychedelic Experience*. London: Turnstone, 1973.

Mendelson, W. B. *The Use and Misuse of Sleeping Pills*. New York: Plenum, 1980.

Mikuriya, T. H. Physical, mental, and moral effects of marihuana: the Indian Hemp Drugs Commission Report. *International Journal of the Addictions*, 3 (1968), 253-270.

Musto, D. F. *The American Disease*. Yale University Press, 1973.

Nyswander, M. *The Drug Addict as a Patient*. New York: Grune & Stratton, 1956.

Pahnke, W. N., *et al*. Psychedelic therapy utilising LSD with cancer patients. *Journal of Psychedelic Drugs*, 3 (1970), 63-75.

Patrick, C. H. *Alcohol, Culture and Society*. Durham, North Carolina: Duke University Press, 1952.

Preventative Medicine Report, Vol. 1. First report from the Expenditure Committee. House of Commons, 17 Feb 1977, 88-89.

Robins, L. N. *The Vietnam Drug User Returns*. Washington: US Govt. Printing Office, 1974.

Robinson, J. T., Chitham, R. G., Greenwood, R. M. and Taylor, J. W. Chromosomal aberrations and LSD. *British Journal of Psychiatry*, 125 (1974), 238-244.

## Selected Bibliography

Royal College of Physicians. *Smoking and Health Now*. London: Pitman Medical and Scientific Publ. Co., 1971.

Royal College of Physicians. *Smoking or Health*. London: Pitman Medical, 1977.

Royal College of Psychiatrists. *Alcohol and Alcoholism*. London: Tavistock, 1979.

Saper, A. The making of policy through myth, fantasy and historical accident: the making of America's narcotics laws. *British Journal of Addiction*, 69 (1974), 183-193.

Schachter, S. and Singer, J. Cognitive, social and physiological determinants of emotional state. *Psychological Review*, 69 (1962), 379-399.

Seltzer, C. C. Coronary heart disease and smoking. *Journal of the American Medical Association*, 203 (1968), 193-200.

Seltzer, C. C. Critique of the Royal College of Physicians report. *Lancet* vol.1 (1972), 243-248.

Shafer Report. *Marihuana: A Signal of Misunderstanding*. Washington: US Govt. Printing Office, 1972.

Sharples, A. *The Scorpion's Tail*. London: Elek, 1975.

Snyder, C. R. *Alcohol and the Jews*. Illinois: Free Press, 1958.

Stafford, P. *Psychedelics Encyclopedia*. Berkeley: And/Or Press, 1977.

Stimson, G. V. *Heroin and Behaviour*. Shannon: Irish University Press, 1973.

Suedfeld, P. *Restricted Environmental Stimulation: Research and Clinical Applications*. New York: Wiley, 1980.

Szasz, T. *Ceremonial Chemistry*. London: Routledge & Kegan Paul, 1975.

Tjio, J. H., Pahnke, W. N. and Kurland, A. A. LSD and chromosomes: a controlled experiment. *Journal of the American Medical Association*, 210 (1969), 849-856.

Trethowan, W. H. Pills for personal problems. *British Medical Journal*, 2 (1975), 749-751.

Trocchi, A. *Cain's Book*. London: Calder, 1960.

United Nations Conference on Trade and Development. *Marketing and Distribution of Tobacco*. United Nations, 1978.

Weil, A. *The Natural Mind*. London: Cape, 1973.

Wenger, J. and Einstein, S. The use and misuse of aspirin. *International Journal of the Addictions*, 5 (1970), 757-775.

Wikler, A. *Opioid Dependence*. New York: Plenum, 1980.

Willis, P. *Profane Culture*. London: Routledge & Kegan Paul, 1978.

## Selected Bibliography

Wolfe, T. *The Electric Kool-Aid Acid Test*. New York: Bantam, 1969.

Wootton Committee. *Cannabis: Report by the Advisory Committee on Drug Dependence*. London: HMSO, 1968.

Yablonsky, L. *The Hippie Trip*. New York: Pegasus, 1968.

Young, J. *The Drugtakers*. London: Paladin, 1971.

Yudkin, J. *Pure, White and Deadly: The Problem of Sugar*. London: Davis-Poynter, 1972.

# INDEX

# Index

# *Index*